Muslims of Central Asia

The New Edinburgh Islamic Surveys
Series Editor: Carole Hillenbrand

Contemporary Issues in Islam Asma Asfaruddin
Astronomy and Astrology in the Islamic World Stephen P. Blake
The New Islamic Dynasties Clifford Edmund Bosworth
Media Arabic Julia Ashtiany Bray
An Introduction to the Hadith John Burton
A History of Islamic Law Noel Coulson
Medieval Islamic Political Thought Patricia Crone
A Short History of the Ismailis Farhad Daftary
Islam: An Historical Introduction (2nd Edition) Gerhard Endress
A History of Christian–Muslim Relations Hugh Goddard
Shiʿism (2nd Edition) Heinz Halm
Islamic Science and Engineering Donald Hill
Muslim Spain Reconsidered Richard Hitchcock
Islamic Law: From Historical Foundations to Contemporary Practice Mawil Izzi Dien
Sufism: The Formative Period Ahmet T. Karamustafa
A History of Islam in Indonesia Carool Kersten
Islamic Aesthetics Oliver Leaman
Persian Historiography Julie Scott Meisami
The Muslims of Medieval Italy Alex Metcalfe
The Archaeology of the Islamic World Marcus Milwright
Twelver Shiism Andrew Newman
Muslims in Western Europe (4th Edition) Jørgen S. Nielsen and Jonas Otterbeck
Medieval Islamic Medicine Peter E. Pormann and Emilie Savage-Smith
Muslims in Eastern Europe Egdūnas Račius
Islamic Names Annemarie Schimmel
The Genesis of Literature in Islam Gregor Schoeler
The Qur'an: A Historical-Critical Introduction Nicolai Sinai
Modern Arabic Literature Paul Starkey
Islamic Medicine Manfred Ullman
A History of Islamic Spain W. Montgomery Watt and Pierre Cachia
Introduction to the Qur'an W. Montgomery Watt
Islamic Creeds W. Montgomery Watt
Islamic Philosophy and Theology W. Montgomery Watt
Islamic Political Thought W. Montgomery Watt
The Influence of Islam on Medieval Europe W. Montgomery Watt
Muslims of Central Asia: An Introduction Galina M. Yemelianova

edinburghuniversitypress.com/series/isur

Muslims of Central Asia

An introduction

Galina M. Yemelianova

EDINBURGH
University Press

Edinburgh University Press is one of the leading university presses in the UK. We publish academic books and journals in our selected subject areas across the humanities and social sciences, combining cutting-edge scholarship with high editorial and production values to produce academic works of lasting importance. For more information visit our website: edinburghuniversitypress.com

Edinburgh University Press Ltd
The Tun – Holyrood Road
12 (2f) Jackson's Entry
Edinburgh EH8 8PJ

Typeset in 11/13pt Baskerville MT Pro by
Servis Filmsetting Ltd, Stockport, Cheshire
and printed and bound in Great Britain

A CIP record for this book is available from the British Library

ISBN 978 1 4744 1632 0 (hardback)
ISBN 978 1 4744 1633 7 (paperback)
ISBN 978 1 47441634 4 (webready PDF)
ISBN 978 1 4744 1635 1 (epub)

Contents

Figures

Acknowledgements

This book would not have been possible without my numerous friends and colleagues in Central Asia, who through many years generously shared with me their invaluable insights on the region and connected me with leading articulators and practitioners of Central Asian Islam. My special thanks are due to Zhulduzbek Abylkhozhin, Bakhtiyar Babadzhanov, Zuhra Halimova, Ashirbek Muminov, Nargis Nurulla-Khodzhaeva, Zumrat Salmorbekova, Suhrat Sirozhiddinov, Anara Tabyshalieva and Zaur Zhalilov. I am especially grateful to Svetlana Zhanabayeva who 'co-opted' me into her wonderful extended family and greatly facilitated my access to and interaction with Kazakh Sufis and other representatives of Kazakh Islam. I am indebted to many of my other contacts in the region who for obvious reasons I cannot name. I am grateful to Carole Hillenbrand for being the first encouraging external reader of my typescript and to the anonymous reviewer of the book's first draft for constructive and improving comments and suggestions. I also want to thank the United Nations Publication Board for permitting me to reproduce the UN map of Central Asia. At Edinburgh University Press I would also like to thank Ellie Bush and Kirsty Woods for their helpful editorial assistance. My particular thanks, however, goes to Nicola Ramsey, who first approached me with the idea of writing this book, and has been terrific through the whole writing journey. I would also like to make special mention of my children Misha, Alex and Katya for counterbalancing my preoccupation with the book and to thank Alex in particular for his assistance with formatting the typescript and sorting out its endnotes. Above all, I thank my husband Brian for being my rock and my most critical reader and editor. I dedicate this book to him.

Birmingham
26 April 2018

Note on transliteration

The use of a consistent system of transliteration has been problematic due to at least four script changes that occurred during the lengthy historical period covered in the book. I have therefore decided to combine more familiar simplified English spellings for the period before the region's Sovietisation and the Library of Congress system of transliteration for most names and terms taken from Russian, Uzbek, Kazakh, Kyrgyz, Turkmen and Tajik. I have, however, retained other transliterations in the case of widely known individuals and places, as, for example, Turajonzoda rather than Turazhonzoda, and Andijan rather than Andizhan. For words in Arabic I have omitted diacritics for long vowels, for example, Bukhara instead of Bukhârâ. I have, however, retained *ayn* and *hamza*, as in *shari'a* and *qira'at.* I have rendered plural forms of foreign words by adding an 's', instead of the form used in the language of origin; thus *oblasts* instead of *oblasti.* The exception to this is words appearing very frequently, like *'ulama'* instead of *'alims.* In most cases I have used place names that were used in the period under discussion; where these have since changed, present-day names are provided in parentheses. For the purposes of simplicity I have not used the *Hijri* (HA) calendar which was prevalent in the region prior to its inclusion within the Russian empire. All dates before February 1918 have been given according to the Julian calendar, which was twelve days behind the Gregorian calendar in the nineteenth century and thirteen days in the twentieth century. Dates after February 1918 have been rendered in accordance with the Gregorian calendar.

Abbreviations and acronyms

ADP	*Azod Dehkonlar Partiiasi* (Party of Free Peasants)
ARA	Agency for Religious Affairs
ATC	Anti-Terrorist Centre
AUCA	American University of Central Asia
AUK	American University in Kyrgyzstan
CARC	Council for Affairs of Religious Cults
CIS	Commonwealth of Independent States
CNS	Committee of National Security
CPSU	Communist Party of the Soviet Union
CPT	Communist Party of Turkmenistan
CRA	Committee for Religious Affairs
CST	Collective Security Treaty
CSTO	Collective Security Treaty Organisation
DMU	Directorate of Muslims of Uzbekistan
DPT	Democratic Party of Tajikistan or Democratic Party of Turkmenistan
DRA	Department for Religious Affairs
DWG	*Dala Wilaiiatining Gazeti* (Newspaper of the Steppe Province)
EABD	Eurasian Bank of Development
EACU	Eurasian Customs Union
EAEC	Eurasian Economic Commonwealth
EAEU	Eurasian Economic Union
Gosplan	*Gosudarstvennyi Planovoi Komitet* (State Commission for Planning)
HCUT	High Council of the 'Ulama' of Tajikistan
HTI	*Hizb al-Tahrir al-Islamii* (Party of Islamic Liberation)
IDB	Islamic Development Bank
IDU	*Islamskoe Dvizhenie Uzbekistana* (Islamic Movement of Uzbekistan)
IIJ	*Ittihad Islamii-Jihad* (Islamic Jihad Union)
IPV	*Islamskaia Partiia Vozrozhdeniia* (Islamic Revival Party)
IPVT	*Islamskaia Partiia Vozrozhdeniia Tajikistana* (Islamic Revival Party of Tajikistan)
ISIS	Islamic State of Iraq and Syria

KAU	Kyrgyz American University
KazASSR	Kazakh Autonomous Soviet Socialist Republic
KazSSR	Kazakh Soviet Socialist Republic
KBTU	Kazakh–British Technical University
KDM	Kyrgyzstan Democratic Movement
KGB	*Komitet Gosudarstvennoi Bezopasnosti* (Soviet secret police)
Kolkhoz	*Kollektivnoe khoziaistvo* (collective farm)
KRSU	Kyrgyz–Russian Slavic University
KyrAO	Kyrgyz Autonomous *Oblast'*
KyrASSR	Kyrgyz Autonomous Soviet Socialist Republic
KyrSSR	Kyrgyz Soviet Socialist Republic
LDPU	Liberal Democratic Party of Uzbekistan
MGB	*Ministerstvo Gosudarstvennoi Bezopasnosti* (Ministry of National Security)
MNST	Ministry of National Security of Turkmenistan
Narkomats	*Narodnyi Komissariat po Natsional'nostiam* (Ministry of Nationalities)
NKVD	*Narodnyi Komissariat Vnutrennikh Del* (Soviet secret police)
OIC	Organisation of Islamic Conference/Cooperation
OMON	*Otdel Mobil'nyi Osobogo Naznacheniia* (Special Police Unit)
PDP	People's Democratic Party
PDPT	People's Democratic Party of Tajikistan
PIE	Party of Industrialists and Entrepreneurs
PTA	Pakistan's Tribal Areas
QKAO	Qara-Kyrgyz Autonomous *Oblast'*
RCPb	Russian Communist Party of Bolsheviks
RSFSR	Russian Soviet Federal Socialist Republic
SADUM	*Tsentral'no-Aziatskoe Dukhovnoe Upravlenie Musul'man* (Muftiiate of Central Asia)
SCO	Shanghai Cooperation Organisation
SCRA	State Committee for Religious Affairs
SDMK	Spiritual Directorate of Muslims of Kazakhstan, or Kyrgyzstan
SDP	Social Democratic Party
Sovkhoz	*Sovetskoie khoziaistvo* (state-owned farms)
SredAzBureau	*Sredne-Aziatskoie Biuro* (Central Asian Bureau)
TajASSR	Tajikistan Autonomous Soviet Socialist Republic
TajSSR	Tajikistan Soviet Socialist Republic
TurASSR	Turkestan Autonomous Soviet Socialist Republic
TurSSR	Turkmenistan Soviet Socialist Republic
TV	*Turkistanskiie Vedomosti* (Turkestan News)
TWG	*Turkestan Wilaiiatining Gazeti* (Turkestan's newspaper)
UDOT	United Democratic Opposition of Turkmenistan

UTO	United Tajik Opposition
UzSSR	Uzbekistan Soviet Socialist Republic
WAMY	World Assembly of Muslim Youth
WTO	World Trade Organisation

Glossary

adab	rules of good Islamic behaviour
adat	a customary norm
adiraspan	a Steppe sage
aji/kaji	see *hajjee*
akim	a governor in Kazakhstan and Kyrgyzstan
ala kachuu	a Kyrgyz tradition of kidnapping a girl for marriage
'alim	(pl. *'ulama'/'ulamo'*) an Islamic scholar
amir/emir	lit. 'Ruler' in Arabic
amlak	state land in the Bukhara Emirate
'aqeedah	Islamic creed
aqsaqal / oqsoqol / arbob	a highly respected elder
aqyn	an improvising poet or singer among Kazakhs and Kyrgyz
arwah	spiritual energy
arwah/auraq	pl. spirits
asharshylyk	lit. 'death by hunger' in Kazakh
aul	a social unit consisting of several families among Kazakhs and some other nomads
avliio	Islamic saint
avlod	an extended family
awlat	pl. sacred tribes among Turkmen
ayat	a verse in the Qur'an
azan shakiru	a Kazakh ceremony of name-giving
bai	a local notable of substantial economic worth among Kazakhs and some other Turkic nomads
baltavar	a ruler's title in the Volga Bulgaria
barakah	a hereditary mystic aura/blessing
baqshi	a shaman healer, see *tabib*
batyr	a legendary hero among Kazakhs
baursak	a Kazakh/Turkic pastry
beg/bek/biy	a chieftain among various Turkic nomadic people
beshbarmak	Kazakh/Turkic meat dish with noodles, onions and potatoes
bibi-mullo	see *bibi-otun, bibi-khalfa, otin* and *otincha*

bibi-otun/bibi-khalfa	a female Islamic authority, usually the wife of an imam or mullah, see *otin, otincha* and *bibi-mullo*
bid'a	unlawful innovation in Islam
bliny	'pancakes' in Russian
bomdod	a morning prayer
bubu	a female Kyrgyz healer who is believed to be able to access the past and to foresee the future
caravansarai	roadside trade station
chador/chachvan	a face veil
chaikhona	a tea-house
Dar al-Harb	'Abode of War'
Dar al-Hikma	'House of Wisdom'
Dar al-Islam	'Abode of Islam'
Dasht-i-Qipchak	Great Steppe
dasturkhonchi	a female organiser of communal feasts
dawrah	underground Islamic discussion club
dekhkan/dekhkon	peasants
demchi	a Kyrgyz healer, who cures through chanting prayers
dhikr	a Sufi practice of ritual commemoration of Allah
dhikr-i khafi	silent *dhikr* among Naqshbandiis
dhikr-i zhahri	loud *dhikr* among Qadiriis and some other Sufis
domullo	an Islamic teacher or imam
du'a/duo	an invocation prayer in Islam
emshi	a Kazakh folk healer
eshon	a Sufi sheikh among Tajiks
Fatihat	the first *surah* of the Qur'an
fiqh	Islamic jurisprudence
firman	a religious ruling
folbin	see *tabib*
gap	a social gathering in Uzbekistan (lit. 'conversation' in Uzbek)
gazat/gazawat	an Islamic holy war, synonymous to jihad
glasnost'	lit. 'openness' in Russian
guzar	clan-based solidarity network among Tajiks, see *qavm*
hadith	account of Prophet Muhammad's sayings, or actions
hajj	a pilgrimage to Mecca and Medina
hajjee	a Muslim who conducted *hajj*
hakim	a governor in Uzbekistan
halal	permitted substances and actions in Islam
halaqah	an underground cell
hatna	a circumcision, see *sunnet*

hijab/hijob	a woman's veil covering the head and chest
Hijrah	Prophet Muhammad's flight from Mecca to Medina in 622; the beginning of the Muslim era
Hijri	Islamic lunar calendar
hujrah	underground Islamic school
hujum	a campaign for women's de-veiling (lit. 'attack' in Arabic)
'Id al-Adha	Feast of the Sacrifice, see *Qurban-Bairam* and *Qurban-Hait*
'Id al-Fitr	celebration of the end of the thirty-day fast of *Ramadan*
idtikrar	a compelling duty in Islam
iftar	an evening meal during *Ramadan*
ijtihad	an independent judgement in Islam
imam-khatib	a chief imam
inorodtsy	an official qualification of Central Asian Muslims in tsarist Russia (lit 'alien-born' in Russian)
ishan/ishon/dervish	a Sufi master, see *khoja* and *tura*
Jadidism	Islamic reformism (lit. 'modernism'; 'belonging to innovation' in Arabic)
janazah	an Islamic burial
jinn	a supernatural creature in Islamic mythology
jiziah	an Islamic per capita yearly tax
juz	a horde among Kazakhs
kafir	a non-Muslim
kalam	Islamic scholastic theology
kalym	a bride's price, see also *mahr*
khalifa	a nominated successor to a Sufi sheikh
khanaqah	a Sufi lodge
kharaj	an Islamic land tax
kharijii	(pl. *khawarij*) a follower of extreme Islamic views
khoja/khwaja	a honorific title of a Sufi master
khutbah	Friday prayer in a mosque
kniaz	a prince in Russia and some other Slavic polities
kraii	a province in the Russian Empire/Russia
kufr	non-belief in Islam
kulak	a Bolshevik term for an allegedly wealthy peasant (lit. 'fist' in Russian)
kuurdak	a Turkic dish made of mutton/sheep's liver, fat and onions
likbez	lit. 'liquidation of illiteracy' in Russian
madhhab	a juridical school in Sunni Islam

madrasah	Islamic secondary school
mahallah	a neighbourhood community among sedentary people
mahdi	the prophesied redeemer of Islam
mahkama-i shari'a	*shari'a* court
mahr	a bride's price, *see* also *kalym*
mahsum	an hereditary Islamic authority
maktab	Islamic primary school
Manas	Kyrgyz epic
manty	Kazakh/Turkic dumplings
Mavlud	celebration of the Prophet Muhammad's birthday
mazar/mozor	Sufi graveyard or other sacred site of pilgrimage
mihrab	a niche in the wall directed towards the Kaaba in Mecca
moldo	an unofficial Islamic authority among Kyrgyz
mudarris	a teacher in a *maktab* or a *madrasah*
muftii	head of the muftiiate
muftiiate	Spiritual Directorate of Muslims
mujahid	(pl. *mujahideen*) an Islamic warrior
mul'k	private land in the Bukhara Emirate
murid	a Sufi disciple
murza	a Genghizid noble
mutavalli	a *waqf*'s trustee
non	Uzbek round flat bread
Nowruz	an ancient holiday of spring (lit. 'new day' in Persian)
oblast'	a region
obshchina	a peasant community in Russia
oralman	an ethnic Kazakh repatriate
Oraza-Bairam	see *Uraza-Bairam*
Oraza-Tutu	see *Uraza-Bairam*, *Uraza-Hait* and *'Id al-Fitr*
Orozo-Ait	see *'Id al-Fitr*
otin/otincha	see *bibi-otun/bibi-khalfa*
padishah	a ruler in Iran
paranja	a body veil
perestroika	lit. 'restructuring' in Russian
pir	Sufi sheikh, especially among Tajiks
polovtsy	Qipchaks, in Russian sources
porhan	a shaman among Turkmen
propiska	a registration of address in a person's internal passport (ID)
purdah	a seclusion

qadi/qazi	an Islamic judge
qadimism	Islamic traditionalism
qavm	see *guzar*
qazi-kolon	supreme Islamic authority in Tajikistan
qaziiat	a regional branch of the muftiiate
qira'at	recitation of the Qur'an
qishlaq/qishloq	a large agricultural settlement
qur'anist	a Muslim who relies exclusively on the Qur'an as the source of faith
Qurban-Ait	see *'Id al-Adha*
Qurban-Bairam	see *'Id al-Adha* and *Qurban-Hait*
Qurban-Hait	see *'Id al-Adha* and *Qurban-Bairam*
Qurbonlik	Islamic sacrifice of an animal
qurultai	a congress among the *Qipchaq* people
Ramadan	the ninth month of the *Hijri* calendar and a month of *sawm*
razmezhivanie	Bolsheviks' national delimitation of Central Asia
ru	a clan among Kazakhs
ruqyah	*jinn's* exorcism
sabr	a patience
Sahib	(pl. *sahaba*) Prophet Muhammad's companion
salat	five daily prayers
Salem Qilu	Islamic greetings among Kazakhs
samsa	a Kazakh/Turkic meat pastry
sawm	Islamic fasting
Sayyid	a descendant of the Prophet Muhammad
seerah	Prophetic biography
shahadah	affirmation of the Islamic faith
sheikha-ul-Islam	an Islamic jurist
shezhere	genealogies among some Turkic people
shirk	heresy
silsilah	a spiritual chain of succession in Sufism
sunnet/sundet	a circumcision, see *hatna*
surah	a chapter in the Qur'an
tabib	a shaman healer, see *baqshi*
tafsir	exegesis of the Qur'an
taipa	a tribe among Kazakhs and some other nomads
tajdeed	a renovation in Islam
tajweed	art of recitation of the Qur'an
takfir	excommunication
Taliban	lit. 'Students' in Arabic
tarawih-namaz	a prayer which follows the night prayer

tariqat	a Sufi brotherhood
tawheed	strict monotheism
tire	a social unit consisting of several families among Turkmen and some other nomads
to'y	a communal celebration
tugra	an Islamicised heraldic sign
tumar	an amulet among Kazakhs and some other nomads
tura	Sufi master, see *ishan* and *khoja*
Turki	Turkic language
uiezd	a secondary-level administrative unit in Tsarist Russia, the Russian Empire and the USSR until 1929
ukaz	a tsar's decree
uki	owl feathers
ummah	community of Muslims
'umrah	small *hajj*
Uraza	fast of Ramadan, one of the five pillars of Islam
Uraza-Bairam	see *'Id al-Fitr* and *Uraza-Hait*
Uraza-Hait	see *'Id al-Fitr* and *Uraza-Bairam*
'urf	a tribal law
Vilaiiat	a province in Uzbekistan
volost'	an administrative unit within *uiezd*
waqf	an Islamic endowment
yasak	an annual tribute
yurt	a nomadic tent
zakat	an Islamic obligatory alms-giving to poor and needy and one of the five pillars of Islam
Zakat al-Fitr	charity given to the poor at the end of Ramadan
Zhen'otdel	a women's department
ziiarat/ziiorot	Sufi visitation

For Brian

Introduction

This book is a product of my lengthy scholarly and personal engagement with Central Asia, which corresponds to the republics of Uzbekistan, Kazakhstan, Kyrgyzstan, Tajikistan and Turkmenistan.[1] It has been driven by my combined interest in the region's fascinating people and their spiritual and material culture, and my frustration at the relative lack of knowledge and understanding of it in the West.[2] Outside the specialised scholarship conducted in 'the ivory tower' the Central Asian states of Uzbekistan, Kazakhstan, Tajikistan, Kyrgyzstan and Turkmenistan remain to some extent terra incognita. The occasional outbursts of media interest in the region have been mainly due to the participation of Central Asian *jihadists* in terrorist attacks in the West. In sociocultural terms, these republics have been perceived as parts of the Muslim world, comparable to Afghanistan, Pakistan and other Islamic 'stans', while at the policy level the region has received attention primarily for its large hydrocarbon reserves and its precarious neighbourhood relations with war-stricken Afghanistan and politically volatile Shi'a Iran. Such a limited and pragmatic approach to Central Asia among Western policymakers and international economic and financial institutions has determined the prevalence in Central Asian studies of political and social scientists dealing with contemporary issues related to regime transition and party politics, regional political and energy security, drug trafficking and Islamicised extremism. They have tended to prioritise theoretical clarity over messy empirics and to rely predominantly on secondary, rather than primary, sources in English, and to a lesser extent, in Russian.

In the last two decades a well-rounded academic understanding of Central Asia has been affected by the disciplinary streamlining of social sciences and humanities, leading to the consistent dismantling of interdisciplinary language-based area studies,[3] including Central Asian studies, and the latter's subsequent dissection into isolated case studies, which were deemed to demonstrate the validity of particular theoretical paradigms. As a consequence, the application to the study of Central Asian Muslims of sophisticated conceptual frameworks has often acquired its own momentum, while obscuring the situation on the ground. Among other implications of theoretical straitjacketing has been a growing disconnectedness between political scientists, on the one side, and social anthropologists, historians and Islamic studies scholars, on the other. The increased fragmentation of scholarly knowledge on Central Asia has adversely affected the understanding of what is actually going on in the region.

This is not to say that there have been no in-depth and primary source-based studies of Central Asia by a relatively small number of Western, Central Asian and Russian area studies scholars, social anthropologists, ethnographers, historians, Islamic studies specialists and linguists. This book has particularly benefited from Devin A. DeWeese's *Studies of Sufism in Central Asia*, Peter B. Golden's *Central Asia in World History*, Adeeb Khalid's *The Politics of Muslim Cultural Reform*, Maria Louw's *Everyday Islam in post-Soviet Central Asia*, Alexei Malashenko's *Islam in Central Asia*, Vitaly V. Naumkin's *Radical Islam in Central Asia*, Oliver Roy's *The New Central Asia*, Sebastien Peyrouse's *Turkmenistan*, Bruce G. Privratsky's *Muslim Turkistan*, Jeff Sahadeo's *Russian Colonial Society in Tashkent*, Svat Soucek's *A History of Inner Asia*, and Sergei Abashin's *Soviet Qishlaq* and Bakhtiyar Babadzhanov's *Kokand Khanate* (both in Russian). Nevertheless, there seems to have been no single text on Central Asian Muslims which would interconnect various periods and aspects of their history and present, transcend the disciplinary cacophony and offer an integrated and plain account of what has happened to them and where and why they are now. I have been acutely aware of this deficiency through many years of teaching an area studies masters course on Central Asia in the United Kingdom, when I had to rely on a variety of thematically and disciplinary disconnected monographs, edited volumes and journal articles, and to navigate between a variety of Orientalist and Occidentalist theoretical perspectives on Central Asian Islam, including Foucault, Bourdieu's 'cultural capital', 'pre-axial and axial soteriology' and 'moral reasoning',[4] while continuing to tell students that one day I would rectify the situation and produce such a book.

What follows is my overdue promise, which seeks to go beyond the prevailing mono-theoretical determinism to generate a history-based integrated overview of the various Muslim peoples of Central Asia. It deliberately does not employ a particular theoretical framework, even as it recognises the usefulness of some theoretical models for better clarity and comparative purposes. Thus, its analysis of the meanings of and reasons for the 'Muslim-ness' of the various peoples of Central Asia is in line with Max Weber's approach outlined in his *Sociology of Religion*. The discussion of the social and institutional implications of the Russia-driven modernisation and secularisation of Central Asia is informed by Jose Casanova's notion of secularisation formulated in his *Public Religions in the Modern World*; while the conceptualisation of post-Soviet Islamic resurgence in the region and the role in this process of globalisation draws on Peter L. Berger's *The Desecularization of the World* and Bryan S. Turner's *Religion and Modern Society*.

The book approaches Central Asia as a historically and culturally self-contained region with its own intrinsic characteristics and dynamics. It situates the region as a whole within the wider Eurasian[5] spatial and cultural context, and assesses the legacy of the Soviet transformation for the region's relations with some other parts of the post-Soviet space, the Middle East and the wider Muslim world. The book's main thesis is that, in cultural, social and political terms, present-day Central Asia is a product of four major factors. One is its pre-Islamic civilisational core, associated with the ancient urbanised and cosmopolitan east Iranian-speaking Sogdians. The second is the region's lengthy domination, along with the wider Eurasia, by Turco-Mongol nomads who laid the foundation for the enduring supremacy of the 'power vertical', embodied by rulers and the prevalence of personal, rather than institutional, mechanisms of social control and governance, subsequently resulting in a civil society deficit. The prolonged nomadic dominance also channelled state formation in the region along the lines of loose multi-ethnic and multi-confessional empires with ill-defined borders, created a common Eurasian political, economic and cultural space, and accounted for the persistence of strong localised and genealogical networks and identities. The third relates to the region's Islamicisation, epitomised in Persianised Islamic scholarship and syncretic folk Islam infused with Sufism,[6] nomadic customary norms and shamanistic beliefs, leading to the emergence of a distinctive Central Asian Islam. The fourth is the late nineteenth-century Russian conquest, followed by the region's comprehensive Sovietisation in the twentieth century. As a result of these factors, the Islamic dynamic in the post-independence Central Asian states has exhibited notable differences from that in the historical Muslim heartland with its centres in Mecca, Medina, Damascus and Baghdad, or in Muslim communities in the West. Nevertheless, since the break-up of the USSR in 1991 and the subsequent transformation of the Soviet Central Asian republics into independent states, it has been affected by other potentially transformative influences related to globalisation and the region's partial material and digitalised reintegration into the wider Muslim world. I deploy the evidence for my argument in what follows.

The book's focus on the Islamic dimension explains its omission of other important factors in the region's history and present.[7] It consists of two parts. Part I, which includes three chapters, deals with the history of the relevant parts of Muslim Central Asia, while Part II, which consists of five chapters, addresses Islam-related developments in the independent republics of Uzbekistan, Kazakhstan, Tajikistan, Kyrgyzstan and Turkmenistan. Chapter 1 discusses the correlation between the narrowly defined Central Asia, containing five post-Soviet republics, and the wider Central Asia, which in different historical periods included present-day northwestern China, Tibet, Pamir, Inner and Outer Mongolia, Afghanistan, northwestern Pakistan, northern India, northern Iran, the southern Caucasus, northern Turkey and eastern Russia. It assesses the role of the ancient Sogdians in the creation of the matrix of Central Asian culture before proceeding to examine the process of Islamicisation of the various sedentary peoples of the Ferghana valley and the nomadic peoples of the Kazakh Steppe, Qarakum desert and southern Siberia. The chapter considers the productive interplay between local pre-Islamic beliefs, *adats*, *'urf* and Islamic doctrine and Sufism. It discusses the specifics of the Central Asian version of the dominant *Hanafi madhhab*[8] and the special role of Abu Mansur al-Maturidi al-Samarqandi (d. 944) in its development. The chapter also examines the particular contributions to the 'making' of a distinctive 'Central Asian Islam' by *Khoja* Ahmad Yasawi (d. 1166), Baha al-Din Naqshband Bukhari (d. 1389) and other great Central Asian Sufis and Islamic thinkers. It dwells upon the emergence of a sizeable Shi'a (*Isma'ili*) community in the Pamir mountains of present-day Tajikistan and its relations with the region's Sunni majority. It pays special attention to the spiritual, social and political role of Sufi authorities and Islamic scholars and their relations with various Central Asian ruling dynasties, including the Samanids, Khwarazmids, Qarakhanids, Ghaznavids, Seljuqids, Genghizids, Timurids, Shaibanids and Kazakh khans.

Chapter 2 begins with an analysis of the spiritual, societal and political role of Islam among Central Asia's various sedentary and nomadic peoples during the time preceding the Russian conquest. It explores the legitimising function of Islam in the Kazakh Small, Middle and Great Hordes and in the Khanates of Khiva and Kokand, as well as the Bukhara Emirate. It discusses the relationship between political rulers and ordinary Muslims and assesses the impact of official and popular Islamic authorities. At the local level, it examines the institution of *mahallah* among sedentary dwellers and the role of Islam in it. The chapter then proceeds to the Russian conquest and its implications for the elites and ordinary Muslims. It is particularly concerned with the effects of the proliferation of Russian education among a fraction of the Central Asian elite. Thus, it discusses Central Asian *Jadidism*[9] and compares it with Tatar-centred *Jadidism* in the Crimea and the Volga region of the Russian Empire, as well as with Islamic reformism in the Middle East and south Asia, pioneered by Jamal al-Din al-Afghani (1839–97), Sayyid Ahmad Khan (1817–98), Muhammad 'Abduh (1849–1905), Khayr al-Din (1820–90) and other leading Muslim reformers.

Chapter 3 addresses the establishment of Bolshevik control over Central Asia. It examines the political, economic and propaganda methods employed by the Bolsheviks to ensure the support of a substantial number of Central Asian Muslims. It considers the variety of responses by local Muslims towards Bolshevik rule, including the *basmachi* movement in the 1920s and 1930s. It pays special attention to the role of the Stalinist national delimitation in the construction of ethnocultural polities, which in 1991 were transformed into independent states. It then analyses the nature and consequences of the seventy years of Sovietisation for Central Asian Muslims. In particular, our discussion looks into the atheistic assault on Islam and the Islamic 'clergy',[10] the *hujum* – the campaign for the forcible unveiling of Muslim women, and the creation of so-called 'official Islam'. It particularly examines the implications of Stalin's nationality and religious policies for local Muslim relations with other Muslim and non-Muslim peoples of the USSR and their ethnic brethren and co-religionists abroad.

Chapters 4–8 of Part II are organised on a country-by-country basis, and are structurally similar. They address various aspects of political, social and religious life in independent Uzbekistan, Kazakhstan, Tajikistan, Kyrgyzstan and Turkmenistan. Given the outlined centrality of political leadership and the weakness of civil society, each chapter begins by examining the distinctive reactions of the five Central Asian leaders to the Gorbachevian *perestroika* and the imminent independence of their republics. All five chapters proceed to discuss the intricacies of post-independence regime formation and the ruling elites' nation-building projects and the role of Islam in them. Each chapter then explores the various manifestations of the so-called 'Islamic revival', while accepting the inadequacy of this notion due to the fact that Islam never died in Central Asia. Here the term 'Islamic revival' is used to describe a dual process: the public resurfacing of 'Central Asian Islam' in the conditions of de-Sovietisation; and Central Asian Muslims' partial re-Islamicisation along the lines of so-called 'normative' or *Salafi* Islam[11] under the impact of globalisation. Each chapter pays special attention to the sources and agencies of the 'Islamic revival', including the ideologies and recruiting tactics of the Islamic Revival Party of Tajikistan, the Islamic Movement of Uzbekistan, *Hizb al-Tahrir al-Islamii* ('Party of Islamic Liberation'), *Jund al-Caliphate* ('Soldiers of the Caliphate') and other Islamist organisations and groupings. The chapters assess the ensuing correlation between 'Central Asian Islam' and normative Islam, and address the reasons behind the latter's relatively weak appeal among Central Asian Muslims by elaborating on the popular perceptions and practices of Muslim-ness. The book concludes by analysing the cultural, social and political implications of the partial physical and digital reintegration of particular Central Asian Muslims into the global *ummah* (Muslim community), alongside their post-Soviet de-industrialisation, re-traditionalisation, trans-regional drug trafficking and, in the case of Uzbekistan, Tajikistan and Kyrgyzstan, their substantial labour emigration.

Notes

1. There is a geographical and geopolitical fluidity and definitional complexity attaching to the very notion of 'Central Asia', which is discussed in detail in Chapter 1.
2. For my fuller elaboration on the state of knowledge and understanding of Central Asia in the West, see Yemelianova 2017.
3. The decline of language-based area studies has occurred against the background of the increasing 'marketisation' of higher education, which has deemed them as being insufficiently 'profitable' and too labour-intensive. As a result, the number of area studies departments has been drastically reduced. For example, in the United States and the United Kingdom there are now only a few universities that provide training in some of the languages of the

peoples of Central Asia. Among them in the United States are the Center for Languages of the Central Asian Region, Indiana University, Bloomington, and the Center for Russia, East Europe and Central Asia, University of Wisconsin-Madison, which offers courses in Kazakh, Tajik, Uzbek and Uighur; and in the United Kingdom the Faculty of Asian and Middle Eastern Studies, University of Cambridge, which provides training in Kazakh.

4. See, for example, Khalid 1998; Montgomery 2016; Rasanayagam 2011; Sartori 2013.
5. I use the term 'Eurasia' to denote the sociocultural area, rather than the much wider geographical region of Eurasia or the Eurasian ideologies of the post-Soviet Russian, Tatarstani and Kazakhstani political elites. See more on Eurasianism in Laruelle 2008; Bassin 2016.
6. Sufism represents a mystical side of Islam which developed in parallel with, or in opposition to, mainstream Islam. The Sufis believe that Sufism is a higher form of Islam because it is based on belief by the heart. By the end of the twelfth century specific Sufi organisations – *tariqats* (a 'way', or a school in Sufism) – had emerged, headed by particular sheikhs who were perceived as intermediaries between God and the individual Muslim. By the fourteenth century there were 12 major *tariqats*: Rifaiia, Yasawiia, Shadhiliia, Suhrawardiia, Chistiia, Kubrawiia, Badaviia, Qadiriia, Mawlawiia, Bektashiia, Khalwatiia and Naqshbandiia. See more on Sufism in Trimingham 1971; Al-Janabi 2000; Bennigsen and Wimbush 1985; Zelkina 2000; DeWeese 2012.
7. Thus, Part I does not address the region's pre-Islamic history; the nineteenth-century Russo-British Great Game; the system of Russian administration; the agrarian colonisation by Russian, Ukrainian and other non-Muslim peoples; the East Turkistan Republic of 1933–4; Stalinist deportations in the region of various Muslim and non-Muslim peoples; or economic and ecological changes. In a similar way, Part II does not consider economic, ecological, water-sharing problems, army and police restructuring or the Central Asian republics' external economic, political and security engagements.
8. *Hanafi maddhab*, or *Hanafism*, is one of the four main *madhhabs* within Sunni Islam. It is named after Abu Hanifa al-Nu'man ibn Thabit (699–767). The other three *madhhabs* are *Malikism*, *Shafi'ism* and *Hanbalism*, which were named after Malik ibn Anas (713–795), Abu 'Abdullah Muhammad ibn Idris al-Shafi'i (767–819) and 'Abdullah Ahmad ibn Hanbal al-Shaibani (780–855), respectively.
9. *Jadidism* (lit. 'modernism') was a specific Russian Islamic phenomenon. It was generated by the reform-minded Tatar Muslim elite in the 1880s in response to Russia's modernisation initiated by Alexander II (1818–81). It started as a movement for the modernisation of traditional *maktab* and *madrasah* education in the Crimea and the Volga region. It was pioneered by Ismail Gasprinskii (Gasparly, 1851–1914), a European-educated Crimean Tatar and the founder of *Tercuman* ('Translator', 1883–1918), the first pan-Turkic Russian Muslim newspaper, which was published in simplified Ottoman Turkish in Bakhchysarai in the Crimea. In 1884, Gasprinskii pioneered a new method (*al-usul al-jadid*, in Arabic) of teaching in the Tatar *maktab* in his home village in the Crimea. Compared to the 'old method' (*al-usul al-qadim*, in Arabic), which was based on memorisation without proper understanding of the Qur'an and other sacred Islamic texts in Arabic; the 'new method' involved the phonetisation of reading in Arabic, the translation of the Qur'an and other texts into simplified Turkish, as well as the introduction into the school curriculum of secular subjects, such as mathematics, geography, history and the Russian language. *Jadidism* soon evolved into a wider sociopolitical and cultural movement that sought both the national enhancement of Tatars and others of Russia's Muslims, and their fully-fledged integration within the socio-economic and political fabric of the Russian Empire. See more on Tatar-centred *Jadidism* in Rorlich 1986 and Yemelianova 1997.

10. Given that, unlike Christianity, Islam does not require an institutionalised hierarchy, I use the Christian term 'clergy' in relation to *'ulama'*, mullahs, imams, muftiis, Sufi sheikhs and other representatives of Islamic authority for the sake of utility and simplicity only.
11. I use the term *Salafi* (lit. 'of ancestors' in Arabic) Islam to describe the views and activities of advocates of the return to the pure, unadulterated Islam of the period of Prophet Muhammad and the Four Righteous Caliphs, which are attributed to the period of the first 400 years after the Prophet Muhammad.

PART I

Central Asia in the pre-Russian, Russian and Soviet periods

CHAPTER 1

Muslims of Central Asia before the Russian conquest

The notion of Central Asia

I begin by accepting the relativism of the concept 'Muslims of Central Asia' for two main reasons. One is the geographical, political and cultural ambiguity of the notion of Central Asia, and the other is the ideational and confessional syncretism and pluralism of its indigenous inhabitants. Historically, the notion of Central Asia as a distinctive geographical and cultural area was born outside the region. Until its ethnonational delimitation by the Bolsheviks in the 1920s and 1930s, various regional rulers (khans, emirs, *begs/beks* and *biys*), as well as ordinary people primarily identified themselves with a particular city, town, village, neighbourhood or tribe and clan. Thus, in the nineteenth century many Iranian- and Turkic-speaking sedentary peoples still perceived themselves as Bukharis (from Bukhara), Samarqandis (from Samarqand), Kokandis (from Kokand), Andijanis (from Andijan) and so on, while Turkic-, Mongolic- and Sintic (Chinese)-speaking nomadic peoples thought of themselves as members of a particular sub-clan, clan or tribe.

In Europe up until the seventeenth century present-day Central Asia, alongside most of Russia, Tibet, Mongolia and western China, were included within a vaguely defined notion of 'Tartary'. The latter's notional delimitation into Russia, Turan and Central Asia/Inner Asia/Upper Asia was done by Prussian geologists and geographers in the eighteenth and early nineteenth century. The leading figures among them were Alexander von Humboldt (1769–1859), Ferdinand Richthofen (1833–1905) and Karl Ritter (1779–1858) who, having travelled extensively throughout the Eurasian expanses, came to the conclusion that Central Asia was characterised by its geographical and cultural *otherness* from the rest of the continent. In 1843, von Humboldt described Central Asia as a geographically landlocked Eurasian region, defined by the Tian-Shan and Pamir-Altai mountains in the east, the Caspian Sea in the west, the Aral Sea and Irtysh river in the north and the Hindu Kush and Kopet Dag mountain range in the south. He distinguished Central Asia from Turan, roughly corresponding to the Kazakh Steppe, and pointed to Central Asia's cultural uniqueness due to its centrality in the trans-Eurasian Silk Road trade, which from ancient times until the end of the eighteenth century acted as a major transmitter and mixer of cultures, beliefs, languages and skills. By comparison, Richthofen and Ritter defined Central Asia as a 'transitional region' which was more centred on von Humboldt's Turan.[1]

Prussian geographers' notions of Central Asia were subsequently appropriated by their Russian colleagues, who for geopolitical reasons 'enlarged' them by uniting von Humboldt's Central Asia with Turan. Throughout most of the nineteenth century the notion of Central Asia was significantly politicised under the influence of the Great Game,[2] the geopolitical rivalry in the region between the British and Russian empires. In 1895, the Great Game officially ended with the signing of the Pamir Boundary Commission Protocols, according to which St Petersburg recognised British control over the Emirate of Afghanistan, while London conceded Russian supremacy over most of today's Central Asia. The eastern border of Central Asia was legitimised by the Sino-Russian Convention of 1898. During that period Russian cartographers introduced the terms 'Middle Asia' (*Sredniaia Aziia*) and 'Turkestan', which were used as synonymous to 'Central Asia' (*Tsentral'naiia Aziia*). In the early 1920s, they began to refer to Xinjiang and adjacent Muslim-populated regions in northwestern China as 'Eastern Turkestan'. The Soviet definition of *Sredniaia Aziia* encompassed the Soviet republics of Uzbekistan, Tajikistan, Kyrgyzstan and Turkmenistan, while excluding the Soviet Republic of Kazakhstan. Subsequently, the whole region was referred to as '*Sredniia Aziia* and Kazakhstan'.

However, outside the USSR this term was used in parallel with 'Inner Asia', or 'Central Eurasia', the boundaries of which varied significantly. Some scholars considered Xinjiang and Mongolia as parts of the region, while others expanded its boundaries even further by including in it eastern Russia, the southern Caucasus, Tibet, northeastern Iran, northern Afghanistan, northern Turkey, northwestern Pakistan and northern India.[3] Like von Humboldt and other Prussian geographers of the past, they emphasised the centrality of the Silk Road in the formation of the region's cultural matrix which synthesised the sophisticated indigenous civilisation and material, ethnocultural and ideational influences emanating from Afghanistan, Iran, India, wider Eurasia, China and the Arab world. Importantly, they regarded the arrival of Islam in the region in the seventh century as an important factor which modified the existing Central Asian culture along Islamic lines, albeit without radically changing it.[4]

Following the disintegration of the Soviet Union in 1991 the Soviet term '*Sredniaia Aziia* and Kazakhstan' was discarded by the political and intellectual elites of independent Uzbekistan, Tajikistan, Kazakhstan, Kyrgyzstan and Turkmenistan and replaced by the term *Tsentral'naiia Aziia* ('Central Asia'), which included all five republics. The new name was officially endorsed by the leaders of these republics at their meeting in Ashgabat in 1993, and since the 1990s it has been used internationally and included in the *Encyclopaedia Britannica*.[5]

Historical setting and the arrival of Islam

Islam was brought to the Ferghana valley of present-day Central Asia by the Arabian Arabs in the mid-seventh century. By the time of the Arab conquest, the Ferghana valley's population included Iranian-speaking urban and agrarian peoples, while the adjacent steppe and desert areas to the west, north and east of the Amu Darya river were dominated by various Turkic-, Mongolic- and Sintic (Chinese)-speaking nomadic peoples, who roamed the vast Eurasian expanses in search of fresh pastures for their horses, camels and cattle. Among the region's largest state formations were Sogdia and Khorezm (Khwarazm). The major divide between the sedentary and nomadic people was reflected in their different political organisations, economic activities, customs and beliefs. It did not prevent, however, the development of a symbiotic and mutually beneficial relationship between them. For centuries more mobile and militarily stronger nomads provided protection for traders and peasants in exchange for artefacts, grain and other agricultural produce and various services. This relationship played a vital role in sustaining the cross-regional Silk Road trade between China and Europe and the Middle East.

The sedentary peoples were engaged in agriculture, trade, metalwork and other crafts. They lived in large houses which hosted extended families, consisting of several generations. In urban areas they formed neighbourhood communities, later on known as *mahallahs*, *guzar* or *qavm*, which were largely organised on the basis of members' common activities. Belonging to a particular territory-based neighbourhood community was central to its members' identity. In terms of religious belief, various sedentary peoples adhered to Manichaeism, Zoroastrianism,[6] Buddhism and Nestorian Christianity. Members of neighbourhood communities shared responsibilities for the maintenance and cleaning of water reservoirs and other communal facilities and were bound to attend individual members' celebrations and funerals, as well as common festivities. Subsequently, in some localities *mahallahs* began to develop on the basis of its members' common belonging to a particular Sufi *tariqat*. In rural areas several *mahallahs* formed larger agricultural settlements, or proto-*qishlaqs*/*qishloqs*. Compared with the urban–rural divide in Europe of the same period, the main divide in Central Asia was between sedentary and nomadic peoples, while the difference between Central Asia's urban and rural settlements was rather blurred since they shared many common characteristics, including the walling along their borders, a common meeting place and, in some cases, a bazaar.

The nomads' livelihood depended on horses, camels, cattle, sheep and yaks. The horses were particularly valued since they were not only the source of nomads' mobility, but also of their meat and dairy products. Nomads lived in *yurts*, which could be easily assembled and transported. The primary unit of nomadic social organisation was the extended family. These were organised into clans, with several clans forming a tribe. For the purpose of military raids several tribes united in confederations. Tribal affiliation was central to the nomads' identity and for the legitimisation of their leaders' authority. It was traditionally expected that a nomad should know his or her ancestors through seven generations, a convention that persisted throughout history and is still widely observed among present-day Kazakhs, Kyrgyz and Turkmen. Nomads differed in terms of their genuine or perceived genealogy and their languages and dialects, as well as their beliefs. Many of them believed in Tengri,[7] the spirit of Blue Sky, and the magic and healing powers of shamans, who were perceived as being able to communicate with spirits and natural forces. The historical resilience of these beliefs is evidenced, for example, in the choice of the Blue Sky background for the flag of independent Kazakhstan and the resurgence of shamanist healing practices among Kazakhs, Kyrgyz and Turkmen.

In 651, the Muslim Arabs conquered Merv (in present-day Turkmenistan), which was one of the main cities of the Sassanid-controlled province of Khorasan, situated in today's northeastern Iran and Afghanistan. From there they attempted to cross the Amu Darya into the Ferghana valley, which they termed *Mawarannahr* (lit. 'What is beyond the River'; referring to the Amu Darya – G.Y.) or what the Romans called Transoxiana. It took the Arabs several decades to establish control over the Ferghana valley, but in the early eighth century under the leadership of Qutaiba ibn Muslim (669–717), an Umaiiad Arab commander of the Bahila tribe, they finally overcame the fierce resistance of Sogdians, Khorezmians and other indigenous sedentary peoples and imposed their control over the region's main cities of Bukhara and Samarqand.

Following the Arab conquest, Central Asia was included in the Arab caliphate, first under the rule of the Umaiiads (661–750) and subsequently under the Abbasids (750–1258). The fact that Islam was introduced to the region by Prophet Muhammad's companions and contemporaries has been of great importance to Central Asia's official and charismatic Islamic authorities, and to Sufi sheikhs in particular, who continue to derive their legitimacy from their either factual or perceived descent from the Prophet and his companions, or Four Righteous Caliphs. Arab expansionism into Central Asia clashed with the inroads into the region by Tang China (618–907). In 751, the Arab–Chinese confrontation culminated in the Battle of Talas (in today's Kyrgyzstan), which ended with Arab victory. This put an end to China's westward expansion and consolidated Arab power in the region. On the other hand, it created contention between China and various Central Asian Muslim rulers over Islamicised Kashgar (Xinjiang).

Still, despite Islam being brought to Central Asia by the first generation of Muslims, the Islamicisation of the region took a different path from other parts of the Arab caliphate. This could be explained by the region's strong Iranian/Persian civilisational core which dated from the third millennium BC. Unlike the

Arabian Arabs, who prior to their adoption of Islam were mostly idol-worshipping nomads,[8] the bulk of the Ferghana valley's dwellers were sedentary. They were either direct descendants of, or borrowers from, the materially, culturally and religiously sophisticated ancient Persian empires, including the Achaemenid Empire (550 BC–330 BC), the Parthian Empire (247 BC–AD 224) and the Sassanid Empire (AD 224–651). The sustainability of this heritage throughout history is manifested, for example, in the wide celebration across present-day Central Asia of the ancient holiday of *Nowruz*,[9] which in terms of its popularity, scale and length of festivities much exceeds the main Islamic holidays of *Qurban-Bairam* (*'Id al-Adha*) and *Uraza-Bairam* (*'Id al-Fitr*). The strong Persian heritage also influenced the development of Central Asian Islamic scholarship and Sufism.

Another shaper of Central Asian Islam was the preponderance in the region of horse-breeding steppe nomads, who, albeit eventually Islamicised, continued to prioritise tribal rather than Islamic norms and practices and to maintain their partial adherence to shamanism. For this reason, their Islamicisation was largely carried out by itinerant Sufis, who, under the influence of Persian culture, employed music and dance in their teaching, as well as nomadic shamanist practices. There were also practical difficulties in the way of the caliphate's government carrying through its policies in Central Asia due to the region's geographical remoteness from Damascus or Baghdad, as well as its political fragmentation and the multi-vector political and commercial engagement of its rulers.

The role of the Sogdians and Samanids

A pertinent political embodiment of Central Asia's Iranian civilisational core was Sogdia, a loose urbanised and trade-centred polyethnic and culturally cosmopolitan polity. Between 1000 BC and the ninth century the eastern Iranian-speaking Sogdians effectively dominated Central Asian culture, trade and politics. During its lengthy existence, Sogdia withstood numerous external invasions, including, in the fourth century BC by Alexander the Great and, in the second century BC, by the Yueji nomads arriving from northwestern China and the nomadic people of Saka (Scythians) coming from the Eurasian Steppe.

For centuries the Sogdian merchants played a pivotal role in the Silk Road trade, which connected China to Khorezm, Balkh, India, Persia and, later, Byzantine and the Hellenised Middle East, on the one side, and to the Eurasian Steppe, on the other. Through their extensive travels across Eurasia and the Middle East, they acted as agents for the exchange and transfer of technical, administrative and scientific skills between different peoples along the Silk Road. Thus, in the sixth century they introduced an alphabet and basic administrative practices among some Turkic nomadic peoples of the Steppe, while in the eighth century they transported paper production technology from China to the Middle East and subsequently to Europe. Their paper-making know-how facilitated the creation of the world's largest library of the Middle Ages – *Dar al-Hikma* ('The House of Wisdom') – in Baghdad, the capital of the Abbasid caliphate. They also acted as cultural ambassadors by introducing Central Asians to music, cuisine, dress and belief systems from other parts of the world. The Sogdians were predominantly Buddhists themselves but they promoted a culture of ethnic and religious pluralism, respect for *the other* and adaptability to a rapidly changing political and economic environment.

The Sogdians created the distinctive Central Asian cultural blueprint which persisted, albeit with significant modifications, after the disappearance of Sogdia as a political entity in the eighth century. It defined the nature, essence and forms of the region's subsequent Islamicisation. Sogdia's fall was precipitated by the advance in the region of the Arabs and the temporary rupture of the Silk Road trade as a result of structural changes in the Chinese imperial economy, triggered by the An Lushan rebellion in China in 755.[10] In the following two centuries most Sogdians and some of Central Asia's other sedentary peoples who also spoke eastern Iranian languages were included in the Persian-dominated province of the Abbasid caliphate and became linguistically Persianised by switching from the eastern Iranian to western Iranian language (Farsi), which is dominant in present-day Iran. However, dwellers of Badakhshan in the Pamiri Mountains retained their eastern Iranian language. Among their contemporary descendants are the eastern Iranian-speaking Yaghnobis, a small community living along the mountain Yaghnob river in present-day Tajikistan.

The inclusion of Sogdia's domain in the Abbasid caliphate was conducive to the proliferation of Islam among its inhabitants. Sunni Islam became the official religion of the Samanid state (819–999), which was founded on the ex-Sogdia's lands, corresponding to present-day Uzbekistan, Tajikistan and northern Afghanistan, by Saman Khuda, a Persian noble of Sassanid heritage. The Samanids, although formally under Baghdad's suzerainty, soon acquired considerable autonomy and at the peak of their territorial expansion they ruled over Islamicised Khorezm which was situated in a large oasis area between the Amu Darya river and the Aral Sea, encompassing most of present-day Uzbekistan and Turkmenistan. The Samanids, like the Sogdians before them, played a central role in the Silk Road trade, encouraging the development of arts and sciences and pursuing a policy of cultural and religious diversity. Their capital cities of Samarqand (819–92) and Bukhara (892–999) began to rival Baghdad in terms of their advances in architecture, artisanship, ceramics and metalwork. They attracted such luminaries of the Middle Ages as Rudaki (858–941), Ferdowsi (940–1020), al-Biruni (973–1048) and Ibn Sina (Avicenna, 980–1037), who made major contributions to the development of medicine, geography, astronomy, physics and mathematics.

Under the Samanids, Bukhara and Samarqand turned into renowned centres of Islamic scholarship in the Muslim world. Bukhara was home to Muhammad ibn Isma'il al-Bukhari (810–69), the author of the Arabic-language compendium of *hadiths*, known as *Sahih al-Bukhari*, which came to be regarded as one of the most authentic *hadith* collections in the Muslim world. Samarqand acquired a special standing in *kalam* due to the contribution of Abu Mansur al-Maturidi (853–944), whose teaching, which became known as *Al-Maturidiia*, was summarised in his *Kitab al-Tawhid* (*Book of Monotheism*). It integrated old Persian dualist religions, local customary norms and beliefs, and the teaching of Abu Hanifa, the founder of the *Hanafi madhhab* of Sunni Islam, with the Basra-centred *Mu'tazilite* Islamic theology.[11] Al-Maturidi's main polemicists within the *Mu'tazilite* School were the Basra-based Abu al-Hasan al-Ash'ari (874–936), who followed the *Shafi'i madhhab*, and Ahmad ibn Muhammad al-Tahawi (d. 933) from Egypt, who, like al-Maturidi, adhered to the *Hanafi madhhab*. The main issues of contention were the meaning of the Islamic creed and the role in it of reason and rational thought, the origins of the Qur'an and the attributes of God. Unlike his opponents, al-Maturidi prioritised an internalised rather than ritualistic Islamic faith, put a stronger emphasis on philosophical reasoning rather than fatalism in Islam, and argued against the eternal nature of the Qur'an. Although al-Maturidi acknowledged the supremacy of God in a person's acts, he also recognised the individual capacity and will to act, and thus provided the doctrinal framework for the flexible, adaptable and syncretic *Hanafism*-based Central Asian Islam.

Compared with the eastern Iranian-speaking Sogdians, the Samanids were passionate Persophiles and promoted western Iranian (Farsi), which subsequently became the dominant language of Central Asian Islamic scholarship and Sufi teaching. The Samanids' linguistic imprint is evidenced by present-day Tajiks,[12] who, like Iranians, speak the western Iranian language. Incidentally, the political and intellectual elite in independent Tajikistan position the Samanids – whose political and cultural centres, Samarqand and Bukhara, are situated on the territory of neighbouring Uzbekistan – at the centre of the Tajikistani nation-building project. By comparison, the Pamiris reinforced their ethnolinguistic *otherness* by converting to *Isma'ili* Shi'a Islam.[13] The important role in the spread and organisational and intellectual consolidation of Isma'ilism in Badakhshan belonged to its renowned resident, Nasir Khusraw (1004–88).[14]

The Turkic nomads

Between the tenth and sixteenth centuries, the ethnolinguistic, socio-economic and cultural evolution of Central Asia, alongside wider Eurasia, was strongly influenced by a succession of militarily superior Turkic- and Mongolic-speaking nomads. Nevertheless, the role of the Turco-Mongol nomads in Central Asian and Eurasian history has not received due recognition among historians, who largely draw on sources[15] created by representatives of urban sedentary culture, who tended to downplay the role of the nomads. The lengthy political supremacy of the nomads in fact had a major transformative influence on the economic, social and political organisation of various peoples across Central Asia and wider Eurasia. It interconnected Central Asians with other Eurasians, including proto-Russians, thus creating notable structural and cultural affinities between them, while further distancing them from Europeans who did not have such experience.

Among the first major nomadic forces that swept across Central Asia in the tenth century were the Turkic (Uighur)-speaking Qarakhanids.[16] They put an end to the Samanid state and established their statehood formation – the Qarakhanid Khaganate (940–1040) with its centre in Kashgar – which absorbed most of the Samanid and Khorezmian territories. The Qarakhanids consisted of Qarkuqs, Yaghmas, Chighils and other Turkic-speaking tribes who originated in the western Altai region. In terms of their beliefs most Qarakhanids were originally Tengians, but in the middle of the eleventh century the Qarakhanid rulers adopted Islam, which they made the official religion in the Khaganate. They patronised Islamic scholarship and became renowned for their deference to *'ulama'* and their generous endowments on *madrasahs* and hospitals, as well as their confessional tolerance. In the middle of the eleventh century, the Qarakhanid Khaganate split into two parts – the western Qarakhanid Khanate (1040–1212), with its centre in Samarqand, and the eastern Qarakhanid Khanate (1040–early thirteenth century), with its centre in Taraz in present-day Kazakhstan.

The arrival of nomadic Qarakhanids in Central Asia marked the beginning of the shift from a town-centred Arab–Persian political and ideational culture towards the steppe-centred Turkic-Persian and nomadic–urban cultural and religious fusion. This shift was accompanied by the creeping ethnolinguistic Turkicisation of the region and the strengthening of shamanism and vernacular Sufism in Central Asian Islam. An important role in this process belonged to *Khoja* Ahmad Yasawi (1093–1166), a Turkic Sufi teacher and poet of the *Hanafi* School, who followed the teaching of *Khwaja* Yusuf Hamadani (1062–1141)[17] via *Khwaja* 'Abd al-Khaliq Gijduvani (d. 1179) from Bukhara. Residing in the town of Yasi (present-day Turkistan in southern Kazakhstan), which was part of the eastern Qarakhanid Khanate, Ahmad Yasawi introduced an oral, rather than book-based, version of Sufism, which was infused with elements of Turkic shamanist and musical traditions. He was also the first Sufi authority to use Turki (a local Turkic language) rather than Farsi in his Sufi teaching and poetry. After his death his followers formed the Yasawi *tariqat*, turning it into the agency of Islamicisation among various Turkic peoples. *Khoja* Yasawi was venerated by many Central Asian Turkic rulers, including Timur (Tamerlan, 1336–1405), who erected a magnificent mausoleum over his grave in Yasi. Ever since, Yasawi's tomb has been a major *ziiarat* among various Turkic peoples, who have regarded it as *Ekinshi Mekke* ('Second Mecca').

During the eleventh and twelfth centuries, the Qarakhanid domination in Central Asia became weakened by the increasing inroads by the Ghaznavids, the Persianised Turks and the Oghuz Turkic-speaking Seljuks in the west, and the Mongolic- and Sintic-speaking Qara Khitais in the east. In 977, the Ghaznavids, who were Islamicised Mamluks, broke away from Samanid rule and created the Ghaznavid Empire (977–1186), with its capital in Ghazni in eastern Afghanistan, which encompassed present-day Afghanistan and Pakistan. The Seljukid Empire (1037–1194) was established by Tughril Beg (1016–63) who adopted Sunni Islam. It was centred on Khorasan and stretched from the Hindu Kush to eastern Anatolia and the Persian Gulf. The Seljukids also adopted Persianised culture and patronised Islamic scholarship and *madrasahs*.

Of particular significance for Central Asia was Tughril Beg's assumption of the title of *Malik al-Mashriq wa-al-Maghrib* ('King of the East and West'), which he received in 1055 from the Abbasid caliph as a reward for the latter's liberation from the control of Shi'a Buyids (934–1062). This act, which symbolised the effective transfer of temporal power in the Muslim world from the Arabo-Iranian to the Turkic elites, provided Islamic consecration of Turkic political dominance in Central Asia. The ethnocultural impact of the Seljukid domination over western areas of present-day Central Asia is evidenced in Oghuz-speaking Turkmen and the magnificent mausoleum of Seljukid sultan Ahmad Sanjar (1085–1157) in Merv. The Seljukid presence in the region also encouraged the spread there of Sufism, especially of the Mawlawi *tariqat*, founded by the mystic and poet Jalal al-Din Muhammad Rumi (1207–73), a resident of Balkh, and of the *Khwajagan*, the spiritual forefathers of the future Naqshbandiis, whose leading representative was the aforementioned 'Abd al-Khaliq Gijduvani.

The Mongol nomads

In the early twelfth century the positions of Islamicised Qarakanids and Seljukids in Central Asia were shaken by the Buddhist Qara Khitai, the Khitan (Mongolic)-speaking nomads, who arrived from northern China. In 1124, their leader, Yelu Dashi (1094–1143), established the Qara Khitai Empire (1124–1218) on the territory corresponding to present-day Kyrgyzstan and northern Tajikistan. In the early thirteenth century, the Mongol presence in Central Asia received a powerful boost as a result of the invasion from northern Mongolia of nomadic troops under the leadership of Genghis Khan (1162–1227). Within a short period of time Genghis Khan conquered most of Central Asia, western China, Kievan Rus, the Caucasus, Turkey, Iran, Iraq, western Afghanistan and southwestern Pakistan which were incorporated into the vast Genghizid Empire (1206–1368).

The key to Genghis Khan's remarkable military success lay in his organisation of Mongol nomads from different tribes into a centralised professional army, consisting of military units of 10, 100, 1,000 and 10,000 men, and answerable directly to him and members of his family. He also integrated a large number of Central Asian and Eurasian nomads into his army and subsequently asserted control over the horse-power of the whole continent. Genghis Khan's military reforms contributed to considerable population shifts across Eurasia. For example, the Qipchak-speaking Kyrgyz[18] nomads, who originated in southern Siberia, were co-opted into the Genghizid army and relocated to western Moghulistan, corresponding to today's Kyrgyzstan. Following Genghis Khan's death the empire was split into four large parts: the Yuan Khanate (1271–1368); the Greater Horde, also known as the Golden Horde (1241–1502); the Ilkhanate (1256–1353); and the Chagatai Khanate (1225–1670). Most of Central Asia was included in the Chagatai Khanate, while present-day Turkmenistan, as well as most of Iran, Iraq, the Caucasus, western Afghanistan, southwestern Pakistan and Turkey became parts of the Ilkhanate. It is also significant that most of present-day Russia became part of the Golden Horde. The unification of Central Asia and the wider Eurasia within the Genghizid Empire had long-lasting implications for the whole continent. The fundamentals of the Genghizid-integrated pan-Eurasian political, economic and cultural system has been mobilised and instrumentalised by subsequent major Eurasian actors, including the Timurids and the Russians/Soviets. They arguably continue to shape socio-economic and political trajectories of post-Soviet Eurasia, including Central Asia and Russia.

Despite their centrality in the history of Eurasia, the Genghizids – like other nomads – have not received a full and balanced recognition of their importance due to the aforementioned prevalence of primary historical sources belonging to the representatives of urban/sedentary culture, which abounded in their largely negative portrayals. Thus, most chronologists from the city-based Turkic-Persian elite depicted them as bloodthirsty killers and plunderers, lacking any morality and cultural sophistication. Such accounts are at odds with the more favourable depiction of the Genghizids provided by Rashid al-Din, a minister under the Ilkhanids, in his *Jami' al-Tavarikh* (*Collection of Histories*). Rashid al-Din's positive portrayal was also echoed by some contemporary foreign explorers and travellers, including Marco Polo, who crossed Central Asia on his way from Venice to China. These suggested that the Genghizids ran their empire as a loose multi-ethnic and polyconfessional confederation. In Central Asia they relied strongly on local Muslim sedentary elites of Turkic, Iranian and Chinese origin. They especially valued multilingual individuals who helped to ensure the smooth functioning of their culturally and linguistically diverse empire. Also, with the passing of time the Genghizids became culturally and linguistically Persianised and Turkicised. Like preceding Central Asian rulers, they began to patronise the sciences, medicine, pharmacology, music, cuisine, the arts and Islamic scholarship.

The early Genghizids did not belong to a single religion, adhering to diverse beliefs which included elements of shamanism, Tengrism and Buddhism. An important principle of Genghizid governance was non-interference in the religious practices and beliefs of the various peoples of their vast empire. The Genghizids safeguarded the privileged positions of religious leaders and exempted them from taxation and public service. They introduced the practice of public debates between leaders of different persuasions.[19] In the middle of the fourteenth century the rulers of the Chagatai Khanate, Ilkhanate and the Golden Horde[20] converted to the Sufi version of Sunni Islam, which they made the official religion in their respective khanates. The Islamicisation of the Genghizid elite facilitated the spread of Islam among rank-and-file Mongols, Qipchaks and other nomadic peoples under their control. The main conduits of Islamic faith were the Sufi teachers and merchants of Bukhara, Samarqand, Urgench, Balkh and Volga Bulgaria. Of particular prominence during that time was the Kubrawi *tariqat*, founded by Najm al-Din Kubra (1145–1221) in Khorezm.[21] Over time, the Genghizids and ordinary Mongol nomads merged with indigenous Turkic and Iranian peoples and absorbed their Persianised Islamic culture.[22] A corollary was the further linguistic Turkicisation and Persianised Islamicisation of the various peoples of Central Asia. The only exceptions were the Tajiks who maintained their western Iranian (Farsi) language, as well as the Pamiris who preserved their eastern Iranian language, although both were often forced into Iranian-Turkic bilingualism.

The Timurids

In the middle of the fourteenth century the Genghizid Empire began to crumble because of its inability to further expand and growing strife within its elite. Among the first challengers to Genghizid supremacy in Eurasia was Muscovy's *kniaz* Dmitrii (1350–89), who in 1380 defeated the Golden Horde on the River Don in today's central Russia.[23] Muscovy's victory triggered the fragmentation of the Golden Horde, which precipitated its final defeat by Muscovy's *kniaz* Ivan III (1462–1505). In the east, the Genghizid Chagatai Khanate broke up into two parts. One, the Chagatai Ulus, comprised much of the Ferghana valley, while the other, Moghulistan,[24] included today's southeastern Kazakhstan, Kyrgyzstan and Xinjiang. Both parts were politically unstable because of inter-clan rivalries and their leaders' shifting alliances.

The situation changed with the ascendance of Timur (Tamerlane, 1336–1405), a Chagatai chieftain of Turkicised Mongol descent.[25] Timur, who lacked a direct blood link to Genghis Khan and therefore could not bear the title of 'khan', assumed the Islamic title of 'amir', which stood for *Amir al-Mu'minin* ('Leader of the Believers'), the once prestigious Arabic title of the caliph.[26] The absence of genealogical ties did not stop Timur from modelling himself on Genghis Khan in terms of imperial ambitions. Indeed, he succeeded in integrating much of the former Genghizid domain within the Timurid Empire (1370–1507), which included most of today's Central Asia, the Caucasus, Afghanistan, Pakistan, northern India, Iran, Turkey, Syria and Iraq. Unlike Genghis Khan, however, Amir Timur failed to subjugate the Moscow Principality, although he made several inroads into it. Amir Timur, like Genghis Khan, combined extreme brutality and ruthlessness towards his enemies and rivals with fairness and

Figure 1.1 Monument to Amir Timur (photograph by author, Tashkent, June 2013)

consideration towards ordinary people. He also made use of a similar practice of relying on indigenous Iranian and Turkic officials to run his vast empire as well as applying a *divide et impera* approach towards the Jalair,[27] the Aq-Qoyunlu,[28] the Qara-Qoyunlu[29] and other major Eurasian nomadic confederations.

Amir Timur succeeded in eclipsing Genghis Khan in his cultural and scientific endeavours. Perhaps for this reason contemporary chronologists and narrators were more sympathetic, or even complimentary, about him and his policies than they were in their accounts of Genghis Khan and his blood-related descendants. Under Timur's rule the capital city of Samarqand became a world centre for the sciences and arts and attracted talent from all over the Muslim world. Timur highly valued both knowledge and meritocracy and created congenial working conditions for gifted scientists, poets, artists and architects. His grandson and Sultan Ulugh Beg (1394–1449), who was himself a brilliant mathematician and astronomer, built the famous Samarqand Observatory, which still today continues to strike its visitors by its scientific advances. Among other magnificent architectural remnants of the Timurid period are the Registan, which is framed by the *madrasahs* of Ulugh Beg, Tilia-Kori and Sher-Dor, as well as the mosque of Bibi-khanym and the necropolis of Shahi-Zinda in Samarqand; Aq-Sarai palace in Shahrisabz in present-day southern Uzbekistan; and the mausoleum of *Khoja* Ahmad Yasawi in Turkistan in southern Kazakhstan.

Amir Timur and his descendants were also noted for their innovative language and religious policies. During the Timurid period the Persian-Turkic bilingualism of the ruling elite became the norm, while Turki was made an official language. Among adamant promoters of Turki was the famous poet Mir Ali Shir Nava'i (1441–1501), a native of Herat in northwestern Afghanistan, who advocated the cultural equality of Persian and Turki and wrote his poetry in both languages. Amir Timur, who adhered to *Al-Maturidiia* and the Kubrawi Sufism, pursued a policy of religious tolerance and encouraged public debates on vital philosophical and theological issues. Thus, Timur was personally engaged in a debate with Ibn Khaldun (1332–1406), a prominent North African Islamic scholar of the Maliki School of Sunnism and a follower of the Ash'ari rationalist school, who is regarded as a forebear of modern sociology and political economy. It is worth noting that the Timurids' culture of religious tolerance and intellectual openness presented a stark contrast to the Catholic Inquisition and, later on, the Catholic–Protestant antagonism in Europe.

At the same time, Amir Timur contributed to the increased role of Islam for political legitimisation purposes in order compensate for his genealogical weakness. For this purpose he brought a number of highly respected *'ulama'* and Sufi teachers into his inner circle. It is no coincidence therefore that during his reign Central Asia witnessed the emergence of the world's largest Sufi *tariqat* – the Naqshbandiia. It was named after *Khwaja* Baha al-Din Naqshband (1318–89), a Persianised Bukharan. He, like Ahmad al-Yasawi, followed the Sufi school

Figure 1.2 Registan (photograph by author, Samarqand, June 2013)

of *Khwaja* Yusuf Hamadani (d. 1147).[30] His teaching, or path, drew on the Central Asian Islamic tradition of flexibility, which enabled his followers to combine Sufi mysticism and asceticism with engagement in various mundane activities. At its core were three main principles: 'reclusion in the community'; 'externally amongst people'; and 'internally with God'. A central element of his

Sufi practice was *dhikr-i khafi*, which contrasted with the *dhikr-i zhahri* practised by other Sufis. Baha al-Din's Sufi teaching and practice allowed his followers to keep their faith in their hearts while participating fully in economic and political life. Subsequently, some Naqshbandiis even formed dynasties of wealthy landowners, merchants and government officials; arguably, this pluralistic and flexible nature of the Naqshbandiia has been behind its continuing global appeal.[31]

The organisational and doctrinal institutionalisation of the Naqshbandii *tariqat* and its political and economic growth occurred under Timur's successors. A key role in this process belonged to *Khwaja* 'Ubaidallah Ahrar (1404–90), a confidant of Sultan Abu Sa'id (1424–69) and his son, Sultan Ahmad (d. 1494). Sultan Abu Sa'id was Timur's great-great-grandson and Ulugh Beg's nephew. Both were also remembered for their sophisticated irrigation and taxation projects, as well as architectural splendour. Ever since, the Naqshbandi *tariqat* has been closely involved with ruling elites and engaged in their major economic and business endeavours. The Timurids, then, infused political loyalty into the key characteristics of a distinctive Central Asian Islam. It is perhaps symptomatic that the post-Soviet leadership of Uzbekistan chose Amir Timur, rather than Genghis Khan or Abulkhair, the first Uzbek khan, as the forefather of the modern Uzbeks.

Uzbeks, Kazakhs and Shaibanids

In the late fifteenth century the Timurid Empire went into decline. The last Timurid ruler, who effectively controlled the Ferghana valley and Khorasan, was the aforementioned Sultan Abu Sa'id. His successors, however, failed to withstand invasions by various Turkic, Kalmyk and other nomads and to prevent the empire's disintegration. Some Timurids migrated to the Indian subcontinent, where they founded the Mughal Empire (1526–1857).[32] Those who remained in Central Asia were forced to succumb to the rule of new nomadic suzerains. Among these was Abulkhair (1412–68), the leader of the Turkic tribal confederation of *Dasht-i-Qipchak* ('Great Steppe'),[33] who claimed his descent from Shaiban, the fifth son of Juchi (1181–1227), the Golden Horde's khan. In 1426, Abulkhair was elected khan of the tribal confederation which came to be known under the general name of the Uzbeks.[34] Under Abulkhair's leadership the Uzbeks first established their control over the southern Urals and Siberia and then began to make inroads into the Ferghana valley, where their advance was countered by the Kalmyk nomads from western Mongolia.[35] Following Abulkhair's defeat in 1456 by the Kalmyks, several Uzbek tribes switched their allegiance to his Genghizid rivals, Girei Khan (r. 1456–73) and Janibeg Khan (r. 1473–80), who asserted their dominance over today's central Kazakhstan (formerly the White Horde). These Uzbek defectors became known as Kazakhs.[36] Significantly, the post-Soviet leadership of Kazakhstan regard Girei Khan and Janibeg Khan as the forefathers of the Kazakh nation.

The Uzbeks' advance into the Ferghana valley acquired a new momentum under the rule of Abulkhair's grandson, Amir Muhammad Shaibani (1451–1510). Having conquered Samarqand in 1501 and Herat in 1507, Shaibani established his control over most of the Ferghana valley and eastern Khorasan. In order to distance himself politically and culturally from the Timurids he chose Bukhara as his capital. After the Shaibanids incorporated northern Afghanistan into their realm, they kept moving their capital between Bukhara, Balkh and Samarqand. Despite the Shaibanids' animosity towards the Timurids, they did not significantly deviate from the latter's political, economic and cultural policies. As in the case of the Timurids and Genghizids, their state presented a loose polyethnic and multi-confessional confederation, and their administrative apparatus was dominated by Persian- and Turkic-speaking urbanites. They also continued with ambitious irrigational and infrastructural projects and patronised scientists, architects, artists, craftsmen and poets. The most notable in this respect were the reigns of Muhammad Shaibani (r. 1500–10), 'Ubaidallah (r. 1533–9) and 'Abdallah (r. 1583–98), which were marked by considerable advances in agriculture, the construction of dams and bridges, and the expansion of trade. The Shaibanids reinvigorated the lucrative Silk Road, which had declined in the second half of the fourteenth century, and extended it to Russia and Mughal India. They also oversaw the building of new *caravansarais* (roadside trade stations).

The Shaibanids' religious policy also drew on the Timurid model of confessional pluralism and religious tolerance. Having converted to Sunni Islam of the *Hanafi madhhab*, they welcomed an intra-Islamic debate between *'ulama'*, Sufi sheikhs and other Islamic authorities. Like the Timurids, they relied on Islamic authorities to strengthen their ideological credentials. The building of the infamous *Mir-i Arab Madrasah* in Bukhara was authorised by Amir 'Ubaidallah, who gave it the name of his Sufi mentor, Mir-i Arab (Sheikh 'Abdullah Yamani). Since then *Mir-i Arab Madrasah* has been the major centre of professional Islamic training in Central Asia and wider Eurasia.

In the Shaibanid period there was further strengthening of the political and economic role of the Naqshbandi *tariqat* and new Naqshbandi dynasties were formed. Although Muhammad Shaibani belonged to the Yasawi *tariqat*, most of his successors were Naqshbandiis. They safeguarded the symbolic centrality of the shrine of *Khwaja* Baha al-Din Naqshband near Bukhara, albeit they favoured the tomb of another great Naqshbandii, *Khwaja* 'Ubaidallah Ahrar near Samarqand. Under their patronage, the latter was de facto elevated to the official centre of the Naqshbandi *tariqat* and the Ahraris turned into a dynasty of politically influential sheikhs, saints, wealthy merchants, manufacturers and *mutavallis* of extensive *waqfs*. Amir 'Abdallah granted the Ahraris the hereditary title of *sheikhs-ul-Islam* of Samarqand.

Among other new influential Naqshbandi dynasties were descendants of Sa'id Ahmad *Khwaja* Kasani (1461–1542) from the town of Kasan in the northern part of the Ferghana valley, who became known as *Makhdum-i Azam* ('The Great Master'). Subsequently, *Makhdum-i Azam* acquired a sizeable following among Uzbeks, Tajiks and Chagataids in Kashgar and his tomb near Samarqand turned into a major *ziiorat.* Another influential Naqshbandi dynasty originated from *Khwaja* Sad (d. 1589), a son and successor of Muhammad Sultan Juibari (1481–1563) and a friend of Amir 'Abdallah. His tomb near Bukhara, later named Char Bakr, became the spiritual centre of the Juibari Naqshbandiis. The Juibaris, like the Ahraris, were granted hereditary rights to the position of *sheikh-ul-Islam* in Bukhara, which they held until the end of the nineteenth century. The Shaibanid-sponsored proliferation of Naqshbandi Sufism occurred alongside the grassroots 'Qipchakisation' of Central Asian Islam, resulting in the strengthening of its shamanist component. Among nomads its main bearers were *khojas*, who embodied the oral, rather than book-based, Sufi Islam, intertwined with shamanism and customary norms.

Central to the subsequently developed Islamic practices were *ziiarats/ziiorots* to *mazars/mozors* related to Sufi sheikhs/*khojas/pirs*, *avliio*, ancestors and natural sacralised objects. Sufi sheikhs and *avliio* became viewed as the Prophet Muhammad's spiritual successors, thus possessing special relations with God. It was widely believed that these perceived relations enabled them to conduct *barakah* and to perform miracles and assist those who appealed to them for help. These beliefs were accompanied by intrinsically shamanist rituals, which appealed to feelings, dreams and revelations and therefore had a stronger hold on people's psyches than mosques. Importantly, these practices provided them with personal exoteric and mystical independence from the harsh natural, economic and political realities.

At the turn of the seventeenth century the Shaibanid state went into decline, prompted by internal strife and changing regional as well as global conditions, including the rise of technologically superior Europe. Of particular significance was the conflict between the Sunni Shaibanids and Iran's ruling Oghuz (Azerbaijani) dynasty of Safavids (1501–1736) who switched from Sunni to Shi'a Islam. The ensuing religious conflict between the Sunni Shaibanids and Shi'a Safavids was aggravated by their rivalry over the control of Khorasan. The antagonism between Shaibanid Central Asia and Safavid Iran outlived both Shaibanids and Safavids. In 1740, Khorezm and some other parts of Central Asia were invaded by Nadir Shah (1688–1747) of Iran and for several decades was part of the Iranian Empire under the Turkoman dynasty of Afsharids (1736–96). The acrimonious relations between Shi'a Iran and various Central Asian polities persisted until the late nineteenth century, when Central Asia succumbed to Russian control. In the long run, the breakdown of the cultural and religious bond between Iran and Central Asia led to their considerable mutual

Figure 1.3 Map of Central Asia in the seventeenth century

isolation. In particular, it triggered the gradual weakening of the Persian book-based component of Central Asian Islam and the corresponding strengthening of its Turkic Qipchak component. It also contributed to the rapprochement between successive Central Asian polities and the Sunni Ottoman Empire, the sultans of which, from the early sixteenth century, assumed the title of caliphs and positioned themselves as champions and defenders of Sunni Muslims across the world.

Notes

1. For a detailed discussion of the emergence, historical evolution and complexities of the notion of 'Central Asia', see Gorshenina 2014.
2. For discussion of the Great Game, see Hopkirk 1992; Sergeev 2013.
3. See, for example, Golden 2011, p. 2; Soucek 2000, p. ix; Privratsky 2001, p. 2; Erturk 1999, p. 3.
4. See, for example, Sinor 1969; Soucek 2000; Golden 2011; Di Cosmo 2009.
5. 'Central Asia', see at: https://www.britannica.com/place/Central-Asia, last accessed 22 September 2016.
6. It is significant that compared with the Persian form of Zoroastrianism, which does not refer to idols, idol-worshipping was an integral part of Central Asian Zoroastrianism, as well as of some other local belief systems.

7. Tengrism or Tengrianism is the ancient belief system among various Turkic- and Mongolic-speaking peoples of Eurasia who seek to achieve harmony with their surrounding world. It has been practiced since the fourth millennium BC. In doctrinal terms it represents a synthesis of shamanism, animism, totemism, and elements of monotheism and polytheism. Its main symbol is the Blue Sky. Following the disintegration of the USSR and the decline of the Communist ideology there has been some revival of Tengrism in Kazakhstan, Kyrgyzstan, Mongolia and Russia's autonomous republics of Tatarstan, Buriatiia, Sakha, Khakasiia and Tuva.
8. The Prophet Muhammad and his close followers, however, originated from the trade communities of Mecca and Medina (Yathrib). See more on the birth of Islam in Kennedy 2015.
9. *Nowruz* (lit. 'New Day' in Persian) is an ancient holiday that marks the day of the vernal equinox. It symbolises the beginning of spring and the cyclic nature of life and the contemplative worldview. It has been widely celebrated for over 3,000 years among various peoples in Central and western Asia, the Caucasus, the Black Sea region and the Balkans.
10. During the An Lushan rebellion in 755–65, the Sogdian ruling elite backed the anti-government forces. For more on the implications of the An Lushan rebellion for the Sogdians, see Pulleyblank 1955.
11. See more on *Mu'tazilites* in Martin, Woodward and Atmaja 1997.
12. The etymology of the name 'Tajik' is ambivalent. Some derive it from the Persian word 'Tazi', meaning 'Arab', which was used by locals to describe all newly arrived Muslims. Others relate it to the word 'Tat', which was used from the eleventh century by various Turkic-speakers to describe Iranian-speakers.
13. *Isma'ilism* is a branch within Shi'a Islam. It was named after Muhammad ibn Isma'il (740–813), who was the seventh imam, after 'Ali (d. 661), and is perceived by his followers as the true imam. For this reason *Isma'ilis* were also called 'Seveners'. They are different from 'Twelvers', who represent the largest branch within Shi'a Islam and who regard the twelfth imam Muhammad ibn Hasan (b. 868) as the true imam, expecting his return as *mahdi* ('a prophesied redeemer of Islam'). The current (forty-ninth) leader of the *Isma'ilis* of Badakhshan is Aga Khan IV (b. 1936), who assumed this position in 1957. See more on *Isma'ilism* in Daftary 1992.
14. Nasir Khusraw, a native of the village Qabodiyon in present-day Tajikistan, was a renowned encyclopaedist and Islamic scholar. He served at the Ghaznavid court and, following the arrival of the Seljuks, embarked on travels across the Middle East. He described his travel impressions and experiences in his famous *Safarnama* (*A Book of Travels*). Nasir Khusrow converted from Sunni Islam to *Isma'ilism* in Egypt which was under the *Isma'ili* Fatimid caliphate (909–1171). See more on Nasir Khusraw in Hunsberger 2003.
15. Among the few exceptions was *Divanu Lugat-it-Turk* (*Dictionary of Turkic Languages*) which was written in the 1070s by the Turkic lexicographer Mahmud al-Kashgari.
16. See more on Qarakhanids in Soucek 2000, pp. 83–92.
17. Sheikh Yusuf Hamadani was born in Merv. He has been one of the most venerated Central Asia's Sufis bearing the honorific title of *khwaja*. Subsequently, this title became the hallmark of Central Asian Naqshbandiis, who were also known under the alternative name of *Tariqa-i-Khwajagan* ('Order of the Khwajas').
18. In Turkic languages 'Kyrgyz' means 'we are forty'. It is believed that the name related to the forty clans of *Manas*, a legendary hero who united forty regional tribes against Orkhon Uighurs, who in 744 established the Uighur Khanate (744–840) with its centre in Mongolia. At the beginning of the ninth century, the Uighurs dominated present-day Kyrgyzstan and the adjacent areas.

19. This policy was implemented in all Genghizid khanates. For example, in the Moscow Principality the political and economic rise of the Russian Orthodox Church occurred during Muscovy's inclusion in the Golden Horde.
20. The first convert to Islam among the Genghizid rulers was the Golden Horde's Khan Berke, who adopted Islam in 1257 under the influence of Saif al-Din al-Bakharzi, a Sufi sheikh from Bukhara. However, only in 1320 was Islam made the official religion in the Golden Horde by Khan Uzbek.
21. See more on the Kubrawi *tariqat* in DeWeese 2012, pp. 58–94.
22. See more on the implications of the lengthy Turco-Mongol rule over Central Asia in Grousset 1970.
23. In appreciation of this victory, which symbolised the rise of Muscovy, *kniaz* Dmitrii became known as Dmitrii Donskoi ('Dmitrii of the Don').
24. The name 'Moghulistan' reflected only the Mongol origins of the ruling elite, while the bulk of its inhabitants were various Turkic peoples, or Turkicised Mongols.
25. See more on Amir Timur in Manz 1989.
26. For the same reasons Timur's descendants, including Babur, the founder of the Mughal Empire (1526–1857), also assumed non-Genghizid titles such as 'amir' or 'sultan'. Later on this was also the case with the Shaibanid and the Bukharan rulers who preferred the title of 'amir'/'emir'.
27. The Jalair were Mongolic-speaking tribal people who inhabited the present-day Zabaikal'skii *kraii* of Russia.
28. Aq-Quyunlu (lit. 'White Sheep', 1378–1501) was a Persianised Sunni Oghuz tribal confederation that dominated northern Iraq, part of Iran, eastern Turkey, Armenia and Azerbaijan.
29. Qara-Qoyunlu (lit. 'Black Sheep', 1375–1468) was the rival tribal confederation to the Aq-Qounlu. In different periods it controlled present-day eastern Iran, Armenia and Azerbaijan.
30. Baha al-Din's immediate Sufi teachers were Muhammad Baba Sammasi (d. 1354) and Amir Kulal (d. 1370), who was *murid* of Baba Sammasi (d. 1370). Sammasi was the fifth *khalifa* to Sheikh Yusuf Hamadani.
31. This assessment is based on my findings within an ESRC-funded research project titled 'Ethnicity, Politics, and Transnational Islam: A Study of an International Sufi Order', which investigated the spiritual, social and political role of the Naqshbandi *tariqat* in Eurasia, the Middle East, Western Europe and the United States, 1999–2001.
32. Babur (1483–1530), the founder of the Mughal Empire, was a Timurid on the agnatic side and a Genghizid on the cognatic side.
33. The name 'Qipchaks' in relation to these Turkic nomads was used in contemporary Arab, Persian and Turkic sources. In Russian sources they were referred to as 'Polovtsy'. Nowadays Qipchaks are represented by Central Asia's Kazakhs, Kyrgyz and Qarakalpaks; the Caucasus' Nogai, Balkars, Karachai and Kumyks; and Russia's Tatars and Bashkirs.
34. The etymology of the name 'Uzbek' is a matter of debate, although it is more likely to derive from Uzbek (d. 1341), khan of the Golden Horde.
35. Although the Kalmyks were Mongolic-speakers, they represented a different group of Genghizids. They are also referred to as western Mongols. Oirats or Jungars are referred to as eastern Mongols.
36. It is believed that the name 'Kazakh' has the same etymology as the Russian 'Kazak' and the English 'Cossack'.

Selected reading

Primary sources

Ibn Battuta (fl. 1303–68) [Rihla; Arabic], ed. and trans. C. Defremery and B. R. Sanguinetti as *Voyages d'Ibn Battuta*, vol. 3, Paris, 1854; English trans. H. A. Gibb as *The Travels of Ibn Battuta*, vol. 3, Cambridge, 1971–95.

Nava'i, Mir Ali Shir (1441–1501), *Muhakamat Al-Lughatain* [Turki] (*Judgement between the Two Languages*), ed. and trans. R. Devereux, Leiden, 1966.

Polo, Marco (1254–1323), *The Book of Ser Marco Polo, the Venetian, Concerning the Kingdoms and Marvels of the East*, ed. and trans. H. Yule, 2 vols, London, 1871.

Rashid al-Din (1247–1318), *Jami' Al-Tavarikh* [Persian] (*The Compendium of History*), trans. J. A. Boyle, New York and London, 1971.

Secondary sources

Barthold, W. (Bartold, V. V.) (1968), *Turkestan Down to the Mongol Invasion*, in C. E. Bosworth (ed.), 3rd edn, Exeter: Short Run Press.

Bosworth, C. E. (1996), *The New Islamic Dynasties: A Chronological and Genealogical Manual*, Edinburgh: Edinburgh University Press.

Bregel, Y. E. (2003), *Historical Atlas of Central Asia*, Leiden: Brill.

DeWeese, D. (1994), *Islamization and Native Religion in the Golden Horde: Baba Tukles and Conversion to Islam in Historical and Epic Tradition*, University Park, PA: Pennsylvania State University Press.

DeWeese, D. (2012), *Studies of Sufism in Central Asia*, Farnham: Ashgate.

Di Cosmo, N. (ed.) (2009), *The Cambridge History of Inner Asia: The Chinggisid Age*, Cambridge: Cambridge University Press.

Frye, R. N. (1975), 'The Sāmānids', in R. N. Frye (ed.), *The Cambridge History of Iran, vol. 4: From the Arab Invasion to the Saljuqs*, Cambridge: Cambridge University Press, pp. 136–61.

Geiss, P. G. (2003), *Pre-Tsarist and Tsarist Central Asia: Communal Commitment and Political Order in Change*, London: Routledge.

Golden, P. B. (2011), *Central Asia in World History*, Oxford: Oxford University Press.

Gorshenina, S. (2014), *L'invention de l'Asie central: Histoire du concept de la Tartarie à l'Eurasie*, Paris: Librarie Droz.

Grousset, R. [1952] (1970), *The Empire of the Steppe: A History of Central Asia*, New Brunswick, NJ: Rutgers University Press.

Manz, B. F. (1989), *The Rise and Rule of Tamerlane*, Cambridge: Cambridge University Press.

Martin, R. C., Woodward M. R. and Atmaja, D. S. (1997), *Defenders of Reason in Islam: Mu'atazilizm from Medieval School to Modern Symbol*, London: Oneworld.

Sinor, D. (1990), *The Cambridge History of Early Inner Asia*, Cambridge: Cambridge University Press.

Soucek, S. (2000), *A History of Inner Asia*, Cambridge: Cambridge University Press.

CHAPTER 2

The Russian conquest and rule of Central Asia

Central Asia and Russia in the Middle Ages

As discussed in Chapter 1, Russians were not complete strangers to Central Asians. Geographically, they inhabited different flanks of the same Eurasian space, centred on the steppe which lacked significant sea or mountain barriers. For this reason, up until the seventeenth century both Russians and various peoples of Central Asia had been similarly affected by regular influxes of Turkic- and Mongolic-speaking nomads, emanating from the Central Eurasian steppes. Among the ethnolinguistic reminders of these pan-Eurasian nomadic migrations are, for example, various indigenous peoples of Mongolian and Qipchak/Turkic origins in today's Russia. The former include Buriats, Tuvans and Kalmyks, who populate Russia's autonomous republics of Buriatiia, Tuva and Kalmykiia and profess Buddhism, Tengrism and shamanism. Russia's Qipchaks are largely represented by Tatars and Bashkirs of the Volga-Urals and the north Caucasus' Karachai, Balkars, Kumyks and Nogai, who are linguistically close to Central Asia's Kazakhs and Kyrgyz and are also similarly affiliated to the *Hanafi madhhab* of Sunni Islam.

The shared historical trajectories of Muscovites/Russians and Central Asians created considerable political, economic and cultural similarities between them. As well as the major regional powers such as the Christian Byzantine and Islamic Abbasid caliphate, a formative influence on the various eastern Slavic peoples who formed the ethnolinguistic core of Russians was their politically and economically more advanced Qipchak/Turkic neighbours. Among them were the Khazars of the Khazar Khaganate (650–1048), situated in the Caucasus and the Caspian Sea basin, and the Volga Bulgars of the Bulgar state (732–1236), which roughly corresponded to present-day Tatarstan and Bashkortostan of the Russian Federation.[1] From 922 onwards Volga Bulgaria was officially Muslim,[2] while various proto-Russian polities still remained pagan. The decision by Volga Bulgaria's *baltavar* (leader) Almush Almas-Khan (d. 925) to convert to Islam was made in order to distance his people from the Judaist Khazar Khaganate and to ensure the support of the Abbasid caliphate. The same geopolitical logic was behind the decision of Vladimir (960–1015), the *kniaz* of Kievan Rus, to adopt Orthodox Christianity in 988 so as to secure the backing of Orthodox Christian Byzantine in his regional rivalry with the Judaist Khazaria and Muslim Bulgaria.

The politically motivated Christianisation of the Russians' ethnic ancestors did not seriously alter their predominant economic, political and military engagement with their Islamicised and pagan Turkic neighbours. Throughout the eleventh and twelfth centuries, their major Eurasian opponents were the Oghuz Turkic-speaking nomadic western Kangars (in Russian, Pechenegs) and the Qipchak Turkic-speaking nomadic Cumans (in Russian, *Polovtsy*). While the former controlled southern provinces of the Khazar Khaganate, the latter effectively dominated the *Dasht-i-Qipchak*, which stretched between the Danube and Irtysh rivers. As discussed earlier, in the early thirteenth century Rus, alongside Central Asian and other Eurasian polities, became constituent parts of the expansive multi-ethnic and polyconfessional Genghizid Empire, which was officially Islamicised in the mid-fourteenth century. Rus constituted the core of the Golden Horde.

The over two centuries-long joint existence of Rus and various Central Asian polities within the Genghizid Islamicised space channelled their political, socio-economic and ethnocultural development along some common lines, which subsequently accounted for notable similarities in their political, military, economic, juridical and tax organisation, court and diplomatic ceremonies, as well as culture and belief systems.[3] These commonalities included the extreme concentration of power at the centre, the merging of the ruling clan with the state, and the supremacy of personal relations between ruler and subject over any other relations. It is symptomatic that the elevation of the Moscow Principality to being Rus' leading polity occurred in 1363 under the Genghizids' watch. Subsequently, and still within the Genghizid political context, the proto-Rus state proper was born, when the Grand Muscovy *kniaz* Ivan III (1440–1505) claimed all-Rus authority, for which he later became known as the *sobiratel'* ('gatherer') of the Rus land. Later on the Genghizid legacy also charted the state-building process in Russia and Central Asia along the lines of polyethnic and polyconfessional empires with ill-defined borders. This was in contrast to contemporary France, England, Spain and some other ethnicity-based European polities with their well-defined borders, which were subsequently enshrined in the Peace of Westphalia of 1648.

The common Genghizid experience of the Rus and Central Asian polities was arguably behind the similar predominantly tribute–redistributory economic relationship between the centre and periphery. The Genghizid nomadic practice of individual ownership of livestock alongside collective ownership of land and water was translated into the extreme, although not stable, power of the state, personified by its ruler, and the relative weakness of both private landowners and cities, which embodied the rulers' power rather than economic activity. This economic model differed from that in contemporary Western Europe, where the economic power of states/monarchs could be, and often was, challenged by the Church and regional gentry, as well as by politically and economically strong cities, which enjoyed considerable autonomy from monarchs in the form of their representative bodies – the early precursors of civil society.

In the ethnocultural sphere, the common Genghizid legacy accounted for a strong Turkic component, as well as a notable Mongol element, in the ethnic identities of Russians and Central Asians. In the case of Russians, these were fused with the dominant eastern Slavic component, along with Finno-Ugric and Varangian/Viking ethnic influences. With Central Asians, the dominant Turkic component was combined with Iranian (Sogdian and Samanid) and Mongol ethnocultural influences. In the ideational sphere, both proto-Russians and Central Asians retained common pagan and shamanist practices despite their official adherence to different religions – Orthodox Christianity and Islam. At the grassroots level, the common Genghizid tutelage was conducive to the better mutual awareness of various peoples of Rus and Central Asia, as well as their mutual borrowings in the field of language, behavioural norms, architecture, arts, music, entertainment, cuisine and costume. The Genghizid khans' non-interference in the religious affairs of their multi-confessional subjects created a relative religious pluralism across Eurasia. It is indicative that it was during the Genghizid reign that the Rus Orthodox Church acquired its economic and political prominence. It was also not unusual for Genghizid Muslim khans to ally with Rus Orthodox *kniazes* against their common Muslim adversaries.[4] Such religious relativism in favour of political expediency was in contrast to the political centrality of religion in contemporary Europe, which witnessed Crusades, the Catholic Inquisition and protracted Catholic–Protestant internecine warfare and which was culturally poised in opposition to Asia and Islam.

Muscovy's break away from Genghizid tutelage in 1480 marked the birth of proto-Russia as a state with its capital in Moscow. In their quest to culturally distance themselves from their former Muslim masters, Rus' rulers began to invoke their Christian Orthodox *otherness*. In 1511, the Pskovian monk Filofei in his letter to the Grand Muscovy *kniaz* Vasilii (1479–1533) introduced the idea of Moscow as the 'Third Rome' after the fall of Constantinople (the 'Second Rome') to the Ottoman Turks in 1453.[5] In 1547, Vasilii III's son Ivan IV (Ivan the Terrible, 1530–84) adopted the Byzantine title of 'tsar' and embarked on Rus' symbolic Byzantinisation. Among the implications of this policy was the strengthening of the political role of the Rus Orthodox Church and the Rus state's assault on Genghizid dignitaries and the Islamic clergy. In 1552, Ivan the Terrible conquered the neighbouring Genghizid principality, the Kazan Khanate,[6] populated by the Tatars.[7] In 1556, he defeated the Genghizid Astrakhan Khanate. In 1557, the Rus troops crushed the Genghizid Nogai Horde (Khanate),[8] situated between the Volga river and the Urals, and in 1598 they defeated the Genghizid Khanate of Siberia.

The territories of these khanates were subsequently transformed into Rus' provinces, while many *madrasahs* and mosques were either destroyed or converted into Orthodox churches. Muslim clergy were subjected to persecution, while Tatars and other Muslims were exiled from Kazan and other major cities. To some extent Muscovy's demonstrative attack on the Genghizid elite, Muslim clergy and ordinary Muslims symbolised Rus' assertion of its political and religious superiority over its recent Muslim suzerains. A few decades after the conquest of Kazan, when the Russian tsars had consolidated their military and political rule, they significantly moderated their anti-Genghizid and anti-Islamic stance. They restored land and other ownership rights to a large number of Genghizid descendants and co-opted many Tatars into the Russian hereditary nobility. It is emblematic that the Russian Tsar Boris Godunov (1551–1605), unlike his Rurik predecessors,[9] was a descendant of a Genghizid *murza*. Overall, Rus' conquest of the Genghizid khanates represented the geopolitical rearrangement of western Eurasia in favour of the Russian state.

Russia's inroads into Central Asia

In the sixteenth and seventeenth centuries the Russian state, in spite of its official Byzantinisation, remained Eurasia-centred and continued to function largely along Genghizid political and economic lines. Internationally, it prioritised its relations with various ex-Genghizid Muslim polities, as well as with the Muslim Ottoman Empire and Safavid Iran.[10] Russia's political Eurasianism was mirrored in her continued cultural distancing from Europe, the Russian political and, to a considerable degree, intellectual elite, like their Central Asian and other post-Genghizid counterparts, missing out on the Renaissance experience which contributed much of the basis for modern Western ideas of liberty, progress, human rights and civil society. This was reflected in the differing Russian and European historiographies which emerged in that period. Thus, contemporary Russian historiographers tended to emphasise the Scythian (Iranian),[11] nomadic Turkic, Slavic and Byzantine ingredients of Russian cultural identity, while their Central Asian counterparts similarly referred to the Iranian, Turkic or Mongolic cultural core of Central Asians. By contrast, European historiographers tended to culturally anchor Europeans in the ancient Greek and Latin heritage and perceived both Orthodox Muscovites and Muslim Asians as exotic and inferior *others*.

However, Russia's political and cultural Eurasianism stumbled in the early eighteenth century with the advent of Tsar Peter the Great (1672–1725), a passionate and determined Europhile. Peter's quest to break Russia away from her intrinsic Eurasian-ness and bring her into civilised Europe was accompanied by the move of the Russian capital from Moscow, located in Russia's heartland, to newly founded St Petersburg, situated on Russia's northwestern frontier. Peter the Great's pro-Europe drive introduced an existential duality into Russia's political and cultural identity, encouraging the adoption by the Russian elite of European superiority attitudes towards Central Asian, Caucasian and other Eurasian Muslims. This civilisational discourse became a factor in the Russian advance into the Kazakh-dominated Great Steppe and into Central Asia, centred on the historical *Mawarannahr* and Khorezm.

Russia's annexation of these regions was preceded by her gradual territorial expansion towards the Urals and beyond. As noted earlier, in the course of the sixteenth century the Russian state absorbed the Urals and Siberia. Its eastward advance was consolidated through the building of a sequence of fortification lines which linked newly founded militarised towns: Troisk (1583), Yaik (1584, Ural'sk from 1775), Tumen' (1586), Tobol'sk (1587) and Tomsk (1604). Russia's next major thrust eastwards occurred in the eighteenth century and was marked by the establishment of the Orenburg, Irtysh and Yaik (Ural'sk) fortification lines which linked the towns of Omsk (1717), Semipalatinsk (1718), Ust'-Kamenogorsk (1720) and Orenburg (1734). Finally, the completion in 1811 of the Iletsk fortification line enabled Russia to encroach on the traditional habitat of the Kazakh nomads in the Great Steppe, which they preferred to call the 'Kazakh' or 'Kirghiz' Steppe.

By that time the Kazakhs, who largely adhered to *khoja*-based Sufi Islam, were divided into three major tribal confederations: the *Ulu Juz* (the Great Horde), the *Orta Juz* (the Middle Horde) and the *Kichi Juz* (the Small Horde). The largest was the *Orta Juz* which roughly included around 40 per cent of Kazakh nomads, the *Ulu Juz* about 35 per cent and the *Kichi Juz* around 25 per cent. The migration area of the *Ulu Juz* roughly corresponded to present-day southern Kazakhstan, the *Orta Juz* dominated central Kazakhstan and the *Kichi Juz* western Kazakhstan. Within each *Juz* Kazakhs were sub-divided into *taips*, each of which in turn included several clans-*rus*, linked by common genealogy. Each clan consisted of several *auls*, which represented self-sufficient mobile social units, the size of which varied from a few extended families to several dozen families, and the members of which had a common herd and shared the same migration routes and grazing areas.

The Russian expansion into the Kazakhs' domain was made easier by the latter's conflict with the nomadic Oirats of the Jungar Khanate (1635–1758), the centre of which was in Xinjiang. In the early eighteenth century, the Jungars, who were western Mongolian Buddhists, dominated the Steppe expanses between the Great Wall of China and southern Siberia. In the face of the Jungar threat some Kazakh chieftains turned for protection to Russia. In 1731, Abu Khair-khan (d. 1748) of the *Kichi Juz* agreed to be Russia's protectorate in exchange for military assistance against the Jungars; in 1732 he was followed by the *Orta Juz*'s Khan Semeke (d. 1738) and in 1740 by the *Orta Juz*'s Khan Ablai (d. 1781). In recognition of Russian tutelage they agreed to pay *yasak* to St Petersburg, though these arrangements were short-lived and only valid during the life-time of the khans who agreed to them. In contrast, the *Ulu Juz*'s khans initially rejected Russian protection in favour of being a Chinese protectorate.

Russia's next and more concerted inroad into the Great Steppe occurred during the reign of Catherine the Great (1729–96), who combined military advance into the region with agrarian colonisation by Cossacks and Russian peasants and Islam-friendly diplomacy. In parallel, Catherine was politically and militarily engaged in the Muslim north Caucasus and the Crimea.[12] In 1784, Catherine issued a decree that allowed the building in the Great Steppe of mosques, *madrasahs* and *caravansarais* along the route of the ancient Silk Road. In 1789, she introduced the institution of the muftiiate in Orenburg (later in Ufa) as the agency of state management and control over its Muslim subjects. Of particular importance was Catherine's decision to re-Islamicise religiously syncretic Kazakhs along more orderly mosque-based lines and to involve Muslim Volga Tatars in this undertaking. The relative success of this mission was assured by the common Qipchak ethnolinguistic heritage of both the Tatars and Kazakhs. In addition to their religious function, Tatar merchants also acted as promoters of Russia's economic interests in the Great Steppe and Central Asia.

Parallel to the subjugation of the Kazakhs, St Petersburg attempted economic and diplomatic engagement with Central Asia's Bukhara Khanate (1500–1785), superseded by the Bukhara Emirate (1785–1920),[13] the Khanate of Kokand (1709–1876) and the Khanate of Khiva (1511–1920). All three had comparable political and economic structures and fluid borders, which were at permanent risk due to internecine warfare and external invasions. The Bukhara Khanate/Emirate, with its capital in Bukhara, was situated between the Amu Darya and Syr Darya rivers and included Bukhara and Samarqand with adjacent areas, as well as present-day Tajikistan. Its population included Farsi- and Uzbek-speaking urbanites and peasants[14] who prevailed in Bukhara and Samarqand and surrounding areas, Oghuz-speaking Turkmen, Farsi-speaking Jews as well as various Turkic-speaking nomadic groups.

Until 1785 Bukhara was ruled by the Genghizid dynasty of Janids, who were superseded by the non-Genghizid dynasty of Manghits. Because the Manghits, like the Timurids before them, did not have direct genealogical links to the Genghizids and could not claim the title of khan they adopted the Arabic title of 'emir' ('amir'), which signified a shift from the tribal Turco-Mongol to the Islamic legitimation of their authority. Among implications of this shift was Burkharan emirs' increased reliance on a Farsi-speaking bureaucratic class and troops, who were not linked to powerful Uzbek tribal chieftains; the political elevation of *sheikh-ul-Islam* and *'ulamo'/'ulama'*; and the institutionalisation of Islamic land and other property ownership and taxation norms. Thus, land ownership was divided into three main categories: the dominant state-owned land – *amlak*; private land – *mul'k*; and *waqf*, while the main taxes were *zakat*, *kharaj* and *jiziiah*.

The Khanate of Khiva, with its capital in Khiva, was situated on the irrigated plains of the lower Amu Darya river south of the Aral Sea and included the territories of much of historical Khorezm, corresponding to present-day Turkmenistan, southwestern Kazakhstan (*Ulu Juz*) and western Uzbekistan. The khanate's population was almost equally divided between nomads and sedentary people. The former was largely represented by Uzbeks, Kazakhs and Turkmen, and the latter by Farsi- and Uzbek-speaking urban and rural dwellers. Until 1804 the Khiva Khanate was nominally ruled by the Uzbek dynasty of Yadigarids who were related to both Genghizids and Shaibanids. The Yadigarids were traditionally sponsored by the Genghizid-Turkic tribe of Konrat, albeit in the 1760s the latter were side-lined by non-Genghizid Inakids, who originated from Mehmet Emin, *inak*, that is, 'prime minister', of Temir Ghazi, a Yadigarid (d. 1763). In the mid-nineteenth century, following short reigns by members of the Konrat dynasty, the Inakids established themselves as the new, and the last, ruling dynasty of the Khiva Khanate. They, like the Manghits, were wary of the Genghizid tribal elite and predominantly relied on various Farsi- and Uzbek-speaking sedentary peoples and the Islamic clergy, and particularly on Sufis.

The Khanate of Kokand, with its capital in Kokand, was situated in the southern part of the Ferghana valley. The khanate, like the Bukhara Emirate, had an Islamicised land ownership and taxation system. It was ruled by the Uzbek dynasty of Ming,[15] known for their religious piety and close relations with Sufi *khwajas*. By the early nineteenth century, the khanate had reached its territorial peak and also included Tashkent, Margilan, Namangan and Andijan in present-day Uzbekistan, Chimkent (Shymkent) and Sairam in southern Kazakhstan and Karategin, Darvaz, Kulyab and Khujand in contemporary Tajikistan and some parts of present-day Kyrgyzstan. In the 1820s, Kokand khans also subjugated the Muslims of Kashgar in China's Xinjiang. For decades the Kokand khans and the Bukhara emirs clashed over the control of Jizzakh and Ura-Tepe and for overall supremacy of the region; in their pursuit of regional dominance the Kokand khans resorted to precarious alliances with various Chinese and Afghan rulers.

Like Bukhara and Khiva, Kokand had a mixed nomadic–sedentary population. Of notable significance was the influx into its territory of nomadic Kyrgyz originating from the Tian Shan mountains. Their arrival aggravated the relations between the nomads and sedentary peoples over arable lands and also contributed to some 'kyrgyzisation' of the Kokand ruling elite. Politically, the increase in numbers in the Kokand Khanate and other parts of Central Asia of nomads who did not recognise political borders further undermined the authority of the urban elites, destabilised the existing political alignments and territorial delimitation, and ultimately weakened resistance to external invasions.[16] Culturally, it further strengthened the *adat* and shamanist components of Central Asian Islam.

Among the region's other politically influential actors who also subsequently faced the Russian conquest were Oghuz-speaking Turkmen nomads who inhabited the Qarakum desert to the south of Khorezm and the areas along the fringes of the Kopet Dag and Balkhan mountains, in what is most of present-day Turkmenistan. Turkmen were divided into over thirty tribes, the largest being Tekke, Yomud, Ersary, Chavdur, Saryq, Salar and Goklen. They were fiercely independent and never formed a khanate or any other form of tribal confederation. Nevertheless, they were often involved in regional conflicts and periodically accepted the tutelage of neighbouring polities. Thus, from time to time the northern Turkmen tribes recognised the suzerainty of the Khiva khan, the southern tribes of the Bukhara emir and the eastern tribes of Iran.

By the turn of the nineteenth century, Russia had developed sustainable trade links with the Bukhara Emirate which accounted for 55 per cent of Russia's total exports of sugar, 45 per cent of metals and 33 per cent of processed leather.[17] Russia also exported grain, gold and silver coins and imported Bukharan raw wool, cotton and silk. The trade was conducted along the Eurasian branch of the ancient Silk Road, as well as along the new trade routes from Bukhara to Russia's towns of Semipalatinsk, Orenburg, Tobol'sk and Astrakhan. As mentioned earlier, a central role in the Russo-Bukharan trade belonged to the Volga Tatars.

In contrast, Russia's relations with the khanates of Khiva and Kokand were barely existent. In the case of Khiva, they were haunted by the events of 1717/18, when Peter the Great sent an armed trade expedition to Khiva under the command of Prince Alexander Bekovich-Cherkasskii (Devlet-Girei-*murza*, d. 1717) who, upon his arrival, was treacherously murdered. Later on, the conquest of Khiva by Nadir Shah of Iran in 1740 further deferred any contacts with Russia. The development of relations between St Petersburg and Kokand was also hampered by Kokand's close engagement with China and its opposition to Russia's trade links with its main adversary – the Bukhara Emirate. Kokand and Khiva khans were also suspicious of Russia's undisclosed agenda in the region in the aftermath of the Russian annexation of the Caucasian khanates in the early nineteenth century. These suspicions were also fuelled by Ottoman and especially British emissaries, who frequented the region in the context of the unfolding Great Game between the Russian and British empires for supremacy in Central and southern Asia.

The Russian conquest

Russia's expansionism into the Great Steppe and Central Asia was primarily driven by St Petersburg's geopolitical and security concerns over the insecurity of Russia's eastern borders due to the lengthy history of Turkic and Mongolian invasions into Russia from the east and the absence of a physical geographical barrier between Russia and the Great Steppe. From the mid-nineteenth century Russia's territorial advance eastwards acquired a European and civilisational dimension in the context of the aforementioned Great Game. Its other important triggers were Russia's defeat in the Crimean War (1853/6), which curtailed her territorial ambitions in the Middle East, and the needs of Russia's developing economy, especially her textile industry, which was adversely affected by the rupture in cotton supplies from America as a result of the American Civil War (1861–5).

In the early nineteenth century, Russia asserted its stable control over the Kazakh *Kichi Juz*, which also incorporated the smaller Bukei *Juz*[18] and the *Orta Juz*. The title of khan was abolished and the territory of the *Kichi Juz* became part of Russia's Ural'sk *oblast'* with its centre in the town of Ural'sk. The *Orta Juz* was divided between Russia's Turgai and Akmolinsk *oblasts*. In 1818, St Petersburg finally forced the *Ulu Juz* into submission, and in the 1850s its territory was absorbed into Russia's Semipalatinsk *oblast'*. Governors of these Kazakh-majority *oblasts* became answerable to the Russian Ministry of Interior; and the administrative inclusion of the Kazakh Steppe into the Russian Empire was followed by the introduction there of the all-Russia land, administrative and criminal regulations which paralleled the existing *adat* and *shari'a* courts. It also triggered the steady inflow into the Kazakh territories of Russian, Ukrainian, Belorussian, Polish and German agrarian settlers.

From the late 1850s St Petersburg increased its political and military pressure on the Khanates of Kokand and Khiva.[19] In 1860, Russian troops captured from the Kokandis the towns of Tokmak and Pishkek (Bishkek), which were followed by Chimkent (Shymkent) and Aulie (Taraz) in 1864 and Tashkent in 1865. In the same year they included the conquered territories into the newly established province of Turkestan with its centre in Tashkent. In 1867, it was reorganised into the Governorate General of Turkestan under the rule of Governor General Konstantin von Kaufman (1818–82), who reported to the Russian Ministry of Defence.

In 1868, the Russians began a military campaign against the Bukhara Emirate, in the course of which they occupied Samarqand and forced the emir to renounce his claims on eastern Bukharia in favour of Russia. In 1869, Russian troops, arriving from the Caucasus, founded the fort of Krasnovodsk on the eastern shore of the Caspian Sea in present-day Turkmenistan from where they began attacks on the Khivans, whom they finally defeated in 1873. Russia's last major opponents were the Turkmen tribes. Although the western Turkmen tribe of Yomud submitted to the Russians without much resistance, most of the tribes, and especially the Tekke, fought fiercely against Russia's invasion of their traditional habitat. In 1881, after several setbacks, Russian troops under the command of General Mikhail Skobelev[20] finally defeated the Tekke at Geok Tepe, and the conquest of the region was completed in 1884, when the Russians captured Merv in present-day Turkmenistan.

Following the military conquest of Central Asia, St Petersburg introduced different forms of governance and administrative delimitation which partially preserved the territorial integrity of the Bukhara Emirate and the Khiva Khanate under the condition of protectorates. The status of Russian protectorate was accepted by the Bukhara Emir Muzaffar al-Din (d. 1885) in 1868 and by the Khiva Khan Muhammad Rahim II (d. 1910) in 1873. In 1883, St Petersburg abolished the Khanate of Kokand and included most of its territories into Russian Turkestan, which was initially divided into five *oblasts*: the Semirechie *oblast'* with its centre in Vernyi (Almaty); the Ferghana *oblast'* with its centre in Novyi Margilan (present-day Ferghana in Uzbekistan); the Samarqand *oblast'* with its centre in Samarqand[21]; the Zakaspii *oblast'* with its centre in Ashgabad; and the Syr Darya *oblast'* with its centre in Tashkent, which was also made the governorship's capital.[22]

In the course of the following three decades Russian Turkestan and the adjacent governorships underwent a series of administrative reconfigurations. In 1867, the Great (Kazakh) Steppe was split between the Syr Darya and Semirechie *oblasts* of the Turkestan Governorship, the Ural'sk and Turgai *oblasts* of the Orenburg Governorate General and the Akmolinsk and Semipalatinsk *oblasts* of the Governorate General of Western Siberia. In 1882, most Kazakh-populated areas were reorganised into Akmolinsk, Semipalatinsk and Semirechie *oblasts* of the newly established Governorate General of the Steppe, with its centre in Omsk. The western external borders of Russia's Central Asia were finalised by London and St Petersburg in 1907, when the former recognised Russia's supremacy in present-day Central Asia and the latter accepted British dominance in present-day Afghanistan and Kashmir.

The social order and the role of Islam under Russian rule

St Petersburg's different forms of governance across the Great (Kazakh) Steppe and Central Asia affected the level of its interference in the political, economic and cultural life of the region's Muslim peoples. This was stronger in the Kazakh Steppe, which was administratively integrated into the Russian Empire. From the 1830s, the traditional nomadic lifestyle of Kazakhs had been affected by the Russian authorities' drive towards their sedentarisation and the agrarian settlement of Cossacks, Russians and Ukrainians on Kazakh-dominated fertile lands along the Orenburg fortification lines. From the 1860s, Kazakhs could secure their control of the land only through farming and the building of permanent structures on it. Consequently, by the end of the nineteenth century a considerable number of Kazakh households, especially in the Ural'sk *oblast'*, were forced to move to semi-nomadism by combining livestock breeding with some forms of agriculture. Alongside the Kazakh Steppe, the presence of Russians and other Slavs also became prominent in Tashkent and other urban areas of Russian

Turkestan, where they began to dominate the civil service, transportation, communications, the emerging industries and modern education.

By contrast, St Petersburg's interference in the internal affairs of the protectorates of Bukhara and Khiva was negligible. Still, in comparative terms, even in the Kazakh Steppe and Russian Turkestan the impact of Russian rule on most natives' lives was considerably weaker than in Russia's Muslim-majority regions of the Volga-Urals and southern Caucasus, and was largely restricted to the security, military and political spheres. Thus, following the conquest of the region, St Petersburg retained around 40,000 troops there on a permanent basis. Of particular significance was the regional Muslim clergy's continued independence from the Orenburg muftiiate; St Petersburg's recognition of the centrality of the *shari'a*-based legal system; its safeguarding of the *hajj* and other Islam-related activities[23]; and its proscribing of the Russian Orthodox Church from proselytising in the region. A pertinent indication of Russia's special treatment of Central Asian Muslims, compared with her Muslim subjects in the Volga-Urals and the southern Caucasus, was their legal designation as 'alien-borns' (*inorodtsy*) and the exemption of Central Asian Muslim men from Russian military service.

For these reasons, until the Bolshevik Revolution of 1917 the social order and culture of the bulk of Central Asian Muslims largely persisted along traditional lines, shaped by Central Asian Islam. In the steppe and desert areas their lives were centred on *auls* and *tires* (among Turkmen), and in the rural and urban areas on *mahallahs*. Both represented self-contained communities which enjoyed a significant degree of autonomy from provincial and central administrations. Given the inclusion of much of the nomadic habitat into the Russian Empire, the nomads' social structures were more affected by Russian rule than those of various sedentary peoples in Khiva and Bukhara. The official abolition of the *Juzes* among the Kazakhs and the division of the Kazakh Steppe into Russian *oblasts*, *uiezds* and *volosts* changed the outlook of traditional *auls* because their customary borders did not always correspond to the newly established *volosts* and *uiezds*. Thus, under the new regime, a *volost'* often comprised a larger number of *yurts* than a traditional *aul* and the borders between different *volosts* did not necessarily follow the genealogical principle. As a result, some Kazakhs from unrelated *auls* found themselves within the same *volost*, while some other related Kazakhs ended up in different *volosts* or even *uiezds*. In the case of the Turkmen, the Russian delimitation strengthened the territorial, rather than blood-related, principle in their social organisation. As a result, they began to prioritise their geographical habitat over their genealogical entity – a *taipa* – and to identify themselves with a particular territorial area – Ahal, Merv, Tejen and so on.

In terms of their religious beliefs and practices, Muslim Kazakhs, Kyrgyz, Turkmen and other nomadic peoples continued to rely heavily on their tribal customary norms intertwined with Sufism. Among the Kazakhs, these norms were formalised in the code of Khan Tauke (d. 1718) known as the *Jeti Jarghy* ('Seven Verdicts'), and among the Turkmen in the *Turkmenchilik* ('Law of Ancestors'), which was infused with the Sufism of the Kubrawi and Naqshbandi *tariqats*. The *Jeti Jarghy*, among other practices, legitimised blood vendettas, an individual's right to communal assistance in case of the loss of livestock and his right to relatives' unpaid help in order to complete seasonal works. It also endorsed the supremacy of the tribal authorities over *qazis* in the adjudication of disputes and in other legal issues. The inferior status of mosque-based Muslim clergy compared with that of tribal authorities, traditional healers and Sufi *khojas* was also evidenced by the association of the presence of a mullah in a Kazakh *yurt* with bad luck. In a similar way, Kyrgyz nomads had a higher esteem for shamans – *baqshi* – than for mullahs.

Most *mahallahs*, which had histories extending over several centuries, were territorially defined sedentary communities, consisting of a number of extended families (*guzars*, *qavms*). In eastern Bukharia and some other areas *mahallahs* combined territorial and kinship principles of organisation. A typical Central Asian town consisted of several walled *mahallahs*, some of which contained a bazaar. Some *mahallahs* also acted as professional guilds by monopolising particular crafts. In rural areas several *mahallahs* made up a *qishloq/qishlaq*.[24] Both urban and rural *mahallahs* were headed by an elected *oqsoqol/aqsaqal/arbob*, who was advised by a council of elders and an imam. The *oqsoqol* was the ultimate authority for solving internal disputes and was responsible for communal tax collection, the organisation of communal events and the external representation of the *mahallah*. Relations within the *mahallah* were characterised by patriarchy, the high social status of elders, women's seclusion and compulsory communal solidarity. All of its residents were expected to participate in communal activities and celebrations, while those in need were entitled to its financial and material assistance.

At the heart of a *mahallah* was a mosque, which combined religious and social functions as it acted as the main communal venue as well. The *mahallah* imam, or mullah, led daily prayers and oversaw the residents' major life-cycle events such as circumcisions, marriages and funerals. Imams also acted as teachers in *maktabs* which were attached to the mosque. There, male pupils were taught along Islamic traditionalist lines. They studied the basics of *adab*, Arabic and the Qur'an; as in the past, the most popular *maktab* textbooks were the *Chahar Kitab* (*Four Books*) and the *Haftiek* which was used in memorising basic Islamic expressions in Arabic. A *mahallah*'s girls received their elementary Islamic education at home, from *otins/otinchas/bibi-khalfas*. Particularly large *mahallahs* in Bukhara, Samarqand and some other larger cities had their own *madrasahs*, while the most authoritative among them was the *Mir-i Arab Madrasah* in Bukhara. Some big *mahallahs* had their own *qadis/qazis* who were bearers of the *shari'a*. The correlation between *adats*, *shari'a* and *'urf* norms in legal procedures varied significantly from one *mahallah* to another. Generally, although not everywhere, *adat* norms had priority over *shari'a* rulings and such *shari'a*-based punishments as the stoning of adulterers or the chopping off of the hands of thieves were relatively rare, while Sufi sheikhs/*khojas*/*ishans*/*pirs*/*turas* usually possessed higher social and religious status than imams and mullahs. They also acted as the main hereditary guardians of the Sufi shrines or other *waqf* objects which existed within the confines of some *mahallahs*.

Geopolitical, cultural and religious implications of Russian rule

The conquest of Central Asia represented the next stage in Eurasia's geopolitical shift in Russia's favour which began in the mid-sixteenth century. It was facilitated by centuries of mutual political and military rivalries, trade, cultural borrowing, territorial delimitation and population mixing, which were conducted on level terms. This was in contrast to the largely unequal nature of Europe's engagement with Asia prior to its European colonialisation. Conversely, Russia's absorption of over 18 million Central Asian Muslims transformed her into a major Eurasian and Christian–Muslim empire, reminiscent of Genghis Khan's empire which for more than two centuries united Russia and Central Asia within a single state. Following the Russian conquest present-day Kazakhs, Kyrgyz, Uzbeks, Tajiks and Turkmen were sealed off from their ethnic and religious brethren in Xinjiang, Afghanistan, Iran and Turkey as they came to be included within a Russia-centred political space. It was thus responsible for the emergence of the 'reduced' notion of Central Asia, which has persisted until the present day.

Russian governance over Central Asia drew on practices of the earlier Eurasian powers and empires. Like them, St Petersburg prioritised the political and military aspects of its rule and did not significantly interfere in the socio-economic and cultural life of grassroots communities. For this reason, following the Russian conquest most Central Asian Muslim *'ulama'* and clergy continued to regard the region as *Dar al-Islam*. This is not to say that St Petersburg did not introduce elements of modernisation and did not apply some colonial practices in the region. These included, for example, the enclave agrarian settlers' colonisation, the nomads' sedentarisation, the promotion of cotton monoculture, and Tashkent's architectural and ethnolinguistic Russification. The arrival of Russia in Central Asia also prompted some cultural changes among a relatively small group of the educated urban elite.

One medium of change was the Russian-native periodicals. A leading role among the latter belonged to the *Turkestan Wilaiiatining Gazeti* (TWG, 'Newspaper of Turkestan Province', 1870–1917), which for a long time was edited by Nikolai P. Ostroumov (1846–1930), a distinguished philologist of

Arabic and Turkic languages and a follower of Nikolai I. Il'minskii.[25] Originally, the newspaper was a weekly supplement in Chagatai to the *Turkestanskiie Vedomosti* (TV, 'Turkestan News', 1870–1917), published in Russian, mainly containing decrees and regulations issued by the governor general and aimed at those Central Asians who worked in the various administrative and trade structures of Russian Turkestan. TWG soon evolved into a forum for a wider *Jadidism*-driven political and cultural debate, and diversified its coverage to include political, cultural and scientific news from the region and abroad, as well as essays and poetry by Central Asian and other Muslim authors. The main periodical in the Kazakh Steppe was a weekly Russian/Kazakh newspaper *Dala Wilaiiatining Gazeti* (DWG, 'Newspaper of the Steppe Province', 1888–1902), which was published in Akmolinsk (Akmola). Its readership consisted of the Russian-educated Kazakh elite of the *Orta Juz*. Ismail Gasprinskii's *Tercuman* also had some circulation among the educated elite. Later on, under the influence of the Russian bourgeois-democratic revolution of 1905–7, and in particular of the liberalising Manifesto of 17 October 1905, a few other pro-*jadid* periodicals were established in the region.

Another source of modernising influence was a limited number of Russo-native schools and pro-*jadid* Islamic schools, which, however, were hugely outnumbered by Islamic traditionalist (*qadimist*) *madrasahs*. The Russo-native schools, which taught both in the vernacular and in Russian, were restricted to the Kazakh-majority areas and in Russian Turkestan. Their function was to train local low- and middle-level officials for the Russian imperial administration; most of their graduates were representatives of the tribal and sedentary regional elites. Although Kazakhs prevailed among them, their actual number was small and did not exceed 4 per cent of the total Kazakh population of over 2 million. Some graduates were able to continue their education in Russian gymnasiums in Omsk and other Siberian cities, while a handful did so in the Russian cadet colleges and universities. Among these were, for example, such charismatic Kazakh figures of Genghizid genealogical stock as Chokan Valikhanov (Chokan Shynghysuly Valikhanuly, 1835–65) and Ibrahim Altynsarin (Ibirai Altinsarin, 1841–89).[26] Both were ardent Russophiles and believed in the enlightening influence of Russian culture and education on the basis of the Cyrillic alphabet, as well as the wider benefits of Russian rule for Kazakhs. These views were also shared by some *madrasah* graduates, including Abai Kunanbayev (Abai Konanbai Uli, 1845–1904), another great Kazakh enlightener and poet of Genghizid descent. In Turkestan, the first Russian gymnasium was opened in Tashkent in 1876 and was followed by two colleges, also in Tashkent, and a gymnasium in Samarqand.

Alongside a very small number of secular-minded intellectuals there emerged a considerably larger number of Islam-centred modernisers. They were graduates of *jadid madrasahs* that were opened, alongside Russo-native schools, in the Kazakh Steppe and Turkestan. Due to the special role of Tatars in the institutionalisation of Islam among Kazakhs, Kazakh *jadids* largely shared the views and aspirations of their Tatar counterparts. Thus, Abubakir Kerderi (1858–1903), Shakarim Kudaiberdi Uli (1858–1931), Aqmolla Muhammadiar Uli (1839–95), Mashur Jusup Kopei (1857–1931) and other Kazakh *jadids* were directly involved in the nationwide Russian intellectual and political debate on the future reform of the Russian state and society, and perceived Islamic reform within the wider context of the social and political modernisation of the Russian state. *Jadids* were also either proponents or opponents of close cultural and political links between Kazakhs and Russians. Some Kazakh *jadids*, who were critical of Russian Orthodox rule, allied with Kazakh writers and poets collectively known as the *Zar Zaman* ('Time of Trouble')[27] who used Arabic rather than Cyrillic script. Tatar-driven *Jadidism* also defined the thinking of a few Turkmen Muslim reformers, including Muhamed Geldiyev, Muhametgulu Atabayev and Durdu Gylysh.

In contrast, the Uzbek and Tajik *jadids* were largely disengaged from the all-Russia political debate and Tatar-centred *jadidist* discourse and were more physically and ideationally involved with the Islamic reformist movement in the Middle East and south Asia which developed as both a reaction to and in opposition to the modernity emanating from outside.[28] It was spearheaded by the earlier mentioned Jamal al-Din al-Afghani, Muhammad 'Abduh, Sayyid Ahmad Khan and Khayr al-Din. Among the key representatives of Central Asian *jadids* were Ahmad Makhtum Qalla (Donish, 1826–97), Mahmud Khoja Behbudi (1874–1919), Munawwar Qari (1878–1931), Hamza Hakimzada Niyazi (1889–1929), Sadri Ziye (1867–1932), Naqibkhon Tugral (1864–1919), Zakidjon Furqat (1858–1909), Mahammadjon Muqimi (1851–1903), Sadriddin Ayni (1875–1954) and Abdurauf Fitrat (1886–1938). *Jadids* were largely based in Bukhara and to a lesser extent in Tashkent, where they dominated the Beglarbegi and Kokaldash *madrasahs*.

Despite these manifestations of secular and Islamic reformist thinking the vast majority of the Kazakh and Central Asian elites, as well as ordinary people, preserved their allegiance to Central Asian Islam based on Islamic traditionalism – *qadimism* and local or tribal customs. Its main guardians were Sufi sheikhs, *'ulama'*, mosque mullahs and *otins*. Most Central Asian Muslim clergy were apprehensive of *jadid maktabs* and *madrasahs* and strongly defended the traditional Islamic education based on the *Chahar Kitab*, the *Haftiek*, and the memorising of the Qur'anic verses. Despite the appearance of several female *maktabs*, *otins* remained the main providers of Islamic education to girls. The major centres of Sufi learning remained Sufi *khanaqahs* organised around a particular Sufi teacher. The boundaries between *maktabs* and *madrasahs*, on the one side, and *khanaqahs*, on the other, were not clear-cut and often a *madrasah mudarris* was a *murid* of a Sufi sheikh, while a Sufi teacher may have had a *madrasah* education.

In the Kazakh Steppe, Muslim clergy were dominated by Tatar mullahs who adhered to the Tatar rather than the Bukhara or Samarqand version of Islamic traditionalism. It should be noted that *qadimist madrasahs* were favoured by St Petersburg because of their non-engagement in politics.

In the Bukhara Emirate and Khiva Khanate, as well as in the rural parts of the Russian Turkestan, the supremacy of traditionalist Muslim clergy was assured by their control over the *shari'a*-based legal system and numerous *waqfs*, which included arable land, water canals, *caravansarais*, artisan workshops, shops and *mazars*.[29] As a result, in the aftermath of the Russian conquest the number of *qadimist maktabs* and *madrasahs* across the region continued to grow. In the period between 1901 and 1917, in Russian Turkestan alone their number increased from 5,755 to over 7,000. The continuing legal centrality of the *shari'a* and the prevalence of Islamic education conditioned many *'ulama'* to apply *ijtihad* and to qualify Russia's Central Asia as the *Dar al-Islam* and the Russian tsar as *Ak Padishah*, that is, 'White Sovereign'. For this reason they advised local imams to include the names of the Russian tsars and members of the royal family in their Friday *khutbahs* – an important factor in the widespread popular acceptance of Russian rule. Nevertheless, some *qadimist 'ulama'* reverted to the revivalist interpretation of Islam and treated Russia's Central Asia as the *Dar al-Harb*, therefore justifying *jihad* against the Russian regional administration.[30] This approach was evidenced in several relatively low-scale Islamicised anti-Russian uprisings, including the Andijan revolt in May 1898 under the direction of the Naqshbandi *ishon* Medali ('Dukchi Ishon', 1856–98) of Ferghana.[31]

Overall, the establishment of Russian rule over the Kazakh Steppe and Central Asia had ambivalent and far-reaching implications for the region. It brought to it relative political stability after over two centuries of endemic and devastating internecine warfare and marauding. It triggered the region's partial modernisation through its integration within the all-Russia railway transport[32] and telegraph system, the creation of modern towns, the revitalising of traditional trade, and the introduction of new industrial and agricultural technologies. It precipitated the abolition of widespread slavery.[33] The Muslims in Russian Turkestan, especially the urbanites, acquired access to such vital goods as kerosene, glass, sugar and tea, as well as modern medicine and vaccinations, resulting in a drastic reduction in mortality rates. The opening of veterinary stations in the rural areas revolutionised cattle breeding. The establishment of Russo-native schools facilitated the proliferation of the Russified version of modern European education, architecture and the arts among some members of the local elites.

But, as already noted, Russian rule was accompanied by some colonial practices, which subsequently modified or, in some areas, disrupted existing political, economic and cultural patterns and perceptions. Particularly detrimental was the promotion of the cotton monoculture for the needs of the Russian textile industry and the concomitant decrease in local production of cereals, resulting in the region's dependency on wheat imports from Russia.[34] The traditional way of life of Kazakhs and other nomads was severely distorted by enforced sedentarisation and the seizure of their lands by incoming Slavic and German agrarian settlers. St Petersburg abolished the institution of khans among the Kazakhs and other nomads, thus significantly weakening the role of the traditional genealogical and Islamicised elites. The influx of Russian-speaking military personnel, civil servants, engineers, teachers, transport, communication and industrial workers radically changed the cultural and architectural outlook and ethnic composition of Tashkent and other main cities in favour of the Slavs.[35] As a result, a sizeable Russified urban elite emerged who were largely disconnected from the rural native majority. Also, Russian administrators, in pursuit of imperial objectives, combined reliance on existing multiple social and cultural hierarchies and connections with adherence to Russian Orthodox civilisational discourse towards the Muslim *other*, and encouraged the linguistic and cultural Russification of some local elites. Such enclave-based practices were not dissimilar from those of British, French, Dutch and other European colonisers in India, Africa, the East Indies and some other parts of the world, although in comparative terms their scale was much more limited.

At deeper structural and human levels the relationship between the Russian imperial centre and its Central Asian possessions differed substantially from those of the major European empires with their overseas colonies. This difference derived from the common Eurasian habitat of Russia and Central Asia, and the similarities in their formative influences and cultures. It could be argued therefore that analysis of the nature of the relations between the imperial Russian centre and the Central Asian periphery requires a nuanced approach that transcends the existing theoretical paradigms of colonial and post-colonial studies.[36]

Notes

1. For a fuller discussion of the role of various Turkic peoples in the formation of Russian ethnicity and polity, see, for example, Yemelianova 2002, pp. 1–27; Bariev 2005.
2. Prior to the official Islamicisation of Volga Bulgaria in 922, Islam was adopted by some members of the Bulgar elite, including *baltavars* Aidar (d. 855) and Jilki (d. 882). Islam was brought to the region by Muslim merchants from Khorasan and envoys of the Baghdad-centred Abbasid caliph. On the Islamicisation of Volga Bulgaria, see Miftakhov 1998.
3. Thus, Russian rulers adopted the Genghizid succession tradition which prioritised the right to succession of the son over other male relatives of the ruler. Russian official documents – *gramoty* – and foreign correspondence contained a Genghizid *tugra* – a special Genghizid Islamicised heraldic sign and the universal Islamic formula *Bismillah al-Rahman al-Rahim* 'In the name of God, most Gracious, most Compassionate') in Arabic script. The first Russian criminal court, like the Genghizid criminal court, prioritised the death penalty and

physical punishment. The Russian military elite – *ulans* (from the Genghizid term 'oglans') – comprised commanders of 10,000 men (*temniki*), commanders of 1,000 men (*tysiachniki*), commanders of 100 (*sotniki*) and commanders of 10 (*desiatniki*). The Russian rulers also took over the Genghizid postal service and their regular general census for tax and police purposes. The Russian inauguration and diplomatic ceremonies were modelled on those by the Genghizids as well.

4. For example, in 1446 the Muscovy *kniaz* Vasily II (1415–62) forged an alliance with the Genghizid khan Qasim (d. 1469) against Khan Said-Ahmad (d. 1455) of the Golden Horde, while in 1480 Ivan III allied with the Crimean khan against Ahmad-khan (d. 1481) of the Golden Horde.
5. On the history of the concept of 'The Third Rome', see Østbø 2016.
6. For a detailed discussion of the history of the Kazan Khanate, see Muslimov 1996, pp. 531–758.
7. Tatars were descendants of the Volga Bulgars and Genghizids who historically populated the area between the Volga and Kama rivers. For a discussion on the ethnic origins of the Tatars, see Zakiev 1995.
8. In 1557, the Nogai Horde split into the Volga-centred Great Nogai Horde and the Kuban-centred Small Nogai Horde. Both hordes were further weakened by internal strife and the inroads made by the Kalmyk. In 1634, the last remnants of the Nogai polity were absorbed within the Russian state.
9. Boris Godunov's predecessors belonged to the Varangian dynasty of Ruriks (r. 862–1598).
10. During the discussed historical period Russia's engagement in Europe was limited to its conflict relationship with Sweden and the Polish–Lithuanian Commonwealth.
11. The Scythians, also known as Saka, were Iranian-speaking nomads who created their empire in Central Eurasia between the ninth century BC and the first century AD.
12. In 1783, the Russians finally defeated the last Genghizid outpost in Eurasia, the Crimean Khanate (1441–1783), which was allied with the Ottoman Empire, and annexed its territory.
13. For a detailed account of the Bukharan Khanate and Emirate, see Burton 1997.
14. In the nineteenth century various Iranian- and Turkic-speaking non-tribal rural and urban settled Central Asians were widely referred to as 'Sarts'. See more on the history of the ethnonym 'Sart' and controversies around it in Soucek 2000, pp. 32–3; Geiss 2003, pp. 94–5; Khalid 1998, pp. 199–209.
15. The Ming dynasty of the Kokand Khanate was called after the local Turkic tribe of Ming, which was unrelated to the Ming dynasty in China.
16. It is worth noting that some Central Asian researchers regard the very concept of boundaries and borders in relation to Central Asia and the wider region of Eurasia as an Orientalist construct which allegedly reflects the Eurocentric notion of the nation-state with clearly defined borders. See, for example, Nurulla-Khodzhaeva 2015.
17. See Becker 2004, pp. 13–14; Khidaiatov 1969, pp. 9, 28.
18. The Bukei *Juz*, also referred to as Inner *Juz*, was formed in the area between the Ural and Volga rivers by the *ukaz* of the Russian Tsar Paul of 11 March 1801.
19. For a detailed account of the Russian conquest of Central Asia, see Becker 2004; Crews 2006; Khalfin 1965; Khidaiatov 1969; Saray 1982.
20. Prior to the Geok Tepe battle General Skobelev 'distinguished' himself by his particular brutality against Kokandis in Andijan, Namangan and Margilan, which left over 20,000 people dead.
21. For a detailed discussion of the Russian rule in Samarqand, see Morrison 2008.
22. The Syr Darya *oblast'* also included a significant segment of the Khiva Khanate.

23. The Russian authorities channelled the annual *hajj* of Central Asian Muslims along the designated route from Tashkent to Odessa by rail and from Odessa to Mecca and Medina by sea. The organisation of the *hajj* was entrusted to the newly founded 'Society for Support of Muslim Pilgrims'.
24. On the historical evolution of the Central Asian *qishlaq*, see Abashin 2015.
25. Nikolai I. Il'minskii (1822–91) was the methodologist of the Russo-Tatar schools, based on the teaching of Russian Orthodox Christianity in Tatar. The first such school was founded by him in 1870 in Kazan.
26. Chokan Valikhanov, a graduate of the Omsk cadet college, made a brilliant career as a geographer and was appointed to head the Russian imperial scientific expedition to Russian and eastern Turkestan. Ibrahim Altynsarin, a graduate of the Orenburg gymnasium, became the first Kazakh educator to produce a grammar for the Kazakh vernacular, which he converted into the written language on the basis of the Cyrillic alphabet. He also authored the first Russo-Kazakh dictionary. In 1867, in Turgai, he founded the first co-educational Russo-Kazakh boarding school.
27. The leading figures of the *Zar Zaman* were Shortambai Kanai Uli (1818–81), Dulat Babatai Uli (1802–71) and Murat Monke Uli (1843–1906).
28. Central Asian Turkic-speaking *jadids* were known locally as *ziialilar* ('intellectuals') or *taraqqiparwarlar* ('progressivists'). For a detailed account of Central Asian *jadids*, see Khalid 1998.
29. From the 1890s the Russian authorities began to introduce a selective ban on some types of *waqfs*.
30. See Krivets 1999, p. 84; Babadzhanov 2010, pp. 39, 42, 43, 539.
31. The majority of over 200 rebels were Kyrgyz who played the key role in the collapse of the Kokand Khanate in 1875. The uprising was speedily suppressed by the Russian troops. Soucek 2000, p. 207.
32. By the early 1900s, Tashkent was linked by rail to the Caspian port of Krasnovodsk (in present-day Turkmenistan), from where there was a sea route to Baku in the Russian Transcaucasus. The other major railroad stretched from Tashkent to Orenburg and from Orenburg to Samara, Riazan, Moscow and St Petersburg. Soucek 2000, pp. 204–5.
33. Prior to the Russian conquest, slavery was widespread in the Bukhara Emirate and the Khanates of Khiva and Kokand. Their rulers and dignitaries acquired slaves during armed raids into adjacent regions of Iran, Afghanistan and Russia, as well as at the regional slave markets. In the early 1860s, the number of slaves in the Bukhara Emirate was around 30,000. They were used as soldiers, servants and concubines. Terent'ev 1906, p. 264.
34. By the end of the nineteenth century, 208 out of a total of 220 Russian cotton mills were located in Central Asia. Yemelianova 2002, pp. 97–8.
35. For a detailed discussion of the Russian impact on Tashkent, see Sahadeo 2007.
36. The nature of Russian rule in Central Asia is debatable and some researchers argue in favour of its greater similarities with British, French and Dutch colonialism. For a wider discussion on this issue, see Abashin 2015; Babadzhanov 2004; Ceraci 2008; Eickelman 1993; Erasov 1991; Erturk 1999; Gorshenina 2012; Kappeler 2001; Khalid 1998; Knight 2000; Lieven 2002; Martin 2001; Sahadeo 2007; Tolz 2011; Vulpius 2012.

Selected reading

Primary sources

Behbudi, Mahmud Khoja (1909), *Mukhtasar Tarikh-i Islam* [Chagatai] (*A Short History of Islam*), Samarqand: n.p.

Mulla Muhammad Yunus Dzhan Shighavul Dadhah (2003), *Tarikh-i Alimquli* [Chagatai] (*A History of Alimqul*), ed. and trans. T. K. Beisembiyev, London: RoutledgeCurzon.

Mirza 'Alim, Mahmud-i Khoja (1915), *Tarikh-i-Turkistan* [Chagatai] (*History of Turkestan*), Tashkent: Publishing House of the Governor General of Turkestan.

Munawwar Qori (1912), *Adib-i Awwal* (*Book One*), Tashkent: n.p.

Munawwar Qori (1912), *Adib-i Sani* (*Book Two*), Tashkent: n.p.

Vambery, A. (1864), *Travels in Central Asia, Being the Account of a Journey from Teheran across the Turkoman Desert on the Eastern Shore of the Caspian to Khiva, Bokhora and Samarcand, Performed in the Year 1863*, London: Murray.

Secondary sources

Ahmedzhanov, G. A. (1995), *Rossiiskaia Imperiia v Tsentral'noi Azii* (*Russian Empire in Central Asia*), Tashkent: FAN.

Babadzhanov, B. (2010), *Kokandskoe Khanstvo: Vlast', Politika, Religiia* (*Kokand Khanate: Power, Politics and Religion*), Tokyo-Tashkent: TIAS.

Bassin, M. (1999), *Imperial Visions: Nationalist Imagination and Geographical Expansion in the Russian Far East, 1840–1865*, Cambridge: Cambridge University Press.

Becker, S. (2004). *Russia's Protectorate in Central Asia: Bukhara and Khiva, 1865–1924*, London: RoutledgeCurzon.

Bregel, Y. E. (2003) *Historical Atlas of Central Asia*, Leiden: Brill.

Ceraci, R. P. (2008), *Window on the East: National and Imperial Identities in Late Tsarist Russia*, Ithaca, NY: Cornell University Press.

Crews, R. D. (2006) *For Prophet and Tsar: Islam and Empire in Russia and Central Asia*, Cambridge, MA: Harvard University Press.

Espagne, M., S. Gorshenina, F. Grenet, Sh. Mustafayev and C. Rapin (eds) (2016), *Asie centrale: Transferts culturels le long de la Route de la soie*, Paris: Vendermiaire.

Geiss, P. G. (2003), *Pre-Tsarist and Tsarist Central Asia: Communal Commitment and Political Order in Change*, London: Routledge.

Gorshenina, S. (2012), *Asie centrale: L'invention des frontieres et l'heritage russo-sovietique*, Paris: CNRS.

Khalid, A. (1998), *The Politics of Muslim Cultural Reform: Jadidism in Central Asia*, Berkeley: University of California Press.

Khidaiatov, G. A. (1969), *Rossiia i Tsentral'naiia Aziia vo Vtoroi Polovine XIX veka* (*Russia and Central Asia in the second part of the 19th Century*), Tashkent: TashGU.

Morrison, A. (2008), *Russian Rule in Samarkand, 1868–1910: A Comparison with British India*, Oxford: Oxford University Press.

Olcott, M. ([1986] 1995), *The Kazakhs*, Stanford, CA: Hoover Institution Press.

Sahadeo, J. (2007), *Russian Colonial Society in Tashkent, 1865–1923*, Bloomington: Indiana University Press.

Schimmelpennick, D. (2010), *Russian Orientalism: Asia in the Russian Mind from Peter the Great to the Emigration*, New Haven, CT: Yale University Press.

Sergeev, E. (2013), *The Great Game, 1856–1907: Russo-British Relations in Central and East Asia*, Baltimore, MD: Johns Hopkins University Press.

Soucek, S. (2000), *A History of Inner Asia*, Cambridge: Cambridge University Press.

Tomohiko, U. (ed.) (2012), *Asiatic Russia: Imperial Power in Regional and International Contexts*, London: Routledge.

Yemelianova, G. M. (2002), *Russia and Islam: A Historical Survey*, London: Palgrave.

CHAPTER 3

The Sovietisation of Central Asian Muslims

Central Asia and the Russian bourgeois-democratic revolutions of 1905–7 and 1917

At the turn of the twentieth century Russia strengthened her economic, political and cultural engagement in Central Asia. The needs of the developing capitalist economy stimulated Russian investments in various industries and businesses in Russian Turkestan. The increased presence of Russian industrialists in the region was accompanied by the rise and diversification of trade between Russian and local merchants, including in Bukhara and Khiva. A growing number of immigrant Russian and other non-indigenous workers and professionals were employed at newly founded industries and businesses, including the railway, printing-houses, construction sites, schools and hospitals. Tashkent, in particular, due to its status as the capital of Russian Turkestan, experienced an economic and cultural boom and quickly turned into one of Russia's largest modern cities, which in terms of its population and economic development surpassed all other Central Asian cities. The region's economic and political transformation received a further boost as a result of the Russian bourgeois-democratic revolution of 1905–7, which improved the professional and educational opportunities of local Muslims by enhancing the proliferation of pro-*jadid* schools and widening their access to Russian gymnasia and universities. Among other important implications of these changes was an involvement of some Central Asians – mainly ethnic Russians, but also some natives – in all-Russian intellectual debate and politics.

The main journalistic fora of this debate among local Muslims were the *Turkestan Wilaiiatining Gazeti*, *Dala Wilaiiatining Gazeti* and *Tercuman*, which were discussed in Chapter 2, as well as a plethora of new periodicals which were prompted by the Manifesto of 17 October 1905. Among the new Kazakh periodicals were the *Ishim Dalasi* (*Ishim Steppe*), the *Ay Qap* (*Come On, Kazakhs*), the *Kazakhstan* and the *Kazakh*. In Turkestan, the most popular new periodicals included the journal *Al-Islah* (*Reform*) and the newspapers *Tudjor* (*Merchants*) and *Khurshid* (*Sun*), while in Bukhara it was the newspaper *Bukhara-yi Sharif* (*Noble Bukhara*).[1] These periodicals and newspapers were dominated by news and essays on local and regional history and customs. They largely avoided politically sensitive topics related to pan-Turkism and pan-Islamism and advocated obedience to the tsar. They also reflected the main themes being debated within the Muslim faction of Russia's first parliament, the *Duma*, which was formed during the revolution. Although the faction was dominated by pro-*jadid* Tatars and Caucasian Muslims, it also included a few secular and *jadid*-minded deputies from the Kazakh Steppe, such as Alikhan Bukeikhanov (1866–1937) and Mustafa Chokay (1890–1941).[2] Ideologically, Muslim deputies were close to the *Cadets*[3] and were similarly preoccupied with land reform and equal political and legal rights for all peoples of the multi-ethnic Russian Empire, especially Turkestani Muslims who were not represented in the *Duma*. Additionally, they raised such specifically Muslim issues as the provision of greater autonomy for Russia's Muslims in religious, educational and cultural matters, the institutionalisation of *waqf* and the recognition of Friday as the official weekly holiday for Muslim civil servants, traders and workers.

The Central Asians' rising national awareness acquired new momentum under the influence of the First World War, in which the Russian Empire confronted the Muslim Ottoman Empire. At the beginning of the war Central Asian Muslims were largely apolitical and loyal to the *Ak Padishah*. However, the decision by Petrograd[4] in June 1916 to introduce conscription for Kazakhs and Turkestani Muslims, which was made because of Russia's growing problems at the front, had a catalytic and divisive effect on them.[5] The minority Russian-educated and pro-*jadid* representatives of the local elites backed this decision and even offered their assistance in its implementation, for example, by setting up recruitment committees and organising a propaganda campaign under the slogan 'Fighting for the Dear Motherland is the Sacred Duty of Russia's People, Christians and Muslims Alike'. They were supported by a number of pro-reform local periodicals which circulated patriotic slogans.

However, the majority of the Central Asian elite and ordinary people reacted negatively to the conscription decree, which they regarded as a violation of their centuries-long social order, defined by local *adats* and *shari'a*. Some *qadimist 'ulama'* and imams interpreted it as an unacceptable interference by *kafir* Christian Russia into the life of Central Asian Muslims and therefore called for a *gazat* against the Russian authorities. In July 1916, widespread resentment against the conscription decree provoked an anti-tsarist revolt in Khujand. By November 1916 it had spread further and turned into a mass Islamicised *basmachi*[6] movement, which engulfed a large amount of territory between the Amu Darya river and the Urals mountains. Many *basmachis*, however, were driven more by economic grievances against the seizure of their land by Russian and other Slavic settlers and the excesses of local landowners than by religious motives. They targeted Russian agrarian settlements, military garrisons, administrative and police buildings, and railway stations. *Basmachis* were particularly active in Semirechie *oblast'*, where they destroyed most of the immigrant settlements. Only in January 1917 did Russian troops manage to crush the uprising but in the process hundreds of Russian soldiers were killed, while the losses among the Central Asians, especially the Kyrgyz, amounted to over 200,000 dead. According to some estimates, the Kyrgyz lost over 40 per cent of their total population either directly in fighting or while attempting to escape to neighbouring China.[7] Among the political implications of the *basmachi* revolt of 1916 and its brutal suppression by Russian troops was the weakening of the authority of the tsar among Central Asian Muslims, and their increased receptiveness to the anti-monarchist and Bolshevik messages emanating from the imperial centre.

In February 1917, the Russian Empire was shaken by another bourgeois-democratic revolution, the repercussions of which were felt in Central Asia. Some representatives of the secular and pro-*jadid* Kazakh, Turkestani, Bukharan and Khivan elite welcomed the abdication of the Russian Tsar Nicholas II (1868–1918), the establishment of the Provisional Government and the prospect of some democratisation and increased political participation for the empire's Muslims. As in 1905, the pro-democracy movement among Russia's Muslims was dominated by Tatars and, to a lesser extent, Caucasian Muslims who in July 1917 at the All-Russia Muslim Congress voted in favour of the preservation of Russia as a unitary rather than a federal state.[8] The unitarist leanings of Russia's Muslim leaders alienated Kazakh and Turkestani Muslim politicians, some of whom joined the more nationalist-oriented parties and groups. One of them was the Kazakh national party *Alash Orda* ('Kazakh Horde', 1917–20) under the leadership of Alikhan Bukeikhanov, which advocated the establishment of Kazakh administrative autonomy within a democratic and federal Russian state. In Bukhara and Khiva a group of Muslim reformers, modelling themselves on the 'Young Turks', formed the organisations of 'Young Bukharans' and 'Young Khivans' which sought the removal from power of the emir and khan, constitutional reform, and wider political and cultural autonomy for Bukhara and Khiva within a federalised and democratised Russia. Among their leaders were Abdurauf Fitrat, Mahmud Khoja Behbudi and Munawwar Qari, as well as Faizulla Khojaev (1896–1938), Abdul Qadir Mukhitdinov (1892–1934), Akmal Ikramov (1898–1937) and Mustafa Chokay. The enthusiastic response to the 1917 February Revolution from the pro-reform Muslim minority was paralleled by the dismay and frustration of the *qadimist* majority, who feared that the dismantling of the Russian monarchy and its replacement by a republic might unleash uncontrolled political and social turmoil with dire consequences for all the peoples of the empire.

The establishment of Bolshevik rule in the Kazakh Steppe and Central Asia

On 25 October (7 November)[9] 1917, amid deepening political and economic crisis and military defeats at the front, power in Petrograd was seized by

Marxist-driven Bolsheviks under the leadership of Vladimir Lenin (1870–1924). This event, the 1917 October Socialist Revolution,[10] triggered a devastating civil war that was waged on the territory of the former Russian Empire until 1921. The October Revolution was welcomed by a relatively small number of Kazakh and Central Asian Muslim reformers. It had a catalysing effect on the 'Young Bukharans', who in March 1918, for a short period, established their control over Bukhara. However, most of the Kazakh and Central Asian elites as well as ordinary Muslims responded to it with caution, suspicion or overt hostility.

Initially, therefore, the social base of Bolshevism in the region consisted mainly of Russian and other non-Muslim immigrant professionals, workers and soldiers. This was quite different from the situation in Russia's Muslim-majority Volga-Urals and, to some extent, in the Muslim Caucasus, where there were Bolsheviks among the indigenous elites and a considerable pro-Bolshevik grass-roots movement. At its forefront were Volga Tatar Marxists and left-wing *jadids* such as Mulannur Vahitov (1885–1918) and Mir Sultan-Galiev (1892–1940),[11] as well as the Kazakh Turar Ryskulov (1894–1938). They generated the concept of 'Muslim communism', which drew on the perceived compatibility and mutual reinforcement of Islam and communism, and advocated the creation of a separate Muslim Communist party.

The Bolsheviks' stronghold in Central Asia was Tashkent, where, in the course of the armed uprising in late October 1917, they seized power from the Provisional Government's Turkestan Committee and created a revolutionary government – the Soviet ('Council') of Soldiers' and Workers' Deputies, which unleashed an intensive propaganda campaign aimed at winning the support of local Muslims. Among their first initiatives was the establishment in Tashkent in March 1918 of the Turkestan People's University for Central Asian Muslims. In April 1918, the Soviet under the leadership of Petr Kobozoev (1878–1941) and Fedor Kolesov (1891–1940), both of whom were ethnic Russians, proclaimed the establishment on the territory of the former Governorate General of Turkestan of the Turkestan Soviet Federative Republic (TSFR), which in September 1920 was renamed the Turkestan Autonomous Soviet Socialist Republic (TurASSR). Between 1920 and 1924, the TurASSR was included in the Russian Soviet Federative Socialist Republic (RSFSR).

However, outside Soviet Turkestan the Bolsheviks were faced with opposition from a variety of nationalist, Islamo-nationalist, White Russian and foreign interventionist forces. In December 1917, the leaders of the Kazakh *Alash Orda* established the *Alash Orda* Autonomy (1917–20) in Orenburg, which first allied with the Orenburg Cossacks and then with the White Russians. In summer 1919, the Bolsheviks advanced on the *Alash Orda*'s positions and in March 1920 liquidated its autonomy. Between August 1918 and March 1919 they were also confronted by the British military invasion in the Transcaucasus and present-day Turkmenistan. The official pretext for the British invasion, coordinated by General Wilfred Malleson (1866–1946), was 'the combating of German and Turkish propaganda' in the region.[12] In April 1919, the Red Army, led by Mikhail Frunze (1885–1925), forced the British troops to withdraw and return to their bases in the Punjab and Meshed.

Meanwhile, in the Ferghana valley the Bolsheviks were opposed by the Government of Autonomous Turkestan, which was created in November 1917 in Kokand. It was headed by Mustafa Chokay, who maintained his allegiance to the deposed Provisional Government, and largely comprised Muslim Central Asians. In February 1918, Bolshevik troops stormed Kokand and put an end to the Turkestan autonomy. Mustafa Chokay managed to flee and joined the anti-Bolshevik coalition, which included the White Russians, Cossacks, the *Alash Orda* and the Bashkir nationalists under the leadership of Zeki Velidi Togan (1890–1970).[13] The Bolsheviks' ruthless actions against the Kokand autonomy reignited the *basmachi* resistance, which engulfed a large part of the Ferghana valley. *Basmachis* were joined by troops loyal to Bukhara Emir Alim-Khan (1880–1944), as well as Turkmen tribes under the leadership of Djunaid-Khan (1857–1938). In November 1921, the *basmachi* movement received a boost when it came under the command of Enver Pasha (1881–1922), the former Ottoman Minister of War, who consolidated it and channelled it along pan-Islamic and pan-Turkic lines, though it scaled down following Enver Pasha's death in August 1922. Still, sporadic *basmachi* skirmishes persisted throughout the 1920s and 1930s. Among the *basmachis*' last leaders was Ibrahim Bek (Chokaboyev, 1889–1931), a native of Hissar in present-day Tajikistan, who throughout the 1920s repeatedly invaded eastern Bukharia from the territory of Afghanistan and Iran until in 1930 he was finally defeated by the Bolsheviks and executed in 1931 in Tashkent.

In April 1920, in the midst of fighting the *basmachis* and other opposition forces, the Bolsheviks safeguarded the establishment on the territory of the former Khiva Khanate of the People's Soviet Republic of Khorezm (1920–4) and, in October 1920, of the People's Soviet Republic of Bukhara (1920–4) within the former borders of the Bukhara Emirate as a transitional stage towards their comprehensive Sovietisation. In both republics, therefore, the preservation of *waqfs* and *mahkama-i shari'a* went side by side with Sovietised economic, infrastructural and educational modernisation. The Khorezm and Bukhara republics witnessed the intensive building of modern roads, bridges, telegraph lines and irrigation facilities, the opening of several teacher-training colleges, over fifty schools for children and adults, and the launch of three newspapers and two journals in the Chagatai language.

The consolidation of Bolshevik rule in Central Asia

By the end of 1922 the Bolsheviks had managed to consolidate their control over the Kazakh Steppe, Central Asia, as well as most of the former Russian Empire.[14]

This was achieved under conditions of extreme economic hardship, of civil war, foreign military intervention and international isolation. Arguably one of the crucial factors in the Bolsheviks' initial success was their radical socio-economic and national programme, which was attuned to the core needs and aspirations of the Russian Empire's multi-ethnic and polyconfessional impoverished majority. The Bolsheviks denounced the Russian Empire as the 'prison of peoples', categorically negated 'Great-Russian chauvinism' and promised land, social justice, and national and religious equality to all dispossessed and discriminated peoples of the former empire. Among the first Bolshevik political documents were the 'Declaration of Rights of Peoples of Russia', 2 (15) November 1917, and the 'Address to All Muslim Toilers of Russia and the East', 20 November (3 December) 1917, which were addressed to Muslims and other non-Russian and non-Orthodox peoples of the former Russian Empire. They proclaimed the equality and sovereignty of all peoples of the former empire and their right to national self-determination up to and including secession and the formation of independent states, and abolished all national and national–religious privileges and restrictions.

In Central Asia, as in other parts of the former empire, the Bolsheviks launched attacks on landowners, bankers and money-lenders, and began to distribute expropriated land among the poor and dispossessed, who made up the bulk of the region's population. At the same time they offered amnesty to those *basmachis* who gave up armed resistance. Of particular significance were the Bolsheviks' 'Muslim communism' and their public display of respect for Islam, including the return of the venerated Qur'an of Uthman from Petrograd to Tashkent. It is important to note that the Bolsheviks' conciliatory approach towards Islam and Muslims, which persisted until the mid-1920s, was in stark contrast to its overt assault on the Russian Orthodox Church as one of the pillars of the Russian autocracy and monarchy.

Having crushed the *basmachi* resistance the Bolsheviks were faced with the even tougher task of ensuring the sustainability of their rule over the Kazakh Steppe and Central Asia. A major challenge related to the existing loyalties and patterns of social mobilisation defined by tribal, regional and Islamic solidarities, rather than by national or political affiliation. Another challenge was the controlling of mostly nomadic Kazakhs, Kyrgyz and Turkmen, who did not recognise political borders. An aggravating factor was the region's geographical proximity to and its cultural and religious affinities with Muslim Iran, Afghanistan, Xinjiang and Turkey. Of particular concern to the Bolsheviks were pan-Islamic and pan-Turkic influences emanating from Ottoman Turkey and its successor the Republic of Turkey, despite the initial rapprochement between the Lenin government and the Turkish nationalists under the leadership of Mustafa Kemal Atatürk (1881–1938), the founder of the Turkish republic.[15]

The Bolsheviks dealt with these challenges by generating distinctive Soviet Islamic and nationality policies aimed at the dissolution of Islamic beliefs and practices within various national cultures, the creation of an apolitical 'Soviet Islam' and the forging of new Sovietised nations out of Central Asian Muslims. Initially, the Bolsheviks' Islamic policy resembled that of Catherine the Great. Thus, in the first years after the October Revolution Moscow[16] largely preserved *mahkama-i shari'a* and did not openly interfere in the system of Islamic education, although, compared with the tsarist authorities, they favoured *jadidist* rather than *qadimist madrasahs*. The Bolshevik nationality policy was aimed at the comprehensive integration within the Soviet state of Central Asians, the building blocks of which policy were the region's territorial delimitation, the 'invention' of new nations with their distinctive languages and national cultures, and the creation of sizeable Persian and Slavic enclaves within newly formed Turkic-majority polities.[17] This territorial delimitation (*razmezhivanie*) was implemented in several stages during the period between 1917 and 1936. When, in December 1922, the Lenin government established the Union of Soviet Socialist Republics (USSR), consisting of the Soviet Socialist Republics of Russia, Ukraine, Belorussia and Transcaucasus, the territories of the Kazakh Steppe and Central Asia were only partially included in it. Until 1924, the Turkestan Autonomous Soviet Socialist Republic (TurASSR) continued to be part of the Russian Soviet Socialist Republic (RSFSR), while the Bukhara and Khorezm People's Soviet Republics existed as separate polities.

In 1924/5 the Bukhara and Khorezm People's Soviet Republics were amalgamated into the Uzbekistan Soviet Socialist Republic (UzSSR), which incorporated the Tajikistan Autonomous Soviet Socialist Republic (TajASSR) with its capital in Dushambe (Dushanbe),[18] and the Turkmenistan Soviet Socialist Republic (TurSSR) with its capital in Poltoratsk (Ashgabad).[19] In 1929, TajASSR was upgraded to a union republic: the TajSSR with its capital in Stalinobad (Dushanbe). The Communist parties of Bukhara and Khorezm were transformed into the *SredAzBureau* (*Sredne-Aziatskoie Biuro*) of the Russian Communist Party of Bolsheviks (RCPb). As a result of this delimitation, the culturally and economic integrated Ferghana valley was divided between the republics of Uzbekistan, Tajikistan and proto-Kyrgyzstan, which acquired sizeable Tajik, Uzbek and Kazakh minorities.

In 1920, the Kazakh-dominated Ural'sk, Turgai and Simipalatisk *oblasts* and parts of the Caspian and Orenburg *oblasts* were united within the Kyrgyz Soviet Socialist Autonomous Republic (KyrASSR) within the RSFSR, with its capital in Orenburg. In 1925, the KyrASSR was renamed as the Kazakh Autonomous Soviet Socialist Republic (KazASSR),[20] and its capital was moved to Kyzyl-Orda and in 1927 to Alma-Ata (Almaty). In 1924, the Kyrgyz-dominated areas of the TurASSR were transformed into the Qara-Kyrgyz Autonomous *Oblast'* of the RSFSR with its capital in Pishkek (Bishkek); in 1925, it was renamed the

Kyrgyz Autonomous *Oblast'* (KyrAO) within the RSFSR; and in 1926 it was upgraded to the Kyrgyz Autonomous Soviet Socialist Republic (KyrASSR) within the RSFSR, with its capital in Frunze (Pishkek).[21] In 1936, the KyrASSR and the KazASSR were transformed into the Kyrgyz Soviet Socialist Republic (KyrSSR) and the Kazakh Soviet Socialist Republic (KazSSR), respectively. Since then and until 1991 the region was referred to in Soviet political and academic discourse as 'Kazakhstan and Middle Asia'. Overall, the Bolshevik national and territorial *razmezhivanie* had major and far-reaching consequences for the region. It replaced the centuries-long major divide between sedentary peoples and nomads by divisions between constructed Uzbek, Tajik, Kyrgyz, Kazakh and Turkmen ethnonational entities separated by newly drawn politico-administrative borders. After the dissolution of the USSR in 1991 those borders acquired international status by dividing the newly independent states of Uzbekistan, Tajikistan, Kyrgyzstan, Kazakhstan and Turkmenistan.

Central Asia and the Kazakh Steppe under Stalinism

The death of Vladimir Lenin in 1924 and the ascendance of Joseph Stalin (1878–1953) as the new and more dictatorial Soviet leader introduced considerable changes into the Bolshevik national and religious policy.[22] Stalin, who did not tolerate any criticism, launched a direct attack on those politicians and intellectuals who disagreed with his vision of Soviet state- and nation-building and his style of leadership. Many of them were his former colleagues and associates, who belonged to the first Bolshevik generation. They were accused of constructed 'crimes', such as rightist or leftist leanings, Trotskyism, petit-bourgeois nationalism, religious obscurantism, pro-British, pro-German or pro-Japanese espionage, and were subjected to persecution, imprisonment, exile and execution.[23] High-profile Muslim Bolshevik leaders who were executed by the secret police included Sultan-Galiev; Akmal Ikramov, the first secretary of the Communist Party of Uzbekistan; Turar Ryskulov, the chairman of the Soviet government of Turkestan; and Faizulla Khojaev, the former leader of the 'Young Bukharans' and a key figure in the Communist Party of Uzbekistan. They were replaced by less educated *apparatchiks*, who did not question the validity of Stalin's judgements and policies. Most newly appointed Central Asian Party leaders, except in the UzSSR, were newcomers of Slavic, Jewish and German ethnic origin.[24] The main conductors of Stalin's leadership policy in the region were the aforementioned *SredAzBureau*[25] of the Central Committee of the All-Russia Bolshevik Communist Party (VKP(b)),[26] the Communist parties of the newly formed Central Asian republics and the national branches of the all-Russia secret police – the United State Political Directorate (OGPU, 1923–34), which was followed at first by the People's Commissariat of Internal Affairs (the *Narodnyi Komissariat Vnutrennikh Del*, NKVD, 1934–46), then by the Ministry of State Security (*Ministerstvo Gosudarstvennoi Bezopasnosti*, MGB, 1966–53) and, finally, by the Committee of State Security (*Komitet Gosudarstvennoi Bezopasnosti*, KGB, 1954–91).

A constituent part of the Stalinist radical cadre reshuffle was the training of ideologically reliable indigenous Communist Party and government functionaries.[27] This training was conducted within a wider campaign of 'indigenisation' (*korenizatsiia*), which started in the late 1920s. The goal of *korenizatsiia* was the prevention of the development of nationalism among Central Asians and other non-Russians of the former Russian Empire through the provision of national territories, education, scholarship, languages, cultures and the forging of loyal national elites.[28] The *korenizatsiia* was marked by Moscow's favouritism towards representatives of a particular region or tribal group, tending, for example, to promote to key Party and government positions natives of Khujand in Tajikistan, northerners in Kyrgyzstan, and representatives of the *Ulu Juz* among the Kazakhs.

Stalin's leadership also significantly altered the previously relatively liberal Bolshevik approach to Islam and the Muslim clergy and unleashed a ruthless assault comparable with that against the Russian Orthodox Church. Both were branded as remnants of medieval backwardness and obscurantism, and were deemed to require eventual eradication. In 1925, Stalin initiated the establishment of the 'Union of Godless Militants' (1925–47) under the leadership of Yemelian Yaroslavskii (Minei Gubel'man, 1878–1943). Initially, the Union employed over 16,000 enthusiastic atheists engaged in administrative and propaganda warfare against clergy of various religious persuasions and any religious manifestations across the USSR. The 'Union' acquired its own publishing house *Atheist*, which published anti-religious books, the newspaper *Bezbozhnik* (*Godless*) and the journal *Antireligioznik* (*Anti-Religionist*). By the end of the 1930s the 'Union' had over 96,000 branches and over 3 million activists across the USSR. In Central Asia, its first branch appeared in 1928 in Uzbekistan headed by I. G. Khansuvarov, a close associate of Akmal Ikramov.

A symbol of the Bolsheviks' anti-Islamic drive in Central Asia became the *hujum* campaign for unveiling Central Asian Muslim women, who were perceived as a 'surrogate proletariat'.[29] The Stalinist leadership equated the veiling of women with the alleged backwardness of arranged marriages, child marriages, *kalym*, polygamy and *purdah*. The main targets of the *hujum*, which began in 1927, were sedentary Uzbek and Tajik women, who wore *paranja* and *chachvon*, and were secluded at home. By contrast, most Kazakh, Kyrgyz, Turkmen and other nomadic Muslim women were spared *hujum* because, for practical reasons, they did not wear the veil and only covered their hair. The *hujum* was conducted by Party functionaries and officials of specifically formed *Zhen'otdels* ('Women's departments') dominated by non-Muslim women.[30] They organised public rallies and mosque gatherings in support of unveiling and broader women's rights. *Zhen'otdel* functionaries applied particular pressure on wives and other female relatives of Central Asian men who were members of the Communist Party. The *hujum* split Uzbeks and Tajiks into two camps. One included officials and ordinary members of the Uzbekistani Communist Party, as well as a small number of non-partisan Muslims and even pro-*jadid* Muslim clergy, who argued that veil-wearing was not prescribed by the Qur'an. The other camp consisted of *qadimist* clergy and their numerous following among ordinary Muslims. They fiercely opposed the *hujum* and equated unveiled women with prostitutes, subjecting them to public humiliation, ridicule or even inciting their killing. Widespread resistance to *hujum* persisted through the 1930s and cost hundreds of thousands of female and male lives. But by the late 1930s the Bolsheviks had accomplished the unveiling and de-seclusion of most Uzbek and Tajik women, albeit the number of housewives among them still remained higher than among the Kazakh, Kyrgyz and non-Muslim women of Central Asia. Child marriages were also drastically reduced, while an increased number of weddings came to be conducted at non-religious state registrar offices. Women were also encouraged into professional employment and Communist Party and regional governing structures.

In parallel with the *hujum* the Bolsheviks encroached on the positions of Sufis and *qadimist* clergy. The Stalinists particularly targeted Sufi sheikhs and ordinary Sufis due to the clandestine nature of Sufi networks, which it was impossible for them to infiltrate. In December 1925, the regional Soviet authorities passed a law on confiscation of *waqf* land aimed at undermining the economic independence of Muslim authorities. Under various pretexts *qadimist mullahs*, *qazis* and *mudarrises* were removed from mosques, *mahkama-i shari'a*, *madrasahs* and *maktabs* and replaced by more cooperative *jadid*-oriented clergy. Many *qadimist madrasahs* and *maktabs* which did not pass the Bolshevik registration were shut down. Most remaining mosques and pro-*jadid* schools were first centralised and subordinated to the Ufa-based muftiiate and subsequently closed down. By the end of the 1930s, as a result of this approach, Central Asian Islam and its Muslim clergy had suffered serious losses. Thousands of Sufis and Muslim clerics had perished, Persian-based Central Asian scholarship and publishing were disrupted in the course of the dual alphabet change from Arabic to Latin (and subsequently to Cyrillic),[31] *waqf* property was nationalised and Islamic education had been severely undermined.

By the late 1920s *madrasah* education, which had been available only for boys, was marginalised and superseded by nationwide co-educational secular primary education. The Bolsheviks were particularly concerned with the provision of free education across the country because they regarded it as a major medium of the USSR's sustainable competitiveness in a hostile capitalist international environment. Lenin's slogan 'to study, to study and to study' became the motto of the Soviet educational project. The legal basis for the introduction of Soviet secular education in Central Asia and the Kazakh Steppe was the 1918 Bolshevik decree on the separation of church from state and school from church, which previously had been applied only to Christian Orthodox schools. However, the promotion of Soviet education in the region was hampered by its particularly low level of literacy, which varied between 2.3 and 6 per cent of the total population. Most of those who could read and write studied in *madrasahs*, while a very small minority were graduates of Russo-native schools and gymnasia.

In the context of the Bolsheviks' 'cultural revolution' Moscow dispatched thousands of teachers from European Russia to the cities, towns and villages of the region. They were largely young men, members of the *Komsomol*,[32] who themselves had had between four and seven years of structured education. They created a network of special *likbez* ('liquidation of illiteracy') schools for male and female adults, as well as co-educational primary schools which taught the secular curriculum in Russian and national languages. From 1930, free standardised primary education became compulsory across the USSR. In order to create national Uzbek, Tajik, Kazakh, Kyrgyz and Turkmen school teachers the Bolsheviks established dozens of newly trained teachers across the region who combined educational, ideological and social functions by overseeing children's socialisation through the system of *Little Octobrists*, *Young Pioneers* and *Komsomol* membership.[33] These teachers acquired high social status due to the Central Asian culture of special respect for educated and learned people; among Uzbeks and Tajiks these Soviet teachers were respectfully addressed as *domullos*.

The introduction of Soviet education in the region was complicated by the linguistic diversity of the local population, their poor knowledge of the Russian language and the prevalence among the educated minority of Chagatai and Farsi written languages which used Arabic script. In 1918, Lenin's leadership authorised the establishment in Tashkent of the Turkestan Peoples' University, the idea for which had been promoted by Sergei Oldenburg (1863–1934), Nikolai Mallitskii (1873–1947) and other distinguished imperial Russian Orientalists and geographers. The main aim of the university was to develop vernacular Uzbek, Kazakh, Kyrgyz, Turkmen, Tajik and some other indigenous languages into distinctive national literary languages. In the late 1920s Arabic script was replaced with Latin. A decade later, however, Latin was replaced with Cyrillic as a preventive measure against potential political and ideational influences from neighbouring Turkey, which in 1928 shifted to the Latin alphabet. In parallel, within the wider drive for further centralisation and homogenisation of the USSR and the need for a nationwide lingua franca, the Bolsheviks increased the teaching of Russian and in Russian at school and university levels. Still, the provision of teaching in national languages at schools remained high. For example, at the end of the 1930s in Uzbekistan school education was conducted in twenty-two languages. Each Central Asian republic acquired a set of higher education institutions and academic research institutes which followed the nationwide Russian-based curriculum, a constituent part of which was Marxist–Leninist theory. In the space of decades the Bolsheviks had succeeded in raising the level of literacy among 16–50-year-olds to 90 per cent.[34] Among the implications of mass literacy was the sharp rise in social mobility among Central Asian men and, particularly, women who for the first time in the history of the region acquired access to structured school education and professional employment.

Alongside the educational sphere, Central Asian Muslims were Sovietised through their fully-fledged inclusion into the USSR-wide political, social, economic and information systems. At the political level, along with other peoples of the multinational Soviet Union, they became governed by national Communist Party and Soviet bodies which were directed and controlled by the USSR Communist Party Central Committee, Supreme Soviet and union ministries. Young Central Asian men became internationalised and Sovietised through their compulsory military conscription. At the economic level, Central Asian Muslims were included in the integrated Soviet economy with particular emphasis on cotton and silk growing and processing, mining and the food industry. Economic integration was assured by the region's comprehensive electrification, which covered even the most remote villages and *qishloqs/qishlaqs*, and its inclusion in the USSR-wide transport system.

But the process of Sovietisation of *dekhkon/dekhkan* and nomads, who constituted the bulk of the population, was ambivalent. It occurred within Stalin's collectivisation, launched in 1929 – 'The Year of the Great Turn' – which was implemented in four stages and was completed by the end of 1938. Its proclaimed aim was the USSR-wide nationalisation of most land and livestock and the creation of a network of *kolkhozes* (*kollektivnoe khoziaistvo*) and *sovkhozes* (*sovetskoie khoziaistvo*, state-owned collective farms), consisting of *kolkhoz* and *sovkhoz* members who lacked ownership of land and livestock. In the central and western parts of the USSR the collectivisation effectively destroyed *obshchina*-based traditional farming, but it failed to do so in rural Central Asia. Instead, it led to modification of *mahallah*-based agriculture through the formation of *kolkhozes* and *sovkhozes* either along the borders of existing *mahallahs*, or along the lines of other traditional family- and neighbourhood-based communities and the attributing to them of new administrative functions. Compared with the earlier period, when traditional *mahallahs* were self-sufficient communities with well-defined functions such as the distribution of land and the regulation and maintenance of the irrigation infrastructure, the Sovietised *mahallahs* were integrated within Soviet governance. Nevertheless, the preservation of the institution of *mahallah*, albeit in a modified form, contributed to the retention among rural Tajiks, and to some extent Uzbeks, of Islamicised traditionalism, which would be mobilised in the post-independence period, as will be discussed in Chapters 4 and 7. In 1923, the Bolsheviks subordinated *mahallah* committees to local Soviets and the Interior Ministry's departments, and tasked them with the collection of taxes, census and the preservation of order.[35] Furthermore, in the process of land and water reforms the Bolshevik authorities encouraged the formation of new *mahallahs* which were charged with the maintenance of roads, canals and other items of the newly created infrastructure.

The collectivisation of Central Asia's nomadic and semi-nomadic peoples, especially the Kazakhs, was particularly traumatic and controversial. Within a ruthless campaign against Kazakh *bais*, tribal chieftains and rank-and-file nomads and semi-nomads who were deemed to be *kulaks* the Bolsheviks launched a mass confiscation of 'excessive' livestock,[36] accompanied by land allocation and their compulsory registered attachment to particular *auls* with clearly defined administrative borders. Following the USSR-wide introduction of internal passports with *propiska* Kazakhs and other nomads acquired permanent postal addresses which were recorded in their internal passports. Kazakhs particularly strongly resisted giving up their livestock and coercive sedentarisation and collectivisation. They resorted to mass slaughter of their horses and cattle leading to the severe hunger of 1931–3, known as the *asharshylyk*. Many tried to flee the collectivisation altogether by migrating to Uzbekistan, China, Mongolia, Afghanistan, Iran and adjacent regions of Russia. A cumulative consequence of the *asharshylyk* and migrations was the reduction of the Kazakh population by over 40 per cent.

In the late 1930s, the Stalinist authorities, having achieved the de-nomadisation of most Kazakhs, turned against Kazakh Bolsheviks, many of whom belonged to the *Orta* and *Kichi Juzes* that in the past had better accommodated themselves to Russian rule than the Kazakhs of the *Ulu Juz*. They were purged within the wider Stalinist assault on alleged petit-bourgeois nationalists of all sorts and subsequently replaced by representatives of the *Ulu Juz*. Until the end of the Soviet period representatives of the *Ulu Juz* dominated the Communist Party leadership of Kazakhstan, including Dinmukhamed Kunayev (1912–93) and Nursultan Nazarbayev (b. 1940), while members of the *Kichi Juz* prevailed in the oil industry and members of the *Orta Juz* in metallurgy.

After several decades of Kazakhs' and other nomads' enforced Sovietised agricultural and urban existence their national identity, which previously had been defined by nomadism intertwined with tribal customary law and the Sufi-shamanist belief system, significantly mutated and acquired some new sociocultural features. This identity transformation, which later became known as *mankurtizatsiia*,[37] accounted for their higher level of susceptibility to the Sovietised linguistic and cultural Russification compared with the historically sedentary Tajiks and Uzbeks, who retained their ethnocultural core. In the post-independence period, as will be discussed in Chapter 5, it has also been an important factor in their greater susceptibility to external Islamic and Protestant Christian influences. On the other hand, the de-nomadisation of

Soviet Kazakhs and other Central Asian nomads was accompanied by their unprecedented economic, educational and cultural advance which enabled them to greatly surpass their brethren abroad. This became particularly apparent with the arrival in Kazakhstan in the late 1990s of Kazakh repatriates, *oralmans*, from China, Mongolia, Iran, Afghanistan and Pakistan.

Between the Great Patriotic War and 'mature socialism'

The Sovietisation of Central Asian Muslims, as well as other peoples of the USSR, received a powerful impetus during their fight against the invasion by Nazi Germany in the Second World War (1939–45). The war, in which over 25 million[38] of the USSR's peoples of different ethnic and confessional backgrounds lost their lives, catalysed a nationwide mobilisation and consolidation and turned into the Great Patriotic War (1941–5), which played a pivotal role in the defeat of Nazi Germany. The war enhanced Central Asians' social and cultural mixing with other peoples of the Soviet Union, both Muslims and non-Muslims, while the war-induced relocation of major Soviet military and other industries from the western regions of the USSR to Central Asia accelerated the latter's industrialisation and modernisation: Kazakhstan acquired over 140 industrial enterprises, Uzbekistan over 100 and Kyrgyzstan over 30. The Central Asian republics obtained hydro-electric plants and dozens of research and educational institutions, as well as hospitals.[39] A corollary was the sharp increase in the involvement of Central Asian men and women, in particular, in industrial production and their close professional collaboration with engineers and workers evacuated from European parts of the USSR. Additionally, in the years leading up to and during the war, Central Asians' multifaceted interaction with other peoples was advanced by the arrival in the region of over a million civilian evacuees from the western regions of the USSR, as well as of over a million deportees from the Caucasus, the Volga region, the Baltics and the Far East.[40]

The war had a considerable impact on state–Muslim relations. Given the nationwide anti-Nazi mobilisation the Stalinist leadership moderated its anti-religion stance. In 1941, it dissolved the infamous 'Union of Godless Militants' and gave permission for the organisation in Ufa of the pan-USSR Muslim conference which called on the country's Muslims to fight against Nazi Germany's aggression. In 1943, Moscow also created three more new regional muftiiates in addition to the existing one in Ufa: the Buinaksk-based muftiiate, which dealt with the Sunni Muslims of the North Caucasus; the Baku-centred muftiiate, which administered the Shi'a and Sunni Muslims of Azerbaijan; and the Tashkent-based muftiiate of Central Asia and Kazakhstan (SADUM, *Tsentral'no-Aziatskoe Dukhovnoe Upravlenie Musul'man*).[41] In 1945, the Kremlin permitted the reopening of the *Mir-i Arab Madrasah* in Bukhara; subsequently, in

1971, the Islamic Institute of Imam Bukhari was opened in Tashkent. The number of students in both institutions, which were formally administered by SADUM, was relatively small, albeit sufficient for the needs of the muftiiates' central, regional and local structures.

SADUM, like the other three muftiiates, was closely monitored by a government department – the Council for Affairs of Religious Cults (CARC, 1944–65)[42] – which was infiltrated by the intelligence services. As in the imperial Russian period, the government authorities cultivated a distinctive 'Soviet Islam', which inherited the main features of 'Russian Islam', and were similarly wary of links between Soviet Muslims and their co-religionists abroad. They severely restricted any external engagements by Soviet Muslims or their exposure to foreign Islamic printed and audio messaging. From 1945, Soviet Muslims had been symbolically permitted to conduct *hajj* to Mecca and Medina, though the actual number of carefully selected *hajjees* remained minimal. In 1947, the future Muftii Ziyouddinkhon and a few other graduates of the *Mir-i Arab Madrasah* spent a year of training in the renowned Islamic university of *Al-Azhar* in Cairo.

The doctrinal position of SADUM was affected by the Bolsheviks' preference for *jadids* and Islamic revivalists and their hostility towards representatives of Islamic traditionalism and Sufism. Thus, SADUM's first muftii, Eshon Bobokhon ibn Abdulmajidkhon (1858–1957, in office 1943–57) and members of his inner circle belonged to the Naqshbandi *tariqat*[43] and claimed their adherence to Central Asian Islamic tradition. However, both his son, Muftii Ziyouddinkhon ibn Eshon Bobokhon (1908–1982, in office 1957–82) and grandson, Muftii Shamsuddinkhon Bobokhon (1937–2003, in office 1982–9), were influenced by the pro-*Salafi* teaching of Shami Domullo al-Tarablusi (d. 1932), a native of Lebanon, who came to Central Asia in 1919 via eastern Turkestan. It is symptomatic that Shami Domullo venerated 'Muhammad al-Bukhari, rather than al-Maturidi, Ahmad Yasawi or Baha al-Din Naqshband. He considered al-Bukhari to be the leading representative of authentic Islamic scholarship, refuted Central Asian Islam as *bid'a*, and called for the return to the Islam of the Prophet Muhammad and the Four Righteous Caliphs. He disseminated his ideas through the underground group *Ahl-i Hadith* ('People of *Hadith*').

SADUM's pro-*Salafi* leanings were evidenced in its denouncing as *bid'a* of such manifestations of Central Asian Islam as *ziiarats* to tombs of local Sufi saints and other sacred sites, the authority of *otins*, the customs of *kalym/mahr*, remembrance wakes on the third and seventh days after the death of a Muslim, demonstrative mourning of a deceased that included loud weeping by women, and conspicuous celebrations of the sunnet/*hatna* and other major events of the life circle. It was also symptomatic that the curricula of both the *Mir-i Arab Madrasah* and the Islamic Institute were at dissonance with the Central Asian Islamic tradition and were dominated by the Arabic language, the *tajwid*, the *tafsir* and the *hadiths* from Arabic primary sources rather than Persian- or Chagatai-based medieval commentaries on *fiqh* and Sufi teachings.

In spite of the imposed conformity of SADUM, which by the 1970s had turned into the main representative of 'Soviet Islam',[44] its relationship with the Soviet state was complex. On the one hand, it acted as the medium for state control and management of its Central Asian Muslim citizens, as well as an agency for state foreign policy in the Muslim world. Consequently, it began to apply concepts of *ijtihad* and *idtikrar* and to issue *fatwas* which provided *shari'a*-based rulings aimed at accommodating Muslims' existence within the atheistic framework. For example, some SADUM *fatwas* equated socialist work with an Islamic virtue, allowed for the flexibility in observance of *Uraza-Bairam*, *Zakat al-Fitr* and *Qurban-Bairam*, advised against women wearing the *chador* and *paranja*, and condemned the ancient custom of women's self-immolation. On the other hand, SADUM's muftii and senior clergy retained a considerable degree of autonomy from the Soviet state and wielded respect among *'ulama'* outside the country, who never accused them of *shirk*, *kufr* or *bid'a*. It was also symptomatic that SADUM's formal reaction to the Soviet invasion of Afghanistan in 1979–89 was subdued, while in private many of its representatives were critical of it.

In general, the establishment of SADUM and its elevation to a position at the centre of official Soviet Islam marked the integration of Central Asian Muslims into the nationwide system of state–Muslim relations initiated by Catherine the Great in 1789. As in the imperial Russian period, the institutionalisation of the Soviet version of 'official Islam' was accompanied by the securitisation and criminalisation of 'unofficial Islam', which referred to any unsanctioned manifestations of Islamic beliefs and practices both of a Sufi or a *Salafi* nature. Meanwhile, the dichotomy between the Soviet version of 'official Islam' and 'unofficial Islam' was not clear-cut and it was not always followed even by their leading representatives, who often came from the same venerated Islamic dynasties and substantiated their true Muslim-ness by the same dogmatic references. At the grassroots level, the dominant positions belonged to poorly educated unofficial imams and mullahs, many of whom were itinerant, critical of the state and SADUM, and who insisted on strict adherence to centuries-long Central Asian Islamic beliefs and practices.

Throughout the 1950s and early 1960s, which were dominated by de-Stalinisation and nationwide economic advance under the Communist Party leadership of Nikita Khrushchev (1894–1971, in office 1953–64), the First Secretary of the USSR Communist Party, the Soviet way of life became dominant among Central Asian Muslims, although the level of Sovietised secularisation varied considerably between representatives of different ethnic and social groups. By the 1970s, most of them, as well as other people in Muslim-majority parts of the USSR, were well integrated, in one form or the other, within the economic, social and political fabric of Soviet society. This new reality was endorsed by the Soviet Constitution of 1977 which postulated the beginning of 'mature socialism' and the emergence of that new social entity – the 'Soviet people' (*Sovetskii narod*). Accordingly, it was assumed that, irrespective of their ethnic and religious backgrounds, the various peoples of the USSR, including Central Asians, had acquired some fundamental common characteristics of Soviet-ness which distinguished them from their co-ethnic and co-religious brethren across the border and made them immune to political, nationalist and religious influences emanating from abroad. These generic characteristics were regarded as primary, while ethnonational and religious characteristics were secondary. Under this premise, the Soviet-ness of Central Asian Muslims was deemed to be irreversible.

In the context of 'mature socialism' which was associated with the economic and political stability under the Communist Party leadership of Leonid Brezhnev (1906–82, in office 1964–82), Moscow notably relaxed its control over the Central Asian republics and enabled their leaders to further their national cultures intertwined with Islam. Particularly representative in this respect was Uzbekistan under the leadership of Sharof Rashidov (1917–83, in office 1959–83), which enjoyed a considerable degree of autonomy from the Kremlin. Subsequently, the Rashidov government became associated with widespread corruption, epitomised by the so-called 'Rashidov cotton affair'.[45] Additionally, the 'mature socialism' of Uzbekistan and other Central Asian republics allowed them to develop direct economic, educational and cultural links with Libya, Syria, Egypt and some other Arab countries which was conducive to some interaction with *other* Islam. This interaction intensified further during the Central Asian conscripts' involvement in the Soviet invasion of neighbouring Afghanistan between 1979 and 1989.

Among the implications of the relative political liberalisation and the limited exposure of Central Asian Muslims to 'foreign' Islam was the reawakening of Islamic debate among a small pious minority who were linked to underground *hujrahs* and *dawrahs*. The leading participants in this debate were Muhammadjon Rustamov, known as Hajjee Domla Hindustoniy, Rahmatulla 'Alloma-*qori*, 'Abduvali-*qori* Mirzoyev and Hakimjan-*qori* of Margilan, who significantly differed in terms of their doctrinal and political orientations. Thus, Hajjee Domla combined *Al-Maturidiia*-based Central Asian Islamic traditionalism with elements of Islamic reformism. Consequently, he favoured Central Asian Muslims' quietism and *sabr*, while opposing Muhammad Abduh's political stance and regarding Saudi Arabia's *Wahhabis* as *Khawarij*.[46] By contrast, 'Alloma-*qori*, 'Abduvali-*qori*, Hakimjan-*qori* and some representatives of 'unofficial Islam' leaned towards *Salafism*. In this respect they were dogmatically close to the 'official Islamic' leadership of SADUM.[47] During *perestroika*, which will be discussed in Part II, some former pupils of Hajjee Domla preserved their adherence to Central Asian Islam, while others turned towards *Salafism*.

Overall, by the end of the Soviet period most Central Asian Muslims, alongside other Muslim peoples of the USSR, had acquired a distinctive identity as 'Soviet Muslims', which enabled them to reconcile Islam and Sovietised secularism. It also further distanced them from their ethnic brethren and co-religionists abroad, while bringing them closer to other Soviet people of both Islamic and non-Islamic religious background. Although most Central Asians continued to identify themselves as Muslims, they began to treat Islam as part of their distinctive Uzbek, Tajik, Kazakh, Kyrgyz and Turkmen national traditions. As such, Islam continued to be one of the central regulators of their family, communal and social life, while being merged with newly established Soviet patterns of behaviour and socialisation. Most Central Asian Muslims, especially those of working age, ceased to observe four out of the five pillars of Islam, such as *salat*, *hajj*, *zakat* and *sawm*. Muslim-ness was often reduced to the observance of the fifth pillar of Islam, that is, *shahadah*, circumcision and Muslim burial. Central Asian conscripts were forced to eat pork and non-*halal* (forbidden) meat and drink vodka and other alcoholic drinks. The absence of mosques was compensated for by the activities of itinerant 'unofficial' mullahs and the transformation of some *chaikhonas*, bakeries, *Doma Kul'tury* ('Houses of Culture') or other non-religious public places into undercover prayer houses with improvised *mihrabs*. Some Muslims continued to visit in secret both the old and newly formed *mazars*, many of which were disguised as secular cultural objects. It can be argued therefore that Sovietisation has had a major transformative impact on Central Asian Muslims and, as will be explored in Part II, has continued to shape the political, institutional and ideational trajectories of the newly independent republics of Uzbekistan, Kazakhstan, Kyrgyzstan, Tajikistan and Turkmenistan.

Notes

1. Alongside the outlined periodicals, educated Muslim Turkestanis, Bukharans and Khivans acquired access to newly established bookstores which contained volumes on history, literature and contemporary politics published in Kazan, Istanbul, Cairo and Beirut.
2. Mustafa Chokay was a Russian-educated representative of the Kazakh Genghizid elite.
3. *Cadets* is a Russian abbreviation for members of the Constitutional Democratic Party, 1905–17, the leading liberal opposition party, which renounced violence and advocated a peaceful transformation of the Russian autocracy into a democratic and liberal constitutional monarchy.
4. In 1914, during the First World War in which Russia confronted Germany, St Petersburg was renamed Petrograd.
5. Under the tsar's decree of 25 June 1916, 230,000 Muslim men from the Governorate General of the Steppe and 250,000 Muslim men from Russian Turkestan were assigned to various auxiliary works on the front. Olcott [1986] 1995, p. 119.
6. The word *basmach* derives from the Turkic verb *basmak* which means 'to attack'. Originally, it was used by the Russians in relation to Muslim raiders on their positions in Central Asia. See more on the *basmachi* movement in Broxup 1983.

7. For more on the revolt of 1916, see Sokol 2016.
8. The position of Russia's Muslim politicians on the future organisation of the Russian state was not consistent. At the First All-Russia Muslim Congress, which was held in May 1917 in Moscow, they voted for the ethnonational federalisation of Russia, including the formation of Russia's autonomous republics of Kazakhstan and Turkestan, and for the establishment of the *Milli Shuro* ('National Council') to oversee the practical implementation of federalisation. However, the Second All-Russia Muslim Congress, which was held in July 1917 in Kazan, switched its support from the federal to the unitarist principle of Russia's political organisation.
9. From February 1918, the date of the October Revolution shifted from 25 October to 7 November 1917 because of the Bolshevik's switch from the Julian to the Gregorian calendar.
10. The nature of the events in October 1917 in Petrograd remains highly debated among academics in Russia and globally. While some regard them as a genuine social revolution which was hijacked by the Bolsheviks, others are inclined to perceive them as a Bolshevik coup d'état.
11. Vahitov and Sultan-Galiev occupied leading positions in the Bolshevik *Narkomats* (*Narodnyi Komissariat po Natsional'nostiam*, 'Ministry of Nationalities') under the leadership of Joseph Stalin.
12. Molberly 1987, p. 335.
13. For a detailed discussion of the Bashkir national movement, see Validi Togan 1994.
14. Among the territorial losses of the Bolshevik state were Finland and the Baltics in the north and in the south the towns of Kars, Kagyzman, Ardahan, Olty and Artvin, which were transferred to Turkey.
15. From 1919, the Bolshevik government, in its drive to break its international isolation, sided with the Turkish nationalists who, following the Ottomans' defeat in the First World War, fought the war of independence (1919–22) on several fronts, including against the Western-backed Greek and Armenian invasions. Bolshevik Russia's supplies of gold and arms were pivotal in Turkey's survival as an independent state. In March 1921, the Lenin government was the first to recognise the Kemalist government of Turkey. The friendly relations between the two countries were sealed by the Moscow treaty of 16 March 1921 and the Kars treaty of 13 October 1921. From the mid-1930s Soviet–Turkish relations deteriorated due to disagreement over the status and control of the Straits. In the aftermath of the Second World War Turkey aligned with the anti-Soviet bloc and in 1952 it joined NATO.
16. On 5 March 1918, the Lenin government moved the new state's capital from Petrograd to Moscow.
17. The process of the Soviet ethno-territorial delimitation of Central Asia was not straightforward and it was aggravated by the ethnic and linguistic intermingling of various peoples and the existence of numerous vernacular languages which lacked written form.
18. The original name of the city was Dushanbe. Between 1924 and 1929 it was known as Dushambe, and from 1924 until 1961 it bore the name of Stalinobad in honour of Josef Stalin. In 1961 it was renamed again as Dushanbe.
19. The original name of the city was Ashgabat. Between 1919 and 1927 it was called Poltoratsk after Pavel Poltoratsky (1888–1918), the Commissar of Labour in Soviet Turkestan, who was executed in Merv by the Bolsheviks' opponents.
20. Between 1925 and 1930 KazASSR included the Qara-Kalpak Autonomous *Oblast'* (QKAO), with its centre in Turt-Kul'. In 1930, the QKAO was moved into the RSFSR and in 1932 into the UzSSR.
21. In 1926, Pishkek (Bishkek) was renamed Frunze in honour of Mikhail Frunze (1885–1925), the Bolshevik military leader who was born there.

22. For an in-depth analysis of the Stalinist policies, see Hosking 1992; Read 2002.
23. On the Stalinist political repressions, see Okhotin and Rogiskii 2016.
24. Between 1937 and 1950, the Communist Party of Uzbekistan was headed by Usman Yusupov (1890–1966); between 1937 and 1946, the Communist Party leader of Tajikistan was Dmitrii Protopopov (1897–1986); from 1939 until 1947, the Communist Party leader of Turkmenistan was Nikolai Fonin (1905–74); between 1938 and 1945, the Communist Party leader of Kazakhstan was Nikolai Skvortsov (1899–1974); and between 1938 and 1945, the Communist Party leader of Kyrgyzstan (Kirgiziia) was Alexei Vagov (1905–71).
25. Between 1922 and 1924 the *SredAzBuro* was headed by Yan Rudzutak (1887–1938), an ethnic Latvian; between 1924 and 1931 by Isaak Zelenskii (1890–1938), a Jew; and between 1931 and 1934 by Karl Bauman (1892–1937), also a Latvian.
26. In 1952 the VKP(b) was renamed the Communist Party of the Soviet Union (CPSU).
27. The training was conducted through short-term courses for Party instructors, as well as longer courses at the newly established Communist Party schools.
28. On different aspects of *korenizatsiia* in Central Asia, see Martin 2001, pp. 125–81.
29. For a detailed discussion of *hujum*, see Keller 2001; Northrop 2004; Kamp 2006.
30. The first *Zhen'otdel* within the *SredAzBureau* was headed by Serafima Liubimova (1897–1958), an ethnic Russian. For more on the activities of the *Zhen'otdel* in Central Asia, see Tursunov 1987, pp. 126–31.
31. The dual alphabet change occurred between 1925 and 1943.
32. *Komsomol* is an abbreviation for All-Russian Leninist Young Communist League, a political youth organisation which was created by the Lenin government in October 1918. It acted as a de facto youth subdivision of the Communist Party.
33. From 1922 all schoolchildren were automatically affiliated to scout-like young people's organisations, such as *Little Oktobrists* (7–9-year-olds), *Young Pioneers* (10–14-year-olds) and *Komsomol* members (14–28-year-olds).
34. *Vsesoiuznaia Perepis' Naseleniia 1939 Goda*, Institut Demografii Natsional'nogo Issledovatel'skogo Universiteta 'Vysshaiia Shkola Ekonomiki', available at: http://www.demoscope.ru/weekly/ssp/sng_nac_39.php?reg=5, last accessed 24 November 2017.
35. The *mahallah*'s status and functions were further codified in 1932, 1941, 1961 and 1983.
36. The Bolsheviks introduced quotas on the permitted size of a Kazakh household's herd. Among nomads it was limited to 400 head, among semi-nomadic Kazakhs to 300 head and among sedentary Kazakhs to 100 head. Olcott [1986] 1995, p. 170.
37. The term 'mankurt', defining a person who lost his or her language and consequently ethnic identity, was first introduced in 1980 by the Soviet Kyrgyz novelist Chingiz Aitmatov.
38. The exact number of Soviet losses during the Second World War remains debated by military historians and varies from over 20 million to over 30 million. See Krivosheev 2001.
39. Hiro 1994, pp. 33–4.
40. Among deportees to Central Asia were Koreans, Germans, Poles, Chechens, Ingush, Karachai, Balkars, Crimean Tatars, Kurds, Kalmyks, Bulgarians and Meskhetian Turks. In Kazakhstan alone deportees made up one-fifth of its total population, while Kazakhs turned into an ethnic minority.
41. For a detailed discussion of Soviet muftiiates, see Ro'i 2000.
42. In 1965, CARC was transformed into the Council of Religious Affairs (CRA, 1965–91).
43. According to some sources, he belonged to the Yasawi *tariqat*. See, for example, Naumkin 2005, p. 39.
44. From the 1960s, SADUM was the only Soviet muftiiate that had the right to send a small number of vetted students to study at Islamic universities and colleges in Egypt, Syria, Algeria and Libya. In 1968, SADUM acquired its own publishing house, which began to

produce its own journal *Muslims of the Soviet East* and other Islamic publications promoting a positive image of Soviet Muslims in the Muslim world. The journal was published in Russian, Uzbek, Persian, Arabic, English and French.

45. At the centre of the 'Rashidov cotton affair' was the falsification of the cotton production figures reported by Tashkent to Moscow with the aim of increasing central funding to the republic. In the late Soviet period, the 'cotton affair' resulted in mass purges in the Party and government structures of Uzbekistan. In post-independence Uzbekistan, Rashidov was rehabilitated and elevated to the status of Uzbekistan's national leader. For more on Rashidov's political evolution, see Critchlow 1991, pp. 39–59.
46. The *Khawarij* were members of a group that broke from 'Ali, the fourth Righteous caliph, when he agreed to arbitration with his rival, Muawiyah, the founder of the Umaiiad caliphate. The *Khawarij* considered arbitration to be a human violation of God's decision to choose the imam. Some *Khawarij* further developed this extreme stand by applying the concept of *takfir* to those Muslims they accused of a lack of Islamic purity.
47. On the complexities of the relationship between representatives of 'official' and 'unofficial' Islam, see, for example, Abashin 2015, pp. 498–9; DeWeese 2002, p. 309.

Selected reading

Primary sources

Hindustani, Muhammadjon (2007), *Al-Shaykh Muhammad ibn Rustam al-Hindustani* (*History of Wahhabis*), in B. Babadzhanov, A. Muminov and A. von Kugelgen (eds), *Disputy Musul'manskikh Religioznykh Avtoritetov v Tsentral'noi Azii v XX Veke* (*Disputes between Muslim Authorities in Central Asia in the 20th Century*), Almaty: Dayk-Press, pp. 105–7, 113–16.

Al-Shami, Sa'id ibn Muhammad al'Asali al-Tarablusi (2007), *Al-Jumal al-Mufida fi Shahr al-Jauhara al-Farida* (*A Useful Summary of the Unique Treasure*), in B. Babadzhanov, A. Muminov and A. von Kugelgen (eds), *Disputy Musul'manskikh Religioznykh Avtoritetov v Tsentral'noi Azii v XX Veke* (*Disputes between Muslim Authorities in Central Asia in the 20th Century*), Almaty: Dayk-Press, pp. 62–71.

Secondary sources

Abashin, S. (2015), *Sovetskii Kishlak: Mezhdu Kolonializmom i Modernizatsiei* (*Soviet Kishlak: Between Colonialism and Modernisation*), Moscow: Novoie Literaturnoie Obozrenie.

Allworth, E. (ed.) (1994), *Central Asia: One Hundred Thirty Years of Russian Dominance: A Historical Overview*, Durham, NC: Duke University Press.

Bennigsen, A. and S. E. Wimbush (1985), *Mystics and Commissars: Sufism in the Soviet Union*, London: Hurst.

Bennigsen, A. and S. E. Wimbush (1986), *Muslims of the Soviet Empire*, London: Hurst.

Bergne, P. (2009), *The Birth of Tajikistan: National Identity and the Origins of the Republic*, London: I. B. Tauris.

Crews, R. D. (2006), *For Prophet and Tsar: Islam and Empire in Russia and Central Asia*, Cambridge, MA: Harvard University Press.

d'Encausse, H. C. (2009), *Islam and the Russian Empire: Reform and Revolution in Central Asia*, London: I. B. Tauris.

Edgar, A. L. (2004), *Tribal Nation: The Making of Soviet Turkmenistan*, Princeton, NJ: Princeton University Press

Hosking, G. (1992), *A History of the USSR: 1917–1991*, London: HarperCollins.

Keller, Sh. (2001), *To Moscow, Not Mecca: The Soviet Campaign against Islam in Central Asia, 1917–1941*, London: Praeger.

Khalid, A. (1998), *The Politics of Muslim Cultural Reform: Jadidism in Central Asia*, Berkeley: University of California Press.

Landa, R. (1995), *Islam v Istorii Rossii* (*Islam in the History of Russia*), Moscow: RAN.

Martin, T. (2001), *The Affirmative Action Empire: Nations and Nationalism in the Soviet Union, 1923–1939*, Ithaca, NY: Cornell University Press.

Masov, R. (1991), *Istoriia Topornogo Razdeleniia* (*History of the Butchered Division*), Dushanbe: Irfon.

Northrop, D. (2004), *Veiled Empire: Gender and Power in Stalinist Asia*, Ithaca, NY: Cornell University Press.

Okhotin, N. and Rogiskii, A. (2016), 'O Mas'shtabakh Politicheskikh Repressii v SSR pri Staline, 1912–53', *Memorial*, Moscow, available at: http://lists.memo.ru, last accessed 12 November 2017.

Olcott, M. ([1986] 1995), *The Kazakhs*, Stanford, CA: Hoover Institution Press.

Poliakov, S. P. (1992), *Everyday Islam: Religion and Tradition in Rural Central Asia*, Armonk, NY: M. E. Sharpe.

Ro'i, Y. (2000), *Islam in the Soviet Union: From the Second World War to Gorbachev*, London: Hurst.

Roy, O. (2011), *The New Central Asia: Geopolitics and the Birth of Nations*, London: I. B. Tauris.

Smith, J. (2013), *Red Nations: The Nationalities Experience in and after the USSR*, Cambridge: Cambridge University Press.

Sokol, E. D. (2016), *The Revolt of 1916 in Russian Central Asia*, Baltimore, MD: Johns Hopkins University Press.

Tolz, V. (2011), *Russia's Own Orient: The Politics of Identity and Oriental Studies in the Late Imperial and Early Soviet Periods*, Oxford: Oxford University Press.

Yemelianova, G. M. (2002), *Russia and Islam: A Historical Survey*, London: Palgrave.

PART II

Central Asian Muslims after independence

CHAPTER 4

Muslims of Uzbekistan

Some general observations

Perestroika and *glasnost'* of 1985–91 and the ensuing dissolution from above of the Soviet Union faced Central Asian leaders and elites with the existential challenge of how to ensure their independent political and economic survival and sustain development detached from the integrated Soviet political and economic system. At the same time, they were forced to consider how to preserve societal cohesion within inherited Soviet politico-administrative borders which often cut across homogeneous ethnocultural communities. Crucial for our consideration of the Muslims of Uzbekistan in this chapter – but also in later chapters on the Muslims of the other four Central Asian republics – is the recognition that personal leadership in these societies is of paramount importance in determining in all their aspects the policies and strategies associated with nation-building. Thus, to analyse what it means to be a contemporary Muslim in the Uzbekistani secular state – indeed, what it means to be Muslim in all the republics – one must first consider the relationship between the leaderships' political reactions to *perestroika* and the consequent meaning and forms of each republic's 'Islamic revival'. In the case of Uzbekistan, this relationship explains how President Islam Karimov's (1936–2016, in office 1989–2016) confrontation with real and imagined Islamists had shaped the country's political system and its official social, ethnonational and religious policies. It is within this larger perspective that we should examine the nature of Muslim experience in Uzbekistan – and with different leaders and specific contexts in other republics – allowing us to more clearly perceive and understand such issues as the factors of continuity and change in state–Muslim relations, the role of so-called 'official Islam' and its relationship with Central Asian Islamic traditionalism.

Initially, all five Central Asian republics responded with a high degree of political and societal congruence to *perestroika* and *glasnost'*. This was largely due to the widespread perception that they represented an intra-system adjustment rather than the centre's conscious drive towards controlled devolution or even dismemberment of the USSR. The first secretaries of the Communist Party across Central Asia thus largely followed the anti-communist and pro-democracy trajectories initiated by the Kremlin. They repackaged themselves as presidents and embarked on some limited liberalisation of the political and economic life of their respective republics. At the societal level there was a rise in popular activism, which was accompanied by the emergence of various democratic, nationalist and Islamic parties and organisations that sought meaningful participation in the political process.

More importantly, all the Central Asian republics witnessed the so-called 'Islamic revival', which was enhanced by the region's reintegration within the wider Muslim world and the influx into Central Asia, as well as into other Muslim-majority parts of the USSR, of Saudi Arabian and other foreign Islamic foundations and missionaries. The rise of Islam was underpinned by the collapse of communist ideology and the severe deterioration in economic conditions as a result of the drastic reduction in the subsidies, investments and other supplies from the centre, which inevitably led to growing unemployment and impoverishment. The level and depth of economic problems differed significantly from republic to republic, correlating with population density and resource availability. Particularly dire were the economic conditions in the Ferghana valley,[1] which coincidentally experienced a more intensive 'Islamic revival'.

In December 1991, the initially unified reaction of Central Asian leaders towards *perestroika* was replaced by their increasing divergence. It was triggered by the unconstitutional dismemberment, in Belavezha, of the USSR,[2] opposed in Central Asia at both the elite and popular levels. Following sudden independence, the heads of state of Uzbekistan, Kazakhstan and Turkmenistan retained their political power and opted for speedy ideological and political disengagement from Moscow, which was in any case embroiled in economic and political chaos under the banners of democratisation and monetarism. In contrast, the Dushanbe-based leadership of Tajikistan was challenged by regional elites, resulting in a bloody civil war. In Kyrgyzstan, the Soviet-era leadership was ousted by new, non-nomenklatura leaders who pursued the Russia-like liberalisation path with equally devastating consequences. What all post-Soviet Central Asian republics had in common, however, was the Soviet-era centrality of their respective leaders in shaping their post-independence transition.

Ramifications of *perestroika*

In Uzbekistan, the advent in 1985 of Mikhail Gorbachev (b. 1931, in office 1985–91) as the reform-minded Communist Party and Soviet leader was met with bewilderment and concern among the ruling elite and for that matter most of the wider population. They feared that the ensuing reforms might unravel the existing centre–periphery relations and create a domino effect with devastating consequences for the whole USSR, including Uzbekistan. In addition, some Uzbekistani officials and the wider public resented the heavy-handedness of the Gorbachev leadership and its protégé, Inomjon Usmonkhojayev (1930–2017, in office 1983–8), the First Secretary of the Communist Party of Uzbekistan,

Figure 4.1 Map of Central Asia after 1991

in dealing with the participants in the aforementioned 'Rashidov cotton affair', which had been initiated by Gorbachev's predecessor, Yurii Andropov (1914–84, in office 1982–4).

Nevertheless, the Moscow-driven pro-democracy impulses were met with enthusiasm by a relatively small group of Tashkent-based intelligentsia, who aspired to democratic and liberal change and who sought greater ethnonational and cultural autonomy for Uzbekistan within the USSR. In 1988, Abdurahim Polat (b. 1945), a computer science professor, founded *Birlik* ('Union'), a party which united some nationalist-minded members of the intelligentsia. *Birlik* organised a series of demonstrations demanding wider national autonomy for Uzbekistan, Uzbek as the sole state language, a ban on Uzbek conscripts serving outside Uzbekistan, the rehabilitation of Uzbek historical figures and the diversification of the cotton-based national economy. In 1990, a group of *Birlik*'s pro-democracy activists under the leadership of Muhammad Solih (b. 1949), a poet, formed an independent political party, *Erk* ('Freedom'), which pursued a more liberal-democratic agenda than the nationalistic *Birlik*.

Though there was widespread discontent with the Gorbachevian leadership among Uzbekistan's political elite, this was not communicated to the Kremlin and there was no attempt at popular mobilisation on an anti-Moscow platform.[3] Instead, the new Uzbekistani Communist Party leaders Rafiq Nishanov (b. 1926, in office 1988–9) and Islam Karimov followed Gorbachev's initiative in moving to dismantle the Communist Party. In March 1990, Karimov became president, while his close ally and the former mayor of Tashkent Shukrullo Mirsaidov (1939–2012, in office 1990–2) was appointed vice-president.[4] In the USSR-wide referendum of March 1991 Karimov ensured the voters' overwhelming support (93.7 per cent) for the preservation of the USSR as a 'reformed federation of equal, and sovereign states'.[5]

Karimov's pro-Union stance was, however, radically altered by the anti-Gorbachev coup d'état in Moscow on 19 August 1991. While Shukrullo Mirsaidov, like other Central Asian leaders, backed the *putchists*, Islam Karimov – who happened to be conveniently 'out of the office' on the day – used the failed coup to swiftly disengage Uzbekistan from the increasingly unstable and dysfunctional USSR. On 1 September 1991 he proclaimed Uzbekistan's independence and in November became the leader of the People's Democratic Party (PDP), the new personalised party of power replacing the Communist Party. On 21 December 1991 Uzbekistan, along with Kazakhstan, Kyrgyzstan, Tajikistan, Turkmenistan, Armenia and Azerbaijan, joined the Russia-speared Commonwealth of Independent States (CIS), followed by its membership in May 1992 of the CIS's military wing – the Collective Security Treaty (CST/CSTO).[6] In May 2001 Uzbekistan joined the Shanghai Five group, the China-led Eurasian security, political and economic organisation, which in June 2001 was renamed as the Shanghai Cooperation Organisation (SCO).[7] At the presidential elections on 29 December 1991, which took place four days after the formal dissolution of the USSR, Karimov, as the PDP candidate, legitimised his rule by receiving 86 per cent of the votes and beating his main rival, Muhammad Solih of the *Erk* party, who obtained 12.7 per cent. Karimov's overwhelming victory was secured by his effective deployment of the old Soviet 'administrative resource', which was inaccessible to his political rival. Another considerable factor behind Karimov's victory was his skilful channelling of the popular grievances about economic and social hardships against the leaders of Russia, Ukraine and Belorussia (Belarus), who violated the Soviet Constitution of 1977 by excluding Central Asian leaders from decision-making regarding the future of the USSR, thus causing the political and economic destabilisation leading to its fatal collapse.

Islam Karimov remained in control of Uzbekistan until his death in 2016, having been re-elected as president by overwhelming majorities three times – in 2000, 2007 and 2015. To his credit was the preservation of Uzbekistan's territorial integrity and political stability, as well as its considerable economic diversification and international assertiveness, all of which were achieved despite extremely difficult political, ethno-religious, economic and regional circumstances. The key ingredients of Karimov's political survival and the sustainability of his authoritarian rule were his strong Communist and Soviet credentials, his reliance on the powerful security services, his political shrewdness and his ability to effectively balance the interests of regional elites, as well as his personal charisma.

Meanings and forms of the 'Islamic revival'

Having won the presidential elections in 1991 Karimov had to consolidate his power base and preserve social and political order in conditions of economic collapse and rising interethnic and religious tensions.[8] Furthermore, he had to create an Uzbek nation-state within borders which were imposed from above and which often cut across homogeneous ethnic communities,[9] as well as generating a new integrating and legitimising ideology that would replace the supranational Communist and Soviet ideology. Of particular concern to Uzbekistan's secularist leader was the rise of Islam, boosted by the Gorbachevian *perestroika* and the new liberal Religious Law of 1990, in particular. The Law guaranteed freedom of conscience and religious activities, prohibited persecution on religious grounds and legalised Soviet Muslims' links with their foreign co-religionists.

The political liberalisation prompted a rapid shift in many people's self-identification, from being 'Communist' and 'Soviet' to 'Islamic' and 'Uzbek', though this arguably reflected the changed political discourse rather than a profound transformation of their worldview. The country, and the Ferghana valley in particular, witnessed an Islamic construction and publishing boom,

Figure 4.2 Boys of Samarqand (photograph by author, Samarqand, June 2013)

and the influx of foreign Islamic funders and proselytisers who freely distributed copies of the Qur'an and other Islamic publications. Alongside the registered new mosques and *madrasahs* numerous unregistered mosques and *madrasahs* also opened. Thus, by the mid-1990s there were around 6,000 mosques compared with 300 mosques in 1989.[10]

Perestroika affected SADUM as well. In 1989, Muftii Shamsuddinkhon Bobokhon was forced out of office by Muhammad Sodiq ibn Muhammad Yusuf (Mamayusupov (1952–2015, in office 1989–93),[11] an ethnic Uzbek, a charismatic representative of the 'young imams'[12] and subsequently the first muftii of independent Uzbekistan. He challenged the allegedly ineffective, servile and conformist SADUM leadership, and called for its cadre rejuvenation and its greater say in the political and social life of Uzbekistan. Muhammad Sodiq's views were shared by other Central Asian 'young imams', including Akbar Turajonzoda, Ratbek Nysanbai-uly and Nasrullah ibn Ibadullah, who subsequently became the muftiis of independent Tajikistan, Kazakhstan and Turkmenistan, respectively.

The movement of 'young imams' within 'official Islam' was paralleled by the movement of 'unofficial' *Salafi*[13] preachers and activists in the Namangan, Andijan and Margilan *oblasts*. Although *Salafis*, many of whom had *hujrah*-based Islamic backgrounds, made up only a small fraction of the Islamic activists, they had a greater impact on some young people because of their educational capacity, as well as their engaging and socially and politically relevant sermons. They were also more visible and effective due to their Islamic, rather than Central Asian, dress code as well as their organisational and financial advantages. Some local *Salafi* preachers became known as *hajjees* because of their dress and their positioning of themselves, on the basis of their *hajj* experience, as the bearers of 'true Islam'. They criticised traditionalist imams and mullahs for their allegedly poor knowledge of Islamic doctrine, their inability to conduct prayers correctly, their condoning of local 'non-Islamic' funeral and wake practices, as well as for attributing magic to *mazars*. Compared with elderly traditionalist imams, many of whom were *mahsums*, *hajjees* and their like were religious neophytes who rediscovered Islam through their interaction with 'true Muslims' from the Middle East. Unlike impoverished traditionalist imams, who made their living from ritual payments by equally poor congregationists, *hajjees* were well off due to their engagement in various lucrative businesses in Russia and other parts of the former USSR. They were therefore able to fund the building of mosques and to influence the decision-making process regarding the new mosques' imams.

Alongside financially self-sufficient *hajjee* imams some other *Salafi* preachers were funded by various official and non-government Islamic funds and organisations, based in Saudi Arabia, the Gulf, Egypt, Turkey, Iran, Pakistan and Afghanistan. The competition between these funds sometimes led to the bizarre situation where, within the same *mahallah*, one mosque was controlled by a local *mahsum*, the second by Saudi missionaries, the third by *Tablighis*[14] from Pakistan and the fourth by *Salafis* from Afghanistan. Both foreign and local *Salafi* preachers introduced some innovative Islamic practices such as allowing men to pray without skullcaps, or permitting women, contrary to the Central Asian Islamic tradition, to attend mosque in specially designated areas. *Salafis* combined their preaching with the distribution in mosques, *madrasahs*, *chaikhonas* and other public places of audio and video tapes and Islamic literature of a *Salafi* nature. These, along with works by Shami Domullo al-Tarablusi, included classic *Salafi* writings by Ibn Taymiyyah (1263–1338), as well as by his more modern followers such as Hasan al-Banna', Sayyid Qutb, Abu Al'a Maududi, Taqi al-Din al-Nabhani (1909–77), Hassan 'Abdallah al-Turabi (1932–2016) and 'Abd al-'Aziz bin Baz. Such materials implicitly opposed Al-Maturidiia-based Central Asian Islam and promoted non-*madhhab* Islam based exclusively on the Qur'an and Sunnah.

Some *Salafi*-minded local activists began to self-organise into opposition Islamic and Islamo-national parties and organisations. Among these was the Uzbekistani branch of the USSR's *Islamskaia Partiia Vozrozhdeniia* (IPV, 'Islamic Revival Party'),[15] which was formed at the end of 1990 in Tashkent under the leadership of 'Abduvali-*qori* Mirzoyev and 'Abdulla Utayev. From the first days of its existence, however, it was overshadowed by the much larger and more effective Tajik branch of the IPV, which will be discussed in Chapter 7. Of more prominence were a number of small *Salafi* groups such as *Barakah* ('Blessing'), *Tawba* ('Repentance'), *Islam Lashkarlari* ('Warriors of Islam') and *Adolat* ('Justice'), which were active in Andijan and Namangan *oblasts*. Among *Islam Lashkarlari* and *Adolat*'s activists were Tohir Yoldashev (1967–2009) and Juma Khodjiev/ Namangani (1969–2001). Members of these groups considered the establishment of an Islamic state their long-term objective, which they sought to achieve through Islamic education and gradual re-Islamicisation of society. Early on in their existence they opposed violence and focused on day-to-day tasks such as the provision of welfare to the impoverished population, the fight against pervasive crime and corruption, the improvement of safety on the roads, and the monitoring of prices at local bazaars in areas under their control. However, in the early 1990s members of *Adolat* and other Islamists, who numbered between several hundreds and several thousands, began to challenge the ruling secular regime directly by conducting armed attacks on police and local government officials.

The Karimov regime and the Islamic opposition

Throughout the 1990s Islam Karimov's autocratic rule was defined by his confrontation with a relatively small number of Islamists who became active in the Ferghana valley. It is alleged that on a personal level his uncompromising stance towards local Islamists was born out of his humiliation at a meeting in Namangan on 25 December 1991, when he was publicly challenged by Tohir Yoldashev, then the leader of *Islam Lashkarlari*, and made to agree to debate in parliament the establishment of an Islamic state in Uzbekistan. On a political level, Karimov's tough position on Islamists was predicated on their growing popularity, economic resources and military assertiveness in Namangan and Andijan *oblasts*. Between the late 1980s and the early 1990s a growing number of disillusioned and angry young men had become receptive to the Islamists' denunciation of the local authorities and law enforcement agencies as corrupt and self-seeking. The Islamists accused them of *kufr* and called for the replacement of Karimov's regime by an Islamic state. On a geopolitical level, Islam Karimov feared the potential spill-over effect of the Islamist-driven social and political turmoil in neighbouring Tajikistan, where in 1992 the Islamists defeated the pro-Soviet political establishment. Yet another potent Islamist threat emanated from the *Taliban* in neighbouring Afghanistan, with its considerable Uzbek and Tajik population – a threat that only increased after the dismantling of the Soviet security and border structures along the former USSR's southern borders.

These factors predetermined President Karimov's heavy-handed approach to Islamists and their sympathisers. During the Tajik Civil War (1992–7) they formed the so-called 'Namangani battalion' within the Tajik Islamic

Figure 4.3 *Non* traders in Samarqand (photograph by author, Samarqand, June 2013)

opposition, though this alliance was short-lived because of the divergent approaches of Uzbek and Tajik Islamists towards Afghanistan's *Taliban*, who were ethnic Pashtuns. While Uzbek Islamists under the leadership of Tohir Yoldashev and Juma Namangani sought close relations with the *Taliban*, Tajik Islamists under the leadership of Sayyid Abdulloh Nuri[16] sided with the anti-*Taliban* Northern Alliance under the command of Ahmad Shah Massoud (1953–2001), who was an ethnic Tajik. By the mid-1990s Uzbek Islamists, who were led by Juma Namangani and Tohir Yoldashev, had broken away from their Tajik counterparts and formed the *Islamskoe Dvizhenie Uzbekistana* (IDU, 'Islamic Movement of Uzbekistan'), which sought the violent removal from office of President Karimov, whom they stigmatised as *kafir*, and the establishment of an Islamic state in Uzbekistan. The IDU united hundreds of Uzbek guerrillas who underwent military training in Islamist training camps in Afghanistan, Pakistan and Chechnya, allegedly receiving financial and military assistance from the Pakistan-based *Jamiat Ulema-e-Islam* ('Assembly of Islamic Clergy') and Afghanistan's *Taliban*. The other alleged sources of their cash-flow related to their involvement in drug trafficking from Afghanistan to Tajikistan and Kyrgyzstan, hostage-taking for ransom and other forms of criminal activity.

In early 1999, the Uzbekistani authorities finally defeated the IDU in the course of a massive offensive triggered by the Tashkent bombing on 16 February 1999,[17] in which the IDU was implicated. Many Islamic militants were physically eliminated or jailed, while others fled to the Tavildara valley in Tajikistan or to northern Afghanistan. On two separate occasions, in August 1999 and August 2000, the IDU Islamists attempted a comeback from Tajikistan via southern Kyrgyzstan but were defeated by the joint Uzbek and Kyrgyz armed forces. In early 2001 some IDU affiliates joined the *Taliban* in Afghanistan and following the US-led invasion of Afghanistan in October 2001, triggered by the 9/11 attacks, they retreated to Pakistan's Tribal Areas (PTA) alongside the *Taliban*. Since then the IDU's militants have been concentrated around the town of Wana in south Waziristan of the PTA, from where they have conducted incursions into Afghanistan but have stayed away from Uzbekistan.

Since the 2000s, some younger IDU recruits have deviated from the movement's original exclusively anti-Karimov agenda towards international *jihadism*. For example, in 2002 Nazhmeddin Dzhalalov, a native of Andijan, and Sukhail Buranov (Sulaiman Abu Hudhaifa), a native of Tashkent, defected from the IDU and formed a separate international *jihadist* group – the *Ittihad Islamii-Jihad* (IIJ, 'Islamic Jihad Union'), the headquarters of which was in the town of Mir Ali in the PTA's northern Waziristan. It is alleged that the group was largely Uzbek, but also included *jihadists* from elsewhere in the former USSR as well as recruits from Turkey, Germany, Pakistan, Libya and other Arab countries. The leaders of the IIJ accused the IDU of subordination to the *Taliban* and of abandoning *jihad* in Uzbekistan. By contrast, the IIJ prioritised *jihad* against Karimov's regime, although it was also open for business in other parts of the world – for example, when it was involved in planning a series of bombings of an American military base in Rheinland-Pfalts in Germany in 2007. Allegedly the group established close links with *Al-Qaeda* via Abu Laith al-Libii (d. 2008) from Libya, who was an influential field-commander in *Al-Qaeda*. The IIJ's other regional ally was the *jihadist* Haqqani network,[18] which also had links to *Al-Qaeda*. According to some reports, since 2014 a number of IDU and IIJ fighters have joined ISIS in Iraq and Syria.[19]

Having crushed or expelled IDU militants from the country, the Karimov government turned its attention to another Islamist opposition organisation, *Hizb al-Tahrir al-Islamii* (HTI, 'Party of Islamic Liberation'), and its affiliates which were also active in the Ferghana valley.[20] Compared with the IDU, which originated in Uzbekistan and consisted mainly of ethnic Uzbeks, the HTI was an international and multi-ethnic Islamist organisation founded in 1953 in Jordan by a Palestinian judge, Taqi al-Din al-Nabhani (1909–77), a member of the Muslim Brotherhood. Among the first HTI leaders in Central Asia were 'Isam Abu Mahmud Qiyadati and 'Abd al-Qadim Zallum, both Jordanians, who arrived in the region in the early 1990s. In Uzbekistan the leading figures of the HTI were Abdulhafiz Nasyrov and Mamasadyk Kadyrov, who combined the HTI's general denunciation of the Western political, economic and cultural model with the exposure of corruption, bribery, arbitrariness, extortion and other malpractices of regional police and other government and law-enforcement agencies, and called for the creation of a caliphate on the territory of a unified Central Asia as the panacea for political fragmentation and economic hardship. They propagated their ideas through preaching and the dissemination of printed, audio and video materials, which were produced abroad and locally. *Tahriris* organised their supporters in a network of underground *halaqats* which were created in Andijan, Surkhan Darya and Namangan *oblasts*. It is alleged that by the early 2000s there were several thousand HTI members and sympathisers, most of them young Uzbeks but also Tajiks, Uighurs, Kyrgyz and other representatives of Muslim ethnic minorities. Among the reasons for the *Tahriris*' appeal were their offers of material support and the 'nativisation' of their ideological message. Unlike *jihadists*, at least until the US-led invasion of Afghanistan in 2001, *Tahriris* denounced violence and repeatedly expressed their willingness for dialogue with the authorities.

In 1996, there emerged an HTI affiliate group, *Al-Akromiia*, which was named after its founder, Akrom Yuldashev (1963–2011), a local mathematics teacher. The group catered for the interests of local Uzbek communities in Andijan, Namangan and Kokand *oblasts*, as well as in the Osh region of Kyrgyzstan. The strategy of *Al-Akromiia*, which was outlined in Akrom Yuldashev's book *Iymonga Yul* (*Path to Faith*), consisted of five stages towards the establishment of an Islamic state. *Al-Akromiia*'s cells were organised along family and *mahallah* lines. At the end of the 1990s another HTI splinter group, the *Hizb al-Nusra* ('Party of Victory'), was operating in the Ferghana valley. In 2001, in response to the US-led Western invasion of Afghanistan and Uzbekistan's alliance with the West against the *Taliban*,[21] the HTI and their affiliated groups embraced violent *jihad* against the Karimov regime.

In late May 2005, the Karimov government escalated its crack-down on real and perceived Islamists, triggered by the Andijan revolt which began as a peaceful demonstration demanding the release from jail of twenty-three local businessmen accused of membership of, or links with, *Al-Akromiia*. The demonstration soon evolved into a wider protest against dire socio-economic conditions and endemic corruption, and on 13 May 2005 President Karimov authorised the Interior Ministry and National Security troops to fire at the unarmed crowd. According to official sources, 187 people were killed, while unofficial sources estimated the death toll to be between 700 and 1,500.[22] Following the Andijan massacre thousands of suspected Islamists and their family members were jailed or subjected to various forms of persecution. *Mahallah* committees were obliged to reveal, name and shame potential *Akromites*, *Tahriris* and their relatives and sympathisers. Alleged Islamists were subjected to public trials reminiscent of the

Stalinist purge trials of the 1930s. This ruthless stance on political Islam has not changed under the new President Shavkat Mirziyoyev (b. 1957, in office since 2016), who was in any case closely involved in the suppression of the Andijan revolt.[23]

Islam Karimov leadership's regime- and nation-building

Islam Karimov's suppression of both Islamic and secular opposition went on side by side with intensive nation-building. In early 1992, Karimov removed his former ally and potential challenger Shukrullo Mirsaidov from office. In order to further weaken the powerful Tashkent and Ferghana regional elites Karimov increased the number of representatives of the Samarqand faction in the top posts as well as co-opting some influential members of the Tashkent and Ferghana factions into his close circle and forging trans-factional and trans-regional networks which were directly linked to him. In the aftermath of the presidential elections in December 1991, *Birlik* and *Erk* were politically marginalised and in December 1992 Muhammad Solih was charged with 'betraying the independence', put under house arrest and in April 1993 forced to flee the country.

Any attempts to form viable pro-democracy opposition parties or movements were suppressed. A case in point was *Azod Dehkonlar Partiiasi* (ADP, 'Party of

Figure 4.4 Samarqand street traders (photograph by author, Samarqand, June 2013)

Free Peasants'), which was established in 2003 under the leadership of Nigora Khidoyatova. During the critical period in the aftermath of the Andijan events the ADP formed the core of the pro-democracy *Serkuyesh Uzbekistonim* ('Sunny Coalition'), which was supported by the United States and other Western donors, and which attempted to campaign for political change in Uzbekistan. However, like its predecessors, it was eliminated by the authorities. Furthermore, President Karimov responded to the US critique of his handling of the Andijan events and their pro-ADP position by evicting American troops from the Karshi-Khanabad air-base, where they had been stationed since 2001 in order to facilitate American military operations in Afghanistan. The eradication of viable political opposition was accompanied by the formation of 'managed' opposition represented by various parties which could not threaten the party of power. Among these were, for example, the People's Democratic Party of Uzbekistan, the *Milli Tiklanish* Party ('National Renaissance' Party), the Social-Democratic Party *Adolat* ('Justice') and the Ecological Movement of Uzbekistan, which nominally competed with President Karimov's Liberal Democratic Party of Uzbekistan (LDPU) during the parliamentary elections in December 2014.

Karimov combined this consolidation of his authoritarian rule with the shaping of the Uzbekistani state and nation, albeit in conformity with the Soviet template with ideology at its core. The new legitimising ideology consisted of the rhetorical negation of the Soviet past and the promotion of an Islamicised Uzbek ethnonationalism alongside the constitutionally endorsed principles of state-framed nationalism. Uzbekistan's de-Sovietisation entailed the rehabilitation of those Uzbek leaders who were subjected to prosecution or were demoted by Moscow, a change in the naming of political and administrative structures and public bodies from Soviet and Russian to Uzbek, the introduction of a national currency, and the switching of the alphabet from Cyrillic to Latin. A powerful symbol of Tashkent's political distancing from Moscow was Karimov's rehabilitation of Sharof Rashidov and his elevation to the status of national hero. Under the nationwide renaming campaign what used to be Communist Party secretaries were turned into *hakims*, *oblasts* into *vilaiiats* and the Supreme Soviet (parliament) into the *Oliy Majlis* ('Supreme Assembly'). In 1994, Uzbekistan acquired its own currency, the *som*.

Karimov's leadership incorporated the concept of the traditional *mahallah*, based on principles of mutual cooperation, into the national ideology. The 1992 Constitution defined *mahallah* as a distinctly Uzbek traditional self-governing body and a citizen's service to the country, and its president was equated with the ethics of the *mahallah*. In the same year, President Karimov created the charity fund 'Mahallah', which was authorised to provide financial and material assistance to existing *mahallahs* and to support the formation of new ones. *Mahallahs* were thus integrated within state structures and turned into agencies of surveillance of their members in the name of fighting 'Islamic extremism'.

Mahallah imams and mullahs/*domullos* were to be appointed and controlled by local or provincial branches of the muftiiate and were expected to combine religious and political functions. Due to such intrinsically Soviet state intervention into the *mahallahs*' activities, they lost their traditional internal dynamism and flexibility, while acquiring some qualitatively new characteristics that distinguished them from both the Soviet-era *mahallahs* and *mahallahs* in neighbouring Tajikistan and Kyrgyzstan.

This distinctly Uzbek 'mahallisation' was supplemented by Soviet-era ethnic primordialism rooted in the theory of *etnos*,[24] which in a bizarre way was intertwined with a social constructivist notion of the nation. As in the Soviet period, scores of archaeologists, historians and ethnographers were mobilised to provide 'historical evidence' for the 'legitimate' rights of post-Soviet Uzbekistan to the territory within its existing borders, which run across the culturally and economically integral Ferghana valley and which created substantial ethnic minorities in its constituent polities. Of particular importance to the Karimov government was the safeguarding of its control over the Tajik-majority cities of Samarqand and Bukhara, which represent the historical, cultural and Islamic centre of the Ferghana valley. Perhaps for this reason the Karimov leadership chose to derive the Uzbeks' ancestry from the Samarqand-centred Timurids rather than from the ethnically closer Shaibanid Uzbeks, who, as we saw in Chapter 1, were also ethnic ancestors of present-day Kazakhs.

The role of Islam in the moulding of the Uzbekistani nation was ambivalent. On the one hand, President Karimov emphasised the centrality of Islam for Uzbek culture and identity and regarded it as a powerful symbol of independence from historically Christian Orthodox Moscow. He took his presidential oath on the Qur'an, positioned himself as an organic part of the Islamised Uzbek cultural heritage and welcomed the formation of the independent muftiiate of Uzbekistan as a marker of Uzbekistan's sovereignty. The Islamic holidays of *Uraza-Hait* (*'Id al-Fitr*) and *Qurban-Hait* (*'Id al-Adha*) were made public holidays. In 1992, President Karimov conducted *hajj* to Mecca and Medina during an official visit to Saudi Arabia and initiated Uzbekistan's joining of the Organisation of Islamic Conference (OIC).[25] The newly introduced currency – the *som* – contained images of Sherdor, Shahi Zind, Gur Amir in Samarqand, Chamsha-Ayub in Bukhara and other famous *madrasahs* and Islamic mausoleums; and the National University of Uzbekistan, which was founded in 1918, was renamed after the Timurid ruler and astronomer Ulugh Beg.[26]

On the other hand, from the first days of his presidency Islam Karimov drew a clear distinction in his public addresses and writings between 'Uzbek Islam' and 'Arab Islam'. The former was portrayed as a product of the particular Uzbek ethical and cultural heritage linked to the great Central Asian scholars, Sufis and *avliio*, while the latter was associated with the Arab Middle East and especially with *Salafism* and *Wahhabism*. The astronomers Ahmad al-Ferghani

(d. 861) and Ulugh Beg, the Islamic theologian al-Maturidi, and the great Sufi sheikhs of the past Ahmad Yasawi, 'Abd al-Khaliq Gijduvani and Baha al-Din Naqshband Bukhari, were singled out by the Karimov leadership as the great forefathers of the Uzbek nation. The government sanctioned the promotion of hagiographic works related to Naqshband and other distinguished 'Uzbek' Sufi sheikhs and incorporated into the official national discourse such Sufism-related virtues as service to society and state, honest labour, the listening to 'ancestors' and anti-individualism.

Accordingly, the practice of *ziiorat/ziiarat*, which is regarded as *shirk* or *bid'a* by *Salafis*, has been elevated into a historical symbol of Uzbek-ness. The authorities depicted *ziiorats* as an individual religious duty, and emphasised their apolitical nature compared with increasingly politicised 'foreign' Islam. The government has granted the status of the state's principal *avliio* site to the grave of *Khoja* Baha al-Din Naqshband in the village of Qasri Orifon near Bukhara. It may be that the state-endorsed glorification of *Khoja* Baha al-Din is linked to his being the spiritual mentor of Amir Timur, the proclaimed forefather of all Uzbeks. In 1993, official Tashkent staged a nationwide celebration of Baha al-Din Naqshband's 675th birthday[27] and opened a lavishly renovated shrine complex consisting of Baha al-Din's tomb, a mosque, a *khanaqah* and a *madrasah*. In addition to the Baha al-Din complex the authorities encouraged pilgrimages to several dozen other major Sufi and non-Sufi shrines[28] scattered over the territory of Uzbekistan and other parts of the Ferghana valley, so it is not surprising that since independence the number of people conducting regular *ziiorats* has kept on rising.

Nevertheless, the institutionalisation of 'Uzbek Islam' has occurred within a Sovietised version of secularism enshrined in the 1992 Constitution of Uzbekistan[29] and the 1998 Law on Freedom of Conscience and Religious Organisations. The latter made it illegal for women to wear the veil and for both men and women to wear Islamic dress in public places, with the exception of those working in registered Islamic institutions. The study of the Qur'an and *shari'a* were prohibited at schools. Instead, Uzbek traditional Islamic values and norms were integrated into various courses on religious history, ethics and morality, based on the *Odob-Noma* (*Book of Ethics*) and propagated through the TV Islamic channel that was launched in 1996. All university students were required to take a semester-long course on 'Freedom of Conscience in Uzbekistan' which outlined the status of religious organisations in secular Uzbekistan. It is also symptomatic that having demonstratively switched from the Cyrillic to Latin alphabet, the authorities nevertheless decided to preserve the Russified endings of -'ov'/-'ova' in their citizens' surnames and to keep Russian patronymics, rather than revert to pre-Soviet Islamicised Uzbek names.

During the 1990s, faced with the Islamist upsurge in the Ferghana valley and in neighbouring Afghanistan, the Karimov government, much earlier than his

Russian as well as other Central Asian counterparts, opted for the blanket securitisation of Islam-related issues. This led, as noted earlier, to the persecution and imprisonment of Islamists of both peaceful and pro-violence orientation, the introduction of surveillance over all observant Muslims through *mahallah* committees, a security crackdown on non-registered Islamic organisations and independent local preachers, and the deportation from Uzbekistan of foreign Islamic activists.[30]

State–Muslim relations and 'official Islam'

The state-driven suppression of Islamists and independent Muslims had significant repercussions for the muftiiate and its relations with both the government and Muslim communities. As noted earlier, in 1989 the last Soviet-era SADUM's Muftii Shamsuddinkhon Bobokhon was replaced by Muhammad Sodiq Yusuf. In 1991, the Tashkent-based and Uzbek-dominated SADUM was transformed into the Directorate of Muslims of Uzbekistan (DMU), headed by Muhammad Sodiq Yusuf (in office 1991–3). Doctrinally, Muhammad Sodiq positioned himself between Central Asian *Hanafism* and *Salafism*. Thus, he recognised the historical role of the *Hanafi madhhab* in the region, while claiming his adherence to *Ahl al-Sunnah wa al-Jama*ʿ ('People of *Sunnah* and Consensus') who opposed *ziiorats* and other Sufi practices. He campaigned for the restoration in the Ferghana valley of *waqfs* on the pre-Soviet scale, the development of Islamic publishing and the introduction of the study of Islam into the state school curriculum, regarding its absence as being a key reason behind young people joining underground Arabic-language study groups and Islamist cells. From the first days of independence Muftii Muhammad Sodiq was openly critical of President Karimov's blanket negative approach to any manifestations of Islamic activism and his suspicion of pious Muslims. His outspoken manner and independent stance inevitably put him on a collision course with the government, and from the beginning of 1992 the authorities began to interfere in the DMU's affairs and increased pressure on the muftii to either cooperate or quit. In 1993, Muhammad Sodiq was forced to resign and flee to Libya, where he remained till 1999 when he was permitted to return to Uzbekistan in a private capacity.[31]

Muhammad Sodiq's successors, including the current Grand Muftii, Usmonkhon Alimov (b. 1950, in office 2006–present), have been obedient implementers of official religious policy. As in the Soviet period, they have been closely supervised by the Government Committee for Religious Affairs (CRA) and the security services. Additionally, in 1995, the authorities set up the International Centre for the Study of Islam under the leadership of official theologian Mahmadud-*hajjee* Nuritdinov. The declared purpose of the centre, which has employed both secular scholars of Islam and Islamic theologians, was to bring together secularism and Islam and to generate 'enlightened Islam'. In

Figure 4.5 At the market restaurant (photograph by author, Tashkent, June 2013)

practical terms, it has provided guidance to the muftii on the contents of the DMU's *fatwas*[32] and other publications, and on acceptable Islamic practices and teaching curricula at the Islamic institute and registered *madrasahs*. In general, the DMU, like the Soviet SADUM, has been encouraged to focus on Islamic rituals such as prayer rules, cleanliness, *hajj* and dietary regulations, rather than on important social or theological issues.

In the aftermath of the 2005 Andijan revolt the authorities prompted the DMU to launch a re-registration campaign aimed at the closure of 'unreliable' mosques and *madrasahs* and to tighten control over the annual *hajj* of Uzbekistani Muslims to Mecca and Medina.[33] The process of selection and nomination of *mahallah* imams and mosque mullahs was tightened and had to be vetoed by local governments, security services and *mahallah* committees. The same procedures applied to the drastically reduced number of Islamic educational institutions, including the Islamic Institute in Tashkent, *Mir-i Arab Madrasah* in Bukhara and nine other registered *madrasahs*. Its *mudarrises* were required to pass a teaching test either at the muftiiate or at *qaziiats*. They taught *'aqeedah, fiqh, tajweed*, Arabic, Persian and English, as well as the history of world religions and IT. Applicants were required to sit an entrance exam in the history of Uzbekistan and in a foreign language and to pass an interview designed to gauge their political views. In 1999, the Karimov government established the Tashkent Islamic University which, unlike the Tashkent Islamic Institute, was staffed by secular specialists in Islamic studies and was not subordinate to the DMU.[34] The university offers programmes in *fiqh*, history, philosophy, economics and natural sciences. Islamic education has noticeably attracted only a very small number of young people, while the majority have favoured university degrees in finance, economics, business, IT, diplomacy, foreign languages and other secular subjects.[35]

Theologically, the DMU, in contrast to SADUM, joined the government in its overt denunciation of *Salafism* and *Jadidism* in favour of Central Asian Islamic tradition, and the conservative teaching of Muhammadjon Hindustoniy, in particular. It is symptomatic that the Uzbekistani official Islamic, as well as national, discourses do not contain any reference to the historical role of Uzbek *jadids*. This might be due to the *Jadids*' pan-Turkist or pan-Islamist tendencies, which are at odds with post-Soviet Uzbekistani nation-building, as well as the pro-*jadid* and pro-*Salafi* leanings of the SADUM leadership. As it happens, the DMU and the government's anti-*Jadidism* is not dissimilar from the position of the Tsarist Russian government, which also favoured Islamic traditionalists. In 2000, the DMU declared Central Asian *Hanafism* the official religious orthodoxy and instructed *mahallah* imams and mosque mullahs to speak out against *Wahhabism* and other non-*Hanafi* Islamic currents, thus jeopardising the religious rights of the Shi'a minority who for several centuries have lived in the Bukhara and Samarqand regions.[36]

In other respects, however, the Karimov government has largely preserved the Soviet model of state–Muslim relations, although adjusted to its nation-building strategy. Thus, it did not in fact revert to the pre-Soviet and pre-Russian period characterised by the existence of *waqfs*, *shari'a* courts and independent Islamic education. Instead, it retained and even further strengthened the muftiiate's dependence on the secular state and blocked its informal interaction with representatives of 'unofficial Islam' and providers of *hujrah*-based Islamic education which had existed prior to independence. Unlike their pre-Soviet counterparts, post-Soviet official Islamic clergy have refrained from any meaningful theological debate and have not participated in the state legal system. A corollary has been the further religious distancing of Uzbekistan from other non-Eurasian Muslim-majority countries, where there has been a link between Islamic law and national jurisprudence. At the same time, the persistence of the Soviet-era state–Muslim relations accounts for considerable similarities with such relations in Russia as well as other ex-Soviet Muslim-majority countries within the Genghizid historical borders.

'Cultural' Muslims?

Thus far official Tashkent has been relatively successful in channelling the 'Islamic revival' within the parameters of apolitical Central Asian Islamic traditionalism while containing the proliferation of 'non-traditional Islam', including that of a *jihadist* nature.[37] Consequently, the vast majority of Uzbekistani Muslims have remained 'cultural' and 'spiritual' rather than consciously religious and practising Muslims. For this reason, many of them do not see any contradiction between their Muslim-ness and the heavy consumption of alcohol at *to'ys* related to Islamic circumcisions, weddings and other major life cycle events. It is also regarded as quite normal for Muslim girls and young women, especially in Tashkent, to wear mini-skirts or tight jeans and not to cover their heads, even though at the same time they are expected to abide by Islamicised gender role patterns at home or to conduct *ziiorat.*

As noted earlier, Islam in Uzbekistan has co-existed with official secularism, important aspects of which have been the considerable epistemological and methodological continuity in Uzbekistan of the Soviet-era secularised academic and educational systems, the country's over 1 million-strong Russian minority,[38] the continuing widespread use of the Russian language, which is taught in many urban schools, and Uzbekistanis' exposure to Russian-language TV, digital media and online social media and networks, such as *VKontakte* ('In Contact') and *Odnoklassniki* ('School Friends'), as well as the existence of the over 3 million-strong Uzbek migrant community in Russia. Islam has remained outside the curricula in schools and universities, and the non-Islamic holiday of *Nowruz* has

Figure 4.6 Tashkent schoolchildren (photograph by one of the pupils, Tashkent, June 2013)

retained its supremacy over the main Islamic holidays of *Qurban-Hait* and *Uraza-Hait* in terms of popularity and its scale of celebration.

The actual correlation between what appear to be secular and Islamic norms and patterns of behaviour has differed considerably among urban and rural populations. It has also been mitigated by people's various kin and Islamicised social networks such as *gaps* (lit. 'conversations'), which unite friends, colleagues, neighbours and classmates who provide mutual social, economic and professional support. The depth of Muslim-ness is also dependent on a person's ethnicity, age, gender, social status and education. Thus, the majority of educated dwellers of Tashkent pursue a cosmopolitan lifestyle which is not so very different from those in Russia, Europe or the United States. A relatively small number of Uzbekistani professionals, who belong to the political and business elite, have in fact been educated in Russia, South Korea, Hong Kong and the West. Historically, an important factor in the cosmopolitanism of Tashkent and some other major cities has been their substantial Russian and other non-Muslim minorities.[39] Some Uzbekistani graduates did not return to Uzbekistan and formed a growing Uzbek diaspora in Russia, the United States and Western Europe, which has nevertheless retained close links with relatives and friends in Uzbekistan.

At the same time, Uzbekistan's 'Islamic revival' and its partial reconnection with the Muslim world have infused a notable diversity in the nature and attributes of people's 'Muslim-ness'. A large part of Uzbekistan's Muslims, especially in urban regions, have remained Muslims at heart while adhering to a minimalist set of Islamic practices, such as Islamic circumcision and burial. In the context of the official endorsement of Central Asian Sufism, it also became not unusual for a person, or a group of people, to perform *ziiorat* at the graves of *avliio*, Sufi sheikhs and at natural sacred sites in the hope of supernatural intercession in resolving various personal or health-related problems, or receiving *avliio*'s blessing prior to important undertakings. *Ziiorats* have become particularly popular among women.[40] Alongside the Sufi complex of *Khoja* Baha al-Din and other state-promoted Sufi sites the popular *ziiorats* have included over 3,500 smaller Sufi and non-Sufi shrines scattered across the Ferghana valley, among which have been the shrines of Imom *Khoja* Baror and *Chashma Ayub* ('Spring of Ayub').[41]

As discussed earlier, there has also been a rise in the 'normative' Islamic observance among young people in the rural parts of the Ferghana valley. However, even the most observant Muslim men usually perform only morning *bomdod* rather than the prescribed five daily prayers, and attend mosque only on Friday, while observant women conduct morning and Friday prayers at home. The increase in Islamic observance has been accompanied by the re-traditionalisation of gender roles, especially among ethnic Uzbeks and Uighurs. Since independence the number of local young men going to mosque and of young men and women holding *Uraza* has risen significantly. For example, in the 2000s young men constituted over 60 per cent of regular mosque attenders and over 70 per cent of young men and women held *Uraza*. There has been some increase in the number of girls aged fourteen and above who have been withdrawn from formal education for early marriage,[42] as well as in polygamous practices among wealthy men. However, these practices are formally illegal and therefore the rights of second, third or fourth wives are not protected by the state in case of divorce, and they cannot access various social benefits and other financial entitlements related to state-registered marriage. A growing number of young women have reverted to wearing the veil and have withdrawn from the public sphere in favour of a secluded existence defined by the socially conservative norms of family and *mahallah* which require their subordination to their husbands and mothers-in-law. These women's lives largely revolve around house, children and small-scale farming on their allotments, although in some cases women are also involved in artisanry, weaving and trading at the market.[43]

Among the implications of the enclave re-traditionalisation has been the greater role in girls and young women's socialisation of *otincha/otins/bibi-otuns* who throughout history have played a central role in the intergenerational transmission of Central Asian Islamic traditionalism. As in the past, *otinschas* combine the functions of religious teachers, imams, masters of ceremonies, moral mentors and healers. Their teaching and practices are informed by national cultural and customary norms, and oral rather than book-based Sufism. Some employ shamanistic practices during their 'interaction' with spirits by invoking their divine assistance in solving women's various personal problems and offering thanks when there are favourable outcomes. *Otinchas* also organise the *Osh Bibiio* events in honour of the female *avliio* Bibi Seshanda, as well as the *Mavlud* ceremonies in honour of the Prophet Muhammad's birthday. In the early post-independence period *otinchas* used to provide individual and group tutorials to *mahallah* girls and young women where they were taught to recite the Qur'anic *ayats* and to conduct basic Islamic rituals related to the major events of the life cycle. However, since the mid-1990s such sessions have been curtailed as a result of the tightening of official control over any Islam-related group gatherings.

Another pertinent marker of creeping re-traditionalisation has been a notable revival, especially among Uzbekistan's Kazakhs, Kyrgyz and other historically nomadic peoples, of shamanist magic healing practices and rituals that evoke *jinns*. These practices combine Islam with elements of local shamanism and biomedicine. Like *ziiorats*, they are not exclusive to Central Asia[44]; in particular, similar practices were widespread among various Turkic and Mongol peoples in those parts of Eurasia that in the past belonged to the vast Genghizid Empire. These forms of traditional healing comfortably co-exist with secular medical treatments and are regarded by some as being superior to normal medicine. It is not uncommon for a person affected by serious illness or other major problems to turn to *tabib/baqshi/folbin* after having exhausted conventional medical treatments.[45] The relations between spiritual healers, who believe that his or her healing power derives from God, and *mahallah* imams and mosque *domullos* are ambivalent and are representative of the flexible and shifting nature of Central Asian Islam. Some local *domullos* regard spiritual healing practices as part of the Central Asian Islamic tradition; other members of the traditionalist Islamic clergy consider them, and especially the interaction with *jinns*, as being outside *shari'a* regulations; while pro-*Salafi* Islamic preachers condemn such activity as *shirk*.[46]

There has also been some resurrection of organised Sufism. Among active Sufi groupings has been the Naqshbandi group of Ibrahim-Hazrat (1928–2009), who represented the *Husainiia* branch of the *Mujaddidi* Naqshbandiia,[47] and whose lodge is located in the village of Qush-Ata in the vicinity of Turkistan in southern Kazakhstan. The group, which numbers over 20,000 *murids* in different parts of the Ferghana valley, holds regular meetings for the purpose of study of the Qur'an and *dhikr*, as well as for an annual celebration of the *Mavlud* at the grave of Sheikh 'Abd al-Wahid (d. 1942), who taught all contemporary representatives of this line. Another relatively large Naqshbandi group of the same succession line, which is present in the Khorezm region, relates to 'Abdalla Qahhar, who was a *murid* of 'Abdalla-Qori (d. 1976), a descendent of 'Abd al-Wahid.[48] Alongside these Naqshbandi groups who practice quiet *dhikr*, several Yasawi and Qadiri groups have resurfaced in the Ferghana valley and in Tashkent which perform loud *dhikr*.

Implications of labour migration

In the last two decades over 10 per cent of Uzbekistan's population of over 32 million have been outside the Central Asian Islamic tradition due to labour emigration. On average, since Uzbekistan's independence over 4 million young Uzbek men and a much smaller number of young women have been based in countries of the former Soviet Union, the bulk of them in Russia, where they number around 3.3 million. Among the factors contributing to the persistent emigration of young people have been the high actual unemployment statistics which exceed 30 per cent among young people, the absence of social mobility, the insufficient state loans for agricultural production, child and forced labour in the cotton fields, state mismanagement of natural and human resources, and widespread corruption among government and police officials.

Men have been predominantly engaged in cyclic or seasonal labour migration which has involved leaving their families at home. Most of them have worked in poorly paid manual jobs on building sites or in municipal and local council services. The lengthy absences of migrant married Uzbek men from home has also adversely affected their families due to the turning of their wives into de facto single parents, although supported by *mahallah* and kinship social networks. The fathers' partial withdrawal from the family hierarchy has produced an increasing number of socially and ideologically disoriented young men, some of whom have turned to radical Islamist groupings inside and outside the country, including ISIS. The institution of the traditional Central Asian family has been undermined by long-term emigration to, or full resettlement in, Russia and elsewhere of some Uzbek women. Most of these women have been employed in the service, community and nursing sectors, as well as in private households, entertainment and agriculture. Only a small proportion of Uzbek labour migrants have been able to settle abroad as whole families.

The migration-related breakdown of the traditional family unit, the withdrawal from the *mahallah* safety net and the syndrome of the cultural *other* have together created fertile ground for the re-Islamicisation and radicalisation along non-traditional lines of a relatively small segment of Uzbek migrants. Their social and cultural alienation has been reinforced by the scarcity or even complete absence in Russia and other host countries of Uzbek-speaking Central Asian imams and, consequently, their exposure to official and unofficial Islamic messaging, including of a *Salafi* and *jihadist* nature, in Russian – the Islamic lingua franca in the post-Soviet space. A contributing factor has been the wider access of migrant Uzbeks to online globalised *Salafi* and *jihadist* Islamic material, which is inaccessible in Uzbekistan. It is indicative that the majority of Uzbek members of *Nurcular, Tablighi Jama'at,* the Islamic Party of Turkestan (successor to the IDU), HTI, ISIS and other international Islamic and Islamist organisations has come from Uzbek migrant communities rather than from Uzbekistan per se. In this respect there are notable similarities between Islamic radicalisation among Uzbek migrants in Russia and other post-Soviet countries and Muslims in France, Belgium, the United Kingdom, Germany and other Western states, although the level of Muslims' cultural and linguistic alienation here has been significantly higher than in Russia and other former Soviet states. Unlike in the West, Uzbek and other Central Asian and Caucasian Muslim migrants in Russia and other former Soviet non-Muslim majority countries have shared with their host countries the Russian lingua franca and centuries-long common political, economic and cultural patterns.

Notes

1. The Ferghana valley includes the Andijan, Namangan and Ferghana regions of southeastern Uzbekistan (18,900 km^2), the Osh, Jalal-Abad and Batken regions of southern Kyrgyzstan (79,895 km^2), and the Sughd and Khujand regions of northern Tajikistan (26,100 km^2). The total population of the Ferghana valley is over 11 million people. The highest density of population, 356 people per km^2, exists in Uzbekistan's part of the valley with a total population of over 7 million. In Tajikistan's part the population density is 71 people per km^2 with

total population of 2.5 million, and in Kyrgyzstan's part, there are 32 people per km^2 with a total population of 1.8 million. Yemelianova 2010, p. 212.

2. On 8 December 1991, presidents Boris Yeltsin, Leonid Kravchuk and Stanislav Shushkevich of Russia, Ukraine and Belorussia (Belarus) signed the Belavezha Accords on the dissolution of the Soviet Union. The three Soviet Baltic republics of Estonia, Latvia and Lithuania had seceded from the USSR in August 1991.
3. The situation was quite different from some other parts of the Muslim world where political independence was achieved as a result of sometimes lengthy and often bloody national liberation movements against the British, French or other European colonial empires. The cases in point are the national liberation wars against the French in Algeria (1954–62) and against the British in South Yemen (1963–7).
4. In terms of regional power networks President Karimov represented the Samarqand and Jizzakh factions and Shukrullo Mirsaidov the Tashkent faction.
5. 'Ob Itogakh' 1991.
6. The CST was signed in May 1992 between the governments of Russia, Kazakhstan, Kyrgyzstan, Tajikistan, Uzbekistan, Armenia and Belarus. In 1999, Uzbekistan left the CST, which in 2002 was renamed the Collective Security Treaty Organisation (CSTO). In 2006, Uzbekistan rejoined CSTO, but withdrew from it again in 2012.
7. The SCO was created in June 2001 by the leaders of China, Russia, Kazakhstan, Kyrgyzstan, Tajikistan and Uzbekistan. It originated from the Shanghai Five group which was established in April 1996 by China, Russia, Kazakhstan, Kyrgyzstan and Tajikistan. In June 2017, the SCO was also joined by India and Pakistan.
8. In 1989/90, the Uzbeks were involved in several ethnic conflicts, including the conflict between Uzbeks and Meskhetian Turks, between Uzbeks and Tajiks in Bukhara and Samarqand, and between Uzbeks and Kyrgyz in the Osh *oblast'* in neighbouring Kyrgyzstan.
9. The Republic of Uzbekistan, which inherited the Soviet borders, is situated between the Amu Darya and Syr Darya rivers covering a territory of 448,978 km^2. It borders Kyrgyzstan, Tajikistan, Kazakhstan, Turkmenistan and Afghanistan. Following the break-up of the USSR Uzbekistan emerged as the most populous Central Asian state. According to the 1989 census, the total population of Uzbekistan was 19.8 million. Over 70 per cent were Uzbeks, while the largest ethnic minorities included: Russians (8.4 per cent), Tajiks (4.7 per cent), Kazakhs (4 per cent), Tatars (2.4 per cent), Qarakalpaks (2 per cent), Uighurs (1 per cent), Koreans (1 per cent), Kyrgyz (1 per cent) and Crimean Tatars (1 per cent). Smaller ethnic groups were represented by Turkmens, Ukrainians, Armenians, Azerbaijanis, Belorussians, Greeks, Bukharan Jews, Germans, Moldovans, Bashkirs, Georgians, Turks, Jews, Mordva, Chuvash, Ossetians, Lezgins, Poles, Mari, Laks, Arabs, Udmurts, Bolgars, Dargins, Kurds and Pashtuns, as well as Iranians who were largely Shi'ites. It is important to bear in mind that the data on the ethnic composition of Uzbekistan, as in other Central Asian republics, are problematic because of the propensity of official statistics to exaggerate the number of the titular ethnic group by registering Tajiks and other representatives of ethnic minorities as 'Uzbeks'. In 2017, Uzbekistan's population was estimated as 32.1 million (*Vsesoiuznaia Perepis': Uzbekistan* 2017; *Republic of Uzbekistan*, available at: www.gov.uz/en/pages/popula tion/territory, last accessed 27 March 2017.
10. Abdullaev 1997, p. 87; Malashenko 1998, pp. 10–13; Muminov et al. 2010, p. 256.
11. Muhammad Sodiq ibn Muhammad Yusuf (Muhammad Sodiq Yusuf), a native of Andijan, was educated at the Bukhara *Mir-i Arab Madrasah*, the Tashkent Islamic Institute and the *Da'wa Islamiia* University in Libya. He was highly respected among Muslim clergy and was addressed as 'sheikh'.

12. The phenomenon of 'young imams' was characteristic of all Muslim-majority regions of the former USSR. 'Young imams' challenged the 'old imams' of the Islamic establishment for their alleged passivity, theological incompetence, low moral standards, collaboration with the KGB and conformity with Soviet atheism.
13. The authorities, media and traditionalist clergy in Uzbekistan, as well as other Muslim-majority parts of the former USSR, referred to all *Salafis* as *Wahhobis/Wahhabis*, thus implying their links with foreign Muslims and funds. The application of this term is factually incorrect because *Wahhabism* represented a politico-religious movement which was founded by Muhammad ibn 'Abd al-Wahhab (1703–87) in Arabia. Doctrinally it was anchored in the *Hanbali madhhab* of Sunni Islam. *Wahhabis* advocated *tawheed* and the purging of Islam of its later accretions, including the worshipping of saints and sacred places. *Wahhabism* is the state religion of Saudi Arabia.
14. *Tablighis* are members of the Islamic organisation *Tablighi Jama'at* ('The Society for Spreading Faith'), an international Sunni missionary organisation, which was founded by Muhammad Ilias al-Kanhlawi (1885–1944) in 1927 in India. It is of *Salafi* orientation since it denies *madhhab* division and regards the Qur'an and *Hadith* as the only sources of faith. Its proclaimed mission is to disseminate proper Islamic behaviour among Muslims through *tabligh* ('proselytisation'). It has a particularly large following among Muslims in south Asia and among the south Asian diaspora. It presently unites over 20 million members in 150 countries. See more on the *Tablighis* in Masud 2002.
15. The IPV of the USSR was created in June 1990 in the Russian city of Astrakhan, the historical centre of the Genghizid Khanate of Astrakhan in the lower Volga region. The IPV included pro-reform, *Salafi*-oriented Islamic intellectuals and activists from the Volga region, Azerbaijan, Daghestan, Tajikistan and other Muslim-majority parts of the USSR. They shared a common aversion towards the allegedly KGB-infiltrated, corrupt and doctrinally rigid 'official Islamic' clergy and campaigned for its replacement by 'young imams' who were not afraid of political engagement in the name of the gradual re-Islamicisation of the traditionally Muslim regions of the USSR along reformist lines. Significantly, they opposed violence, called for the promotion of Islamic values and family ethics through education, and did not question the existence of the Soviet Union.
16. See more on of Sayyid Abdulloh Nuri in Chapter 7.
17. As a result of the 1999 Tashkent bombing sixteen people were killed and more than a hundred were wounded.
18. The founder of the Haqqani network was Dzhalaluddin Haqqani, who controlled northern Waziristan during the Soviet invasion of Afghanistan in 1979–89 and collaborated with Arab *mujahideen*, on the one side, and the Pakistani intelligence, on the other. Since then the Haqqani network has been linked to the Pakistani army and intelligence and indirectly acted as their agency in Afghanistan.
19. See Karin 2016, pp. 61–7; Witter 2011.
20. For more on the HTI in Central Asia, see Naumkin 2005, pp. 127–200; Karagiannis 2010, pp. 58–72; Yemelianova 2010, pp. 211–43.
21. The Islamists especially opposed Islam Karimov's permission for the US air force to use the military base in Karshi-Khanabad, known as K2, for their air raids on the *Taliban*. The American presence at K2 was terminated in 2006, following the deterioration of Uzbek–American relations over the Andijan massacre in 2005.
22. Khalid 2007, pp. 192–200.
23. During the Andijan massacre Shavkat Mirziyoyev, a native of Jizzakh, was prime minister. He succeeded Islam Karimov upon the latter's death in late August 2016.
24. The author of the Soviet theory of *etnos* was academician Yulian Bromley (1921–90), the

leading Soviet ethnologist. He prioritised ethnic, rather than civic, consciousness as the core element of nation-building. Bromley 2008.

25. The Organisation of Islamic Conference (OIC) is an international Muslim organisation which was founded in 1969 in Rabat, Morocco. Its headquarters is in Jeddah, Saudi Arabia. The OIC's proclaimed goal is to preserve Islamic social, cultural and economic values across the Muslim world. In 2008, it changed its name to the Organisation of Islamic Cooperation. By 2017, it consisted of fifty-seven Muslim states with collective population of over 1.6 billion.
26. In the Soviet period the University bore the name of Vladimir Lenin.
27. The high political importance of this event was evidenced by the participation in it of President Karimov, Muftii Mukhtar Abdullaev and numerous Sufi sheikhs from all over the Muslim world. In the same year, Bukhara's main street, which used to bear the name of Vladimir Lenin, was renamed after Baha al-Din Naqshband.
28. Among those in the vicinity of Bukhara alone, in addition to *Khoja* Baha al-Din's complex, there are six other popular Sufi shrines, which together are known as the *Yetti Pir* ('Seven *Pirs*'), relating to other great Naqshbandis: 'Abd al-Khaliq Gijduvani, *Khoja* Orif al-Revgari (d. 1259), *Khoja* Mahmud Anjir Fag'navi (d. 1245), *Khoja* Ali Rometani (d. 1306), Muhammad Boboi Samosi (d. 1340) and Sayyid Mir Kulol (d. 1371). Louw 2007, pp. 65–6.
29. See *Konstitutsiia Respubliki Uzbekistan, 1992*, available at: http://constitution.uz/ru/clause/index#section1, last accessed 13 March 2017.
30. It worth noting that the government's tight control over the religious sphere created a major hindrance to local and especially foreign scholars conducting field work research on Islam and Muslims in Uzbekistan. This, in turn, has had negative repercussions for the quality of Islam-related research, leading to a proliferation of unverified and often politicised data on the subject.
31. Upon his return to Uzbekistan in 1999 and until his death in 2015 Muhammad Sodiq worked as an independent Islamic scholar and was a member of several high-profile international Islamic organisations, including the World Union of Muslim *'Ulama'*, the World Islamic League and the World Council of *Da'wa Islamiia* ('Islamic Call'). It was only after his death that he was officially recognised as an authoritative Uzbek Islamic scholar. This change of heart was replicated in neighbouring Kazakhstan, where President Nursultan Nazarbayev endorsed the naming of a mosque in the city of Shymkent after Sheikh Muhammad Sodiq, as well as in Russia's Chechnya where President Ramzan Kadyrov named a street after him. It is worth noting that Muhammad Sodiq's recorded sermons informally circulated in Uzbekistan throughout the 1990s and 2000s.
32. For example, in 1998, the DMU was advised to issue a *fatwa* banning the use of loudspeakers in mosques on the pretext of the 'non-Muslim' nature of this practice; in 2005, it was recommended that collective *iftars* were forbidden in order to prevent youth gatherings; and in 2014 *tarawih-namaz* and *iftar* in restaurants, cafés and mosques were outlawed.
33. Since then, the DMU has allowed around 4,500 people to conduct *hajj*, which was much below the permitted quota of 7,200 (2017). Since the average cost of *hajj* was around US$1,000 per person – a sum that the bulk of the population could not afford – the *hajj* business became fraught with corruption and most *hajjees* were from wealthy families or were funded by the whole *mahallah*.
34. Similar secular Islamic universities were established in other Muslim-majority regions of the former USSR, including the Russian Islamic University in Kazan, Tatarstan (1998) and the Russian Islamic University of Kunta *Hajjee* in Grozny, Chechnya (2009).
35. This observation is based on the author's visiting lecturing and discussions with students at the University of World Economy and Diplomacy in Tashkent and the Institute of

Economics and Service and the Institute of Foreign Languages, both in Samarqand, April 2013.

36. Most of Uzbekistan's Shi'ites are ethnic Iranians who in 1989 numbered around 25,000. See 'Uzbekistan', *International Religious Freedom Report 2010*, US Department of State, 17 November 2010, available at: https://aoprals.state.gov/content.asp?content_id=184&menu_id=78, last accessed 4 April 2017.
37. For a critique of the academic and media preoccupation with radical Islam in Central Asia, see Heathershaw and Montgomery 2014.
38. As of 2000, there were nearly 1.2 million ethnic Russians in Uzbekistan.
39. As of 2008, Tashkent's population was 2.2 million. Its ethnonational make-up was as follows: Uzbeks 63 per cent; Russians 20 per cent; Tatars 4.5 per cent; Koreans 2.2 per cent; Uighurs 1.2 per cent; and others 7.0 per cent. *Tashkent*, available at: http://dic.academic.ru/dic.nsf/es/89801, last accessed 4 April 2017.
40. The logistics of *ziiorat* include pilgrims' payment of some money to the shrine's *domullo* (*domlo*) for reciting in Arabic the *Fatihat*, followed by a *duo* in Uzbek, and for addressing the *avliio* with a request for intercession on their behalf. Sometimes pilgrims decide to sleep at a shrine in the hope that in their dreams the *avliio* might give them a sign or advice. Some *ziiorats* are accompanied by *qurbonlik* as a gesture of gratitude for the *avliio*'s helpful mediation. Louw 2007, p. 58.
41. It is widely believed that *Khoja* Baror, who allegedly used to cure the disabled and blind by referring to Allah, played a key role in the Bukharans' conversion to Islam in the eighth century. The shrine of *Chashma Ayub* is believed to have emerged in the twelfth century around a spring originally created by Ayub, the biblical prophet. People travel to Ayub's shrine to gain extra patience when they have been particularly struck by bad luck. Some shrines are linked to the patron saints of various professions; for example, *avliio* Usta Ruhi is regarded as the patron saint of metalworkers, Boboi Porado'z of shoemakers and Imom Muhammad G'azzoli of tailors. Louw 2007, pp. 66–7.
42. According to Uzbekistani law the marriageable age for women is seventeen and for men eighteen.
43. The author's findings within the Nuffield Foundation-funded research project on 'Islamic Radicalism in Uzbekistan, Tajikistan and Kyrgyzstan', 2002–5, and the British Council-funded INSPIRE project, 2010–13.
44. On healing practices involving *jinns* in some other parts of the Muslim world, see, for example, Barth 1993; Nourse 1996; Beller-Hann 2001; Lindquist 2001; Bali 2004; Al-Khudayri 2012.
45. A spiritual healer works on the assumption that the cause of a person's illness is the loss of spiritual purity due to pollution by fright or stress, or to possession by an evil *jinn*. The purpose of the 'treatment' is the restoration of the patient's proper blood circulation, which allegedly has been disrupted by stress, or the exorcism of the bad *jinn*. During the 'treatment' healers combine the energy of their hands, herbal medicine, reciting of Qur'anic verses, prayer and 'interaction' with good and evil spirits. Each spiritual healer has his or her own good spirits, who often belong to their ancestors and who were revealed to them in their dreams. Good spirits 'assist' healers in their healing practices and especially in the driving out of evil spirits from affected individuals.
46. See Rasanayagam 2011, pp. 212–15, 221–2, 225.
47. The *Mujaddidi* (lit. 'Renewed') line of the Naqshbandi *tariqat* derived from the teaching of the Indian Sheikh Ahmad Faruqi Sirhindi (d. 1624) who reaffirmed the centrality of *shari'a* against alleged innovations introduced by Sufis. Its *Husainiia* branch originated from the Bukhara Sheikh Khalifa Husain (d. 1834). See more on the evolution of the

Naqshbandi *tariqat* in Algar 1998, and on its *Mujaddidi Husainiia* branch in Babadzhanov 2006.

48. Smaller Naqshbandi groups include those related to Alla Nazar Akhun Kosnazarov (d. 1991) in Qarakalpakistan; Muqim-khan ishan and Gilani ishan, both in the town of Shahrisabz; Sheikh Ishaq-khan ishan near Aqtash in Samarqand region; as well as Dust Muhammad domullo Qonghirat and Ahmadzhan ishan, both in Surkhandaria region. Muminov et al. 2010, pp. 272–3.

Selected reading

Primary sources

Constitution of the Republic of Uzbekistan, available at: http://constitution.uz/en, last accessed 12 May 2017.

Law of the Republic of Uzbekistan on Freedom of Conscience and Religious Organisations (new version), 1 May 1998, available at: http://www.legislationline.org/documents/id/18436, last accessed 12 May 2017.

Salih, M. (2005), *The Opponent*, Bodrum: Komen Publications.

Secondary sources

Abashin, S. (2015), *Sovetskii Kishlak: Mezhdu Kolonializmom i Medernizatsiei* (*Soviet Kishlak: Between Colonialism and Modernisation*), Moscow: Novoie Literaturnoie Obozrenie.

Allison, R. and L. Jonson (eds) (2001), *Central Asia Security: The New International Context*, Washington, DC: Royal Institute of International Affairs.

Khalid, A. (2007), *Islam after Communism: Religion and Politics in Central Asia*, Berkeley: University of California Press.

Laruelle, M. (ed.) (2017), *Constructing the Uzbek State: Narratives of post-Soviet Years*, Lanham, MD: Rowman & Littlefield.

Louw, M. E. (2008), *Everyday Islam in post-Soviet Central Asia*, London: Routledge

Malashenko, A. (2008), *Islam in Central Asia*, Reading: Ithaca Press.

Muminov, A., U. Gafurov and R. Shigabdinov (2010), 'Islamic Education in Soviet and post-Soviet Uzbekistan', in M. Kemper, R. Motika and S. Reichmuth (eds), *Islamic Education in the Soviet Union and its Successor States*, London: Routledge, pp. 223–79.

Naumkin, V. V. (2005), *Radical Islam in Central Asia: Between Pen and Rifle*, Lanham, MD: Rowman & Littlefield.

Rasanayagam, J. (2011), *Islam in post-Soviet Uzbekistan: The Morality of Experience*, Cambridge: Cambridge University Press.

Roy, O. (2000), *The New Central Asia: The Creation of New Nations*, London: I. B. Tauris.

Sultanova, R. (2014), *From Shamanism to Sufism: Women, Islam and Culture in Central Asia*, London: I. B. Tauris.

Yemelianova, G. M. (ed.) (2010), *Radical Islam in the former Soviet Union*, London: Routledge.

CHAPTER 5

Muslims of Kazakhstan

The sovereignisation of Kazakhstan

As in other parts of Central Asia, and for the same reasons, the Kazakhstani ruling elite under First Secretary Dinmukhamed Kunayev (1912–93, in office 1964–86) resented the arrival of Mikhail Gorbachev as the young pro-reform Soviet leader. For his part, Gorbachev regarded the elderly Kunayev, a protégé of Leonid Brezhnev, as the Kazakhstani embodiment of Brezhnevian stagnation. In December 1986, Gorbachev removed the uncooperative Kunayev from his post and replaced him with Gennady Kolbin, an ethnic Russian (in office 1986–9), an appointment that catalysed Kazakh national self-awareness and led to Kazakh mass protests in Almaty and other major cities. Kolbin responded with a campaign of purges against top pro-Kunayev Kazakh Communist Party and government officials. But in the face of a deteriorating situation the Kremlin was forced in June 1989 to replace Kolbin with the young and reform-minded Nursultan Nazarbayev (b. 1940, in office 1989–present), who had previously served as Kazakhstan's prime minister.

Having found himself between the Gorbachevian reformist leadership in Moscow and Kunayev's sympathisers in Almaty, Nazarbayev chose to take a moderate and cautious stance by focusing more on Kazakhstan's economic and political liberalisation than on the promotion of Kazakh ethnonationalism. Protest sentiments were thereby largely channelled into the popular movement known as Nevada-Semipalatinsk which campaigned for a ban on nuclear tests in the northeastern Semipalatinsk region.[1] Kazakhstan also witnessed the emergence of informal national groupings such as, for Kazakhs, *Alash* ('Kazakh Horde'),[2] *Azat* ('Freedom') and *Zheltoksan* ('December'),[3] and, for Russians, *Yedinstvo* ('Unity') and *Vozrozhdenie* ('Renaissance'). The central demand of the Kazakh activists was the elevation of Kazakh to the status of the state language. In the elections of March 1990 representatives of non-government organisations gained 90 out of 360 parliamentary seats.[4] In April 1990, following the general trend, Nazarbayev elevated himself from the First Secretary of the Communist Party to the President of Kazakhstan. However, unlike Islam Karimov in neighbouring Uzbekistan, he did not prevent the Communist Party from retaining its majority in the parliament.

During *perestroika* and afterwards Nursultan Nazarbayev was the most enthusiastic and consistent supporter of the preservation of a reformed and democratic Soviet Union; in the nationwide referendum in March 1991 he ensured endorsement of it by 94 per cent of the votes.[5] Even after the break-up of the USSR he remained committed to Eurasian unity. During the anti-Gorbachev coup d'état in Moscow on 19 August 1991, Nazarbayev initially adopted a position of neutrality, but soon distanced himself from Vladimir Kriuchkov, Gennady Yanayev and other *putchists* and sided with Boris Yeltsin, Russia's president and Gorbachev's arch-rival. In this respect he acted differently from Islam Karimov, who used the coup to break away from Russia. Having been excluded, like other Central Asian leaders, from the Belavezha Accords of 8 December 1991 on the dissolution of the USSR, Nazarbayev had no choice but to proclaim the independence of Kazakhstan on 16 December 1991. However, his reluctance in pursuing comprehensive sovereignisation was reflected in Kazakhstan's preservation for several years after the dissolution of the USSR of many Soviet institutions, including the Supreme Soviet. Thus, in late December 1991 Kazakhstan joined the Russia-speared Commonwealth of Independent States (CIS), followed by its membership in May 1992 of the CIS's military wing – the CST/CSTO. In April 1996, along with Russia, Kyrgyzstan and Tajikistan, Kazakhstan joined the China-dominated Shanghai Five group (SCO).

The impact of *perestroika* on the Islamic dynamic in Kazakhstan was less pronounced than it was in Uzbekistan and Tajikistan. On the surface, as in other Muslim-majority regions of the USSR, there was an increased Islamic presence in the public sphere. By the end of the 1980s there were twenty-five registered mosques in Kazakhstan, while unregistered mosques numbered several hundred.[6] The country became open to the activities of representatives of various foreign Islamic foundations, Islamic preachers and educators who funded the building of mosques, *madrasahs* and other Islamic institutions, and were actively involved in the proselytising of various versions of Islam that were at variance with the Kazakh version of Central Asian Islam.[7]

In general, the rise of Islam in Kazakhstan during *perestroika* was more symbolic than substantive, and most of the newly opened mosques remained sparsely attended. The comparative weakness and slow pace of the 'Islamic revival' in Kazakhstan during *perestroika* can be put down to three main reasons. One was the near loss by Kazakhs of their Islamic heritage as a result of the Stalinist destruction of their nomadism, which was organically intertwined with Islam. Another was the greater degree of ethnic and confessional diversity in Kazakhstan, where ethnic Kazakhs constituted only half of the population, combined with the higher level of supra-ethnic and supra-confessional civic Soviet-ness of Kazakhs, along with the other peoples of Kazakhstan. And the third reason was the Kazakhs' greater cultural and linguistic Russification, and with it their higher susceptibility to the cultural and informational influences emanating from Russia rather than from the Muslim world.

Nazarbayev's Eurasianism, ethnonationalism and Islam

Throughout its independence the political, social and cultural development of Kazakhstan has been strongly influenced by President Nazarbayev's Eurasian vision, which emphasises Kazakhstan's political and civilisational centrality in Eurasia due to its geography and territorial expanses. The other important consideration was the 'kazakhisation' of the Russian-majority in northeastern Kazakhstan. In 1998, Nazarbayev moved the capital from Almaty in the south to Tselinograd (Akmola) in central-north Kazakhstan, now renamed Astana (lit. 'Capital', in Kazakh). Among other manifestations of Nazarbayev's Eurasianist vision have been the promotion of the ethnically and confessionally pluralistic 'people(s)' of Kazakhstan, rather than the Kazakhstani nation,[8] and the positioning of Kazakhstan as being allegedly at the crossroads of world religions. In 1995, Nazarbayev initiated the formation of a consultative state body – the Assembly of Peoples of Kazakhstan – consisting of 384 representatives of various ethnic communities.[9] The Eurasian discourse has also been reflected in the names of various official and non-official organisations and websites, such as Kazakhstan's Eurasian Bank and the Eurasian University of Leo Gumilev, founded in 1996 in Akmola/Astana on the basis of a merger between the Civil Engineering and Pedagogical Institutes.

In 1994, at the peak of the post-Soviet 'parade of sovereignties', President Nazarbayev proposed the formation of the Eurasian Union in the territory of the former USSR. In 2000, following years of intensive lobbying of this idea among his counterparts in the ex-Soviet republics, he presided over the signing in Astana of the Treaty on the establishment of the Eurasian Economic Commonwealth (EAEC) between Kazakhstan, Russia, Belarus, Tajikistan and Kyrgyzstan. In 2006, he played a pivotal role in the creation of the Eurasian Customs Union (EACU) between Kazakhstan, Russia and Belarus. In the same year, he initiated the creation of the Eurasian Bank of Development (EABD), which initially united Kazakhstan and Russia, and by 2011 also included Armenia, Belarus and Kyrgyzstan. Nazarbayev also played a central role in the creation in early 2015 of the Eurasian Economic Union (EAEU) between Kazakhstan, Russia and Belarus; by the end of 2015, the EAEU was joined by Armenia, followed by Tajikistan. However, since the mid-2000s Nazarbayev's leadership in the Eurasian integrationalist project has been increasingly challenged by Russia's President Vladimir Putin, who perceives it as being Russia-centred.

President Nazarbayev's Eurasian perception of Kazakhstan and its people has paradoxically co-existed with his embrace of Kazakh ethnonationalism, which has drawn on Leo Gumilev's theory of ethnogenesis and the concepts of *passionarity* and *superethos*[10] in particular. The Kazakhs' national energy has been linked to their alleged symbiosis with the endless steppe, the blue sky and the horse. Gumilev's ideas have affected some Kazakh 'historical' studies which have stressed the Kazakhs' ethnic distinctiveness and statehood tradition from times immemorial and have claimed their pivotal role in the historical development of Eurasia.[11] The political importance of Gumilev's thinking has been reflected in the creation in Astana of the Eurasian University named after him. Kazakh ethnonationalism has been behind the 'kazakhisation' of the political, economic and military elites, the steady increase in the number of ethnic Kazakhs in the country and the promotion of the use of the Kazakh language at the expense of Russian. Given the post-Soviet exodus from Kazakhstan of ethnic Russians, Germans and other non-titular ethnic groups, the Nazarbayev government sought their replacement by *oralmans* – ethnic Kazakh repatriates. In 1997, the government adopted a programme of repatriation of ethnic Kazakhs to Kazakhstan and established annual quotas. *Oralmans* were offered substantial financial and housing incentives, registration for medical and social care, as well as employment and schooling. By 2016, Kazakhstan had acquired almost a million *oralmans* from Uzbekistan, China, Mongolia, Turkmenistan, Kyrgyzstan and Russia, as well as from Iran, Afghanistan and Pakistan. Most of them (over 65 per cent) came from Uzbekistan and China (25 per cent).[12] By 1999, as a result of state demographic policy, Kazakhs were for the first time since the 1930s the ethnic majority in Kazakhstan. In general, *oralmans* who came from the former Soviet republics have integrated more successfully than the culturally and linguistically different *oralmans* from far abroad. Furthermore, *oralmans* who came from Afghanistan and Pakistan have adhered to 'untraditional' forms of Islam, including *Salafism*, and have thus contributed to the proliferation in Kazakhstan of non-Central Asian forms of Islam.[13]

An important factor of 'kazakhisation' was President Nazarbayev's language policy. The 1989 Language Law named Kazakh as the state language and Russian as the language of interethnic communication, a provision reiterated in the 1995 Constitution of the Republic of Kazakhstan. The 1992 Education Decree stipulated the gradual replacement of Russian-language instruction in schools and universities by Kazakh and the ultimate switch of all state and official communication to Kazakh by 1995. Under this policy, the number of Kazakh-medium schools increased in the period between 1989 and 1996 by 28 per cent, while the number of Russian-medium schools decreased by 37 per cent. For the same period, the number of Kazakh-medium university courses increased from 22 per cent to 31 per cent. The linguistic 'kazakhisation' led to the gradual political side-lining of Russians and other non-Kazakhs who were not proficient in the Kazakh language. As a result, during the period 1985–94 the number of Russians and other non-Kazakhs in high-level government posts dropped from 50 per cent to 25 per cent.[14] However, in 1997, having failed to undermine the Russian language's de facto dominance in both public and private spheres the Nazarbayev government was forced to abandon its earlier strategy of a comprehensive switch to Kazakh. The new Language Law, which was passed that year, legalised Russo-Kazakh bilingualism even in the official sphere. A decade later, in 2007, the authorities yet again modified their language strategy in favour of achieving Kazakh, Russian and English trilingualism in Kazakhstan's population,[15] while from 2017 they have embarked on the Latinisation of the Kazakh language.[16]

Kazakh ethnonational discourse has also involved the revaluation of the historical role of various Kazakh khans, *biys* and *batyrs* depending on their relations with Russian rulers. The significant shift of focus in post-Soviet Kazakh historical studies towards Kazakh khans and the Kazakh Khanate has been accompanied by the downplaying or negating of the Russian and Soviet legacy, on the one hand, and the 'deepening' of Kazakh Islamic history, on the other. For example, some Kazakh authors support their argument in favour of the Kazakhs' lengthy *Hanafi* Islamic tradition through the association of Kazakhstan's Kazakhs with various sedentary inhabitants of present-day southern Kazakhstan who were Islamicised by the Arabs in the early eighth century.[17] Others regard the Qarakhanids as direct ancestors of the Kazakhs, and on this basis date the Islamic history of the Kazakhs from the conversion to Islam of the Qarakhanid ruler 'Abd al-Qarim Satuk Boghra-Khan (901–55).[18] Other writers essentialise the Kazakh belief system of the distant past into Islamic categories.[19] Such 'deepening' of Kazakh *Hanafism* is at odds with the findings of other reputable historians and ethnographers, which point to nomadic Kazakhs' problematic relations with mullahs up to the mid-nineteenth century.[20]

Kazakhstan's relatively successful post-Soviet transition has occurred against serious domestic, regional and international challenges, which have included general post-Soviet economic and political disorder and endemic corruption, the large Russian population in the north of the country, the rise of militant Islamism in neighbouring Uzbekistan and Tajikistan, and the growing pressure from major regional and international actors to bring Kazakhstan into their spheres of influence. It has been achieved through the synthesis of ideological de-Sovietisation, the retention of core components of the Eurasian political and economic model, and a distinctive Kazakhstani ethno-civic national discourse. Of special significance has been the preservation of the executive vertical, safeguarded by the national security forces, successors of the KGB, which have continued to prevail over the constitutionally enshrined principles of the people's sovereignty, the division of powers and government accountability. Another important factor in Kazakhstan's relative success has been its abundant gas and oil resources, which, even after being substantially tapped for its own profit by the ruling elite,[21] have provided a sufficient economic and financial basis for the country's partial economic modernisation and sustainability.

The 'Islamic revival'

As in other Muslim-majority parts of the USSR, the 'Islamic revival' in late Soviet and early post-Soviet Kazakhstan was marked by increased Muslim self-identification among Kazakhs and Kazakhstan's other Muslims and a rise in the number of mosques and other objects of Islamic infrastructure. During that period the number of registered Islamic organisations rose from just over 20 to 2,300, while over 80 per cent of Kazakhs began to identify themselves as Muslims.[22] These changes were part of the broader process of de-Sovietisation and 'kazakhisation' and did not significantly affect the majority's secularised worldview and private and public behaviour. In fact, throughout the 1990s the 'Islamic revival' lacked internal dynamism and to a large extent was shaped by Islamic influences emanating from Turkey, Egypt, Kuwait, Saudi Arabia, the United Arab Emirates and Pakistan. The Saudi-based World Assembly of Muslim Youth (WAMY) and *Al-Waqf al-Islamii*, the Kuwait-based *Al-Khairiia* ('Benevolence') Foundation and other foreign official and non-government Islamic funding and proselytising organisations were behind the rapid construction of mosques, the opening of *madrasahs*, the organisation of summer youth camps and the charity work among disadvantaged children, as well as the development of Islamic publishing and the emergence of informal groups for the study of Islam. Young Kazakhs and others among Kazakhstan's youthful Muslims became recipients of various foreign Islamic scholarships enabling them to study in Islamic universities and colleges abroad. The newly opened Islamic bookshops abounded with Islamic books in Russian, Turkish and Arabic, published in Mecca, Medina, Istanbul, Beirut, Cairo, Karachi and Lahore. Many of these were *Salafi* in nature.[23]

Particularly influential were Islamic proselytisers from Turkey due to the ethnolinguistic and *madhhab* affinities between Turks and Kazakhs. Emissaries of the Turkey-based Fethullah Gulen,[24] with the Nazarbayev government's blessing, began indirectly to promote the Gulen ideology through the state school and university system by offering superior natural sciences and IT courses in Turkish. The foci of Gulen educationalism became the Turkey-funded International Kazakh–Turkish University of Ahmad Yasawi, which was opened in 1991 in Turkistan, and the Suleyman Demirel University, which was established in 1996 in Almaty. Representatives of the Gulen movement also established their control over twenty-five Kazakh–Turkish lyceums, as well as the newly launched Turkish–Kazakh newspaper *Zaman* ('Times').[25]

Kazakhstan also welcomed the influx into the country of Islamic lecturers and preachers from Egypt, Kuwait, Saudi Arabia and some other Arab countries. In 1993, the governments of Kazakhstan and Egypt agreed to jointly fund the creation in Almaty of the Egyptian University of Islamic culture *Nur-Mubarak*,[26] which was opened in 2003. The Kazakhstani government also initially welcomed the involvement of various Arab and Pakistani foundations in secular higher education and specifically in Islamic training. Thus, the Kuwait-based pro-*Salafi Jama'at al-Islah al-Ijtima'i* ('Society for Social Reform') was involved in the establishment in Chimkent (Shymkent) in 1992 of the International Kazakh–Arab University, known as the Otyrar University, which offered courses in Arabic, Kazakh language and literature, history, pedagogy and religious studies; in 1998 the university opened a branch in Taraz. Saudi and some other Middle Eastern charitable foundations provided courses in Arabic, *'aqeedah*, *fiqh*, *adab*, *seerah* and *tajweed*, while the Pakistani International Islamic University offered scholarships for Kazakh students to study there.[27]

Kazakhstan also witnessed, albeit on a much smaller scale, the proselytising activity of members of the Pakistan-based *Tablighi Jama'at*, the UK-based Ahmadiia,[28] as well as of foreign Sufis. *Tablighis*, whose centre was the village of Baiserka, conducted door-to-door *da'wa* across Almaty *oblast'*. Most active among foreign Sufis were the Turkey-based *Suleimancis*, followers of the Naqshbandi *Mujaddidi* Sheikh Suleiman Hilmi Tunahan (1888–1959); by the mid-1990s the *Suleimancis* had acquired a following in Almaty, Chimkent (Shymkent), Pavlodar, Semipalatinsk and Ust'-Kamenogorsk. Kazakhstan was also frequented by the Turkish Naqshbandi sheikhs 'Abd al-Baki Husain, Ahmad Afand and Mahmud Usta Osmanoglu, who acquired a limited number of *murids* among ethnic Kazakhs.[29]

Since the 2000s, the 'Islamic revival' has been affected by the resurgence of traditional Sufism, the small-scale proliferation of *Salafism*, and the limited involvement of ethnic Kazakhs in Central Asian Islamist and *jihadist* networks. Among the notable indigenous Sufi formations have been the aforementioned Naqshbandi group of Ibrahim-Hazrat and the Yasawi/Qadiri group of *pir* Ismatulla Abdugappar, an *oralman* from Afghanistan. The Ibrahim-Hazrat group has been based in the village of Qushi-Ata, not far from the town of Turkistan, as well as the area around the shrines of Ishan-Baba and Abd al-Wahid-*qari* (d. 1967) in southern Kazakhstan. Its followers have led a secluded lifestyle, practised silent *dhikr* and stayed away from politics. Given the secretive nature of the group it is difficult to estimate their number, which might range between several hundreds and several thousands. A considerable proportion of the group's members are ethnic Uzbeks from southern Kazakhstan and adjacent regions of Uzbekistan.[30] The group of *pir* Ismatulla Abdugappar has been active in Almaty and Almaty *oblast'*, as well as in Karaganda, Jezkazgan, Taraz and Kentau. Its members have claimed their spiritual descent from *Khoja* Ahmad Yasawi, but have practised the loud Qadiri *dhikr*. Among *pir* Ismatulla's followers have been representatives of small business, education and the mass media; for a short period of time they even controlled a few cable TV channels.[31]

The embodiment of moderate *Salafism* has been the so-called *qur'anists* who regard the Qur'an as the only source of the faith and thus oppose Kazakh *khoja*

Sufi Islam as *bid'a*. Significantly, *qur'anists* have included Kazakh students, young professionals and even some members of the political, administrative and business elite. They hold regular study gatherings, refrain from alcohol and non-*halal* meat and diligently observe fasting during the month of *Ramadan*. However, in terms of their dress code and social behaviour they have been indistinguishable from their secular colleagues. The main sources of their Islamic education have been online and printed Russian translations of theological works by 'Abdalla bin Baz, 'Abd al-Razzaq 'Afifi, Muhammad bin Jamil Zeno, Salih al-Suheimi, 'Abd al-Razzaq al-Badr, Ibrahim al-Ruheili, El'mir Kuliev and other leading scholars of *Salafi* orientation. It is difficult to assess their number, but it is plausible to suggest that they constitute a substantial part of the worshippers who each Friday overcrowd the 5,000-strong *Nur-Astana* mosque in Astana.[32]

In the early 2000s Kazakhstani officials and media began to admit that there were ethnic Kazakhs among the Islamists operating in the Ferghana valley, although their number remained much lower than that of Uzbeks and Tajiks. These Kazakh Islamists were part of the regional Islamist network consisting of members and sympathisers of the HTI, the IPV, the IDU and the latter's splinter groups. Most active among them were *Tahriris*, who numbered several hundred and who were involved in providing welfare assistance to the most disadvantaged and in distributing Islamist leaflets in Kazakh, Uzbek and Russian.[33] The reasons behind the emergence of Islamism on Kazakhstani soil have been largely similar to those in other parts of Central Asia and wider Muslim Eurasia, including dire socio-economic conditions, endemic corruption, high youth unemployment, the enormous discrepancy between the living standards of the business and political elite and the ordinary people, the lack of social mobility, and post-Soviet ideological confusion, amplified by the young people's exposure to external religious proselytising. A contributing factor has been the shifting geopolitics due to Russia's brutal suppression of the Chechen rebels in 1999–2001 and the US-led invasion of Afghanistan in 2001, conducted in the name of the 'global war on terror' in the aftermath of 9/11. With the state securitisation of Islamism and 'non-traditional' *Salafi* Islam by the leaderships of neighbouring Russia and Uzbekistan the Nazarbayev government has also, in a kind of domino effect, tightened state control over the religious sphere, including the introduction of state registration of religious organisations, the criminalisation of unregistered Islamic and other religious activities, and the expulsion of foreign religious foundations and missionaries from the country. The official persecution of 'non-traditional' Muslims has had in turn a radicalising effect on some *Salafi*-minded Kazakhs, some of whom have adopted violence.

During the 2010s a small number of ethnic Kazakh *jihadists* have been active in Tajikistan, Kyrgyzstan, Daghestan and other Muslim regions of the former USSR. Kazakhs have also been present in *Jama'at al-Mujahideen* ('Community of Islamic Warriors') of Central Asia, the Islamic Party of Turkestan, *al-Takfir va al-Hijrah* ('Excommunication and Exodus'), *al-Qaeda* and ISIS. In 2011 and 2012 western Kazakhstan was shocked by Islamist suicide attacks committed by ethnic Kazakhs from the *Jund al-Caliphate* (JC, 'Soldiers of the Caliphate'), founded by Rinat Habidolla, Orynbasar Munatov and Damir Znaliyev, all ethnic Kazakhs trained in international *jihadist* camps.[34] Since 2014 there have been reports of a growing number of Kazakhs fighting for ISIS. According to official statistics, in 2014, 300 ethnic Kazakhs, including women, were fighting in Syria and Iraq within the *Kazakh jama'at.*[35]

State–Muslim relations

From the first days of Kazakhstan's independence the Nazarbayev government's line on Islam has been shaped by the secularist perception of Islam as an element of the Kazakh ethnocultural tradition. The Constitution of 1995 describes Kazakhstan as a democratic and secular state,[36] and state secularism has been upheld by the atheistic Soviet background of the president and other top government officials who welcomed the formation of the muftiiate of Kazakhstan as a formal attribute of state sovereignty. Islamic symbols have been integrated into Kazakh national and foreign policy discourses; Islamic motifs have been present in the new state architecture and monuments; and the names of Al-Farabi and other renowned Islamic thinkers of the past have been given to universities, while their faces appeared on Kazakh banknotes. The authorities have lavishly invested in the renovation of the mausoleum of *Khoja* Ahmad Yasawi in Turkistan and the hosting of numerous international conferences and symposia on Islam in Central Asia and on inter-confessional dialogue. The government has begun to instrumentalise Kazakhstan's Muslim-ness in order to advance its relations with their counterparts in the Muslim world. In 1994, Nursultan Nazarbayev conducted *hajj* to Mecca and Medina and in 1995 Kazakhstan joined the OIC, chairing it in 2011. Since 2017, it has provided the platform for the internationally pivotal inter-Syrian dialogue mediated by Russia, Turkey and Iran.

Nevertheless, despite its growing symbolic significance Islam remained outside the ruling elite's priorities until the end of the 1990s. These priorities included the privatisation and modernisation of the lucrative gas and oil industries, the country's interethnic stability and the preservation of Kazakhstan's territorial integrity, as well as its so-called 'multi-vector' external engagement. President Nazarbayev and his Soviet-era entourage genuinely believed that, unlike the more religious Tajiks and Uzbeks, Kazakhs were sufficiently secularised to be immune to foreign proselytisers, Islamic and Christian alike. Such an approach was behind the introduction in January 1992 of the liberal Religious Law and the government's *laissez faire* attitude towards the activities of foreign Islamic missionaries, educators, funders and charities, as well as its initially minimal interference in the muftiiate's affairs. According to the Religious Law, Islamic and other religious associations were recognised as legal entities with the right to hold property and conduct financial transactions.[37] But, as noted earlier, from the early 2000s, with changed regional and global conditions, the Nazarbayev government had to make Islam, and Islamism in particular, one of its main political and security priorities. Like its Russian and Uzbekistani counterparts, it established the legally enshrined dichotomy of 'traditional' (that is, indigenous, apolitical and good) Islam and 'untraditional' (that is, foreign, political and bad) Islam, which strongly resembled the previous dichotomy of 'official' and 'unofficial' Islam. 'Untraditional Islam' was securitised and dealt with under anti-terrorist and anti-extremist legislation. In 2003, Astana established the Anti-Terrorist Centre (ATC), tasked with the prosecution of members and affiliates of foreign Islamist and Islamic organisations, the deportation of unregistered foreign Islamic preachers, and the de-legitimisation of most educational and cultural institutions funded by foreign Islamic governmental and non-governmental organisations. From 2004, onwards the Kazakhstani authorities have synchronised with their Russian and Uzbekistani counterparts the banning of various Islamist organisations which had been active across post-Soviet Eurasia, among them the HTI, the Islamic Movement of Eastern Turkestan, the *Jama'at al-Mujahideen* of Central Asia, the Islamic Party of Turkestan, the IIJ, the JC, *al-Takfir va al-Hijrah*, the ISIS and, subsequently, the *Jabhat al-Nusrah* ('Victory Front').[38] Many members of these organisations have been arrested and jailed, while dozens of Islamic preachers have been deported to Pakistan, Turkey, China, Uzbekistan and Russia.[39]

In May 2011, President Nazarbayev authorised the establishment of the Agency for Religious Affairs (ARA) under the leadership of Kairat Lama Sharif (b. 1962, in office 2011–13), a professional diplomat without any background in Islamic theology, to formulate a more restrictive Religious Law. In October 2011, the Kazakhstani parliament adopted a new and restrictive Law which strongly resembled the 1997 Russian Religious Law. Like this, which recognised the special role in Russian history of the traditional religions – Orthodox Christianity, Islam, Buddhism and Judaism – the Kazakhstani Religious Law recognised the special role of traditional *Hanafi* Islam and Orthodox Christianity. The Law prescribed re-registration of all religious organisations and banned prayers and Islamic activities in schools, prisons, the army and other state institutions. It changed registration requirements to 50 in the case of local organisations, 500 for regional organisations and 5,000 for national organisations.[40] As a result, the number of re-registered religious organisations was reduced by a third. The Law enabled the ARA, in coordination with the muftiiate, not only to reduce significantly the number of religious organisations, but also to tighten control over the process of selection and appointment of mosque imams and *madrasah* teachers. The Law has been used broadly against

Islamists and independent Muslims, as well as the politically assertive Yasawi Sufis.[41]

By 2012, as the result of the joint ARA and muftiiate review of Islamic education, there remained only one official provider of higher Islamic education – the *Nur* University (formerly *Nur-Mubarak* University) in Almaty – and five providers of *madrasah* education – in Almaty, Astana, Pavlodar, Shymkent and Aqtobe.[42] The pro-Gulen Kazakh–Turkish University of Suleiman Demirel in Almaty was also spared. In 2016, in order to further strengthen the government's control over the religious and particularly the Islamic situation, the Religion and Civil Society Ministry was formed, headed by Nurlan Ermekbayev (b. 1963), a Sinologist with a military background, who was previously in charge of the Security Council of the Republic of Kazakhstan. In early 2017, the government introduced further restrictions on imports of Islamic and other religious literature for 'personal use' to one copy of any one book and intensified anti-extremist raids on Islamic bookshops.[43] The authorities have mounted punitive and preventive measures against real and potential Islamists, and have developed a de-radicalisation programme aimed at young people in schools, universities and sports clubs. The government has been particularly concerned with stopping young Kazakhs from joining the JC, ISIS and other regional and global *jihadist* networks.

The muftiiate of Kazakhstan

The muftiiate has played an important role in the state's control over the Islamic sphere. It was formed in January 1990 when the Kazakh *qaziiate* under the leadership of the 'young imam' Ratbek Nysanbai-uly (b. 1940, in office 1990–2000) broke away from the Tashkent-based SADUM. In the same month, Kazakhstan's Islamic clergy at their first national *qurultai* proclaimed the establishment of their own muftiiate – the Spiritual Directorate of Muslims of Kazakhstan (SDMK). As noted above, throughout the 1990s the government did not seriously interfere with the muftiiate's cadre, educational and publishing politics or its sources of funding. The post-Soviet relaxation of state control enabled Muftii Ratbek Nysanbai-uly to strengthen his authoritarian grip on the muftiiate and to secure his endorsement as muftii for life at the *qurultai* in January 1990. The *qurultai* formed its new governing body – the Committee – which consisted of ten senior clerics and established five regional *qaziiates* with centres in Alma-Ata (Almaty), Jambyl (Taraz), Chimkent (Shymkent), Ural'sk and Semipalatinsk (Semey). The unlimited power he had acquired allowed Muftii Nysanbai-uly to embark on the 'kazakhisation' of the Islamic clergy, financial and structural separation from the Soviet-era centre in Tashkent, the organisation of *hajj* and *'umrah*, as well as Islamic publishing, and obtaining of external Islamic funding.[44] The SDMK, under different pretexts, began to replace Uzbek and Tatar imams by ethnic Kazakhs. In the same year, the SDMK established in Almaty an Islamic University and a *madrasah* in the village of Merke (Jambyl *oblast'*), both of which proclaimed their curricular and methodological independence from the Tashkent Islamic Institute. Given the scarcity of theologically competent ethnic Kazakhs and the practical non-existence of Islamic educational institutions outside Uzbekistan, such initiatives were more demonstrative than substantive in nature and led to a significant decline in the standards of the mufiiate's staff, Islamic education provision, and the increased cadre and methodological dependence on the Islamic educational institutions of Egypt, Turkey and Pakistan.

By the late 1990s the SDMK acquired all the formal trappings of a muftiiate. It created a system for registration of Muslim communities and *madrasahs*, the selection and appointment of imams and *mudarrises*, and the organisation and administration of *hajj* and *'umrah*. It established annual quotas and organised the selection process for Muslim Kazakh students to be sent abroad for further studies, funded by host institutions. On average eighty Kazakhs were sent to study at *Al-Azhar*, a hundred Kazakhs in various Islamic institutions in Turkey, and twenty Kazakhs in Islamic institutes in Pakistan.[45] The SDMK founded its own Islamic periodicals: *Islam Alemi* (*Islamic World*), *Iman* (*Faith*), *Islam Zhane Orkeniiet* (*Islam and Civilisation*) and *Shapaghat Nur* (*Light of Mercy*).[46] It dealt with the organisation of Islam-related events, including competitions for the best reader of the Qur'an, and with the running of *halal* meat shops. In 1992, it organised a high-profile celebration of the release of the Kazakh-language edition of the Qur'an in Nysanbai-uly's translation; and, in 1997, the SDMK staged the grand opening in Almaty of the new Central Mosque for 3,000 people.

Behind this publicity, the actual role of the SDMK in Kazakhstani society was marginal; in fact, it was significantly weaker, structurally and theologically, than the Soviet-era Uzbek-dominated SADUM. Its authority among grassroots Muslim communities was low for three main reasons. One was the overall complex relations between historically nomadic Kazakhs and the established Islamic clergy, and their preference for unregistered mullahs and *khojas*, rather than for a centralised Islamic administration and mosque-based registered imams. Another was related to the self-centredness of the new muftiiate's clergy and their lack of genuine interest in the life and religious needs of ordinary Muslims. And a third reason was the muftiiate's considerable financial and theological dependence on foreign Islamic sponsors who treated Kazakh Sufi *khoja* Islam as a deviation from 'true' Islam. This was exacerbated by the pro-*Salafi* orientation of the muftii, whose oral presentations and publications were largely based on works by an influential *Salafi* thinker Abu A'la Maududi and *'ulama'* from *Al-Azhar* University, a leading centre of Islamic scholarship. In 1990, President Hosni Mubarak of Egypt decorated Ratbek Nysanbai-uly to celebrate his 'Service to Scholarship and Culture'.[47]

However, in 2000, as part of the tightening of state control over the Islamic sphere, the unpredictable and independent-minded muftii was removed from his post on the grounds of venality and corruption and replaced by a state official, professional diplomat and Arabist Absattar-Hajjee Derbissali (b. 1947). In 2005, Derbissali was re-elected as muftii, despite the fact that he did not have any Islamic education and work experience as a mosque imam, as prescribed in the muftiiate charter. Nevertheless, Muftii Derbissali was successful in employing his political and professional capital and international links to advance the interests of Kazakhstan in the Muslim world. He had less success, however, in the formulation of the muftiiate's policy, its meaningful participation in wider Islamic theological debate and its engagement with grassroots Muslim communities in Kazakhstan. His Islamic credentials also suffered from his Soviet atheism and the absence of any training in Islamic studies despite his fluency in Arabic.

The Arabophile Derbissali was actively involved in the opening in 2003 in Almaty of the Kazakh–Egyptian Islamic University *Nur-Mubarak* under the leadership of Egyptian Professor Mahmud Fahmi Al-Hijazi (in office 2003–14),[48] a professor of *shari'a* law, and of the Institute for the Further Qualifications of Islamic Clergy under the directorship of Deputy Muftii Muhammad Husain Alsabekov, who had returned from Chechnya. The staff at both institutions consisted of Kazakh, Egyptian and Saudi lecturers; in both, the teaching of *madhhabs*

Figure 5.1 Supreme Muftii Absattar-Hajjee Derbissali of Kazakhstan and the author (photograph by the muftii's assistant, Almaty, February 2013)

Figure 5.2 Deputy Muftii Muhammad Alsabekov of Kazakhstan and the author (photograph by Alsabekov's secretary, Almaty, May 2012)

in Sunni Islam tended to favour *Shafiism* and *Malikism*, which are dominant in Egypt, and to downplay or ignore Kazakh Sufi *khoja* Islam. Likewise, the courses on Sufism and Kazakh history and Sufism were only offered on an optional basis.[49]

The muftiiate's de facto elevation of the *Al-Azhar* version of Islam to the status of 'normative' and 'true' Islam, along with its rhetorical trumpeting of allegiance to Central Asian *Hanafism* of the *Al-Maturidiia* School, has accounted for its ambivalence towards Kazakh *khoja* Sufism and other forms of indigenous Islam. This has been evidenced in its hostile position towards members of the Naqshbandi group of Ibrahim-Hazrat and the Yasawi-Qadiri group of *pir* Ismatulla Abdugappar.[50] The muftiiate has sided with the law enforcement agencies in targeting independent-minded Islamic clergy, including imams of the Tatar-Bashkir mosque *Din-Muhammad* in Petropavlovsk and the *Nurdaulet* mosque in Aktoba.[51] In 2013, *Al-Azhar* University's doctrinal supremacy over the muftiiate was reconfirmed by the replacement of the theologically feeble Muftii Derbissali[52] by the doctrinally robust Muftii Yerzhan Mayamerov (b. 1972), who for thirteen years had studied at *Al-Azhar*, from which he graduated in 2006.[53] In December 2017, he was succeeded by Muftii Serikbai-*hajjee*

Figure 5.3 At the *Nur* Islamic University (photograph by VC's assistant, Almaty, May 2011)

Oraz (b. 1975), another graduate of *Al-Azhar*, as well as the pro-*Salafi*-oriented International Islamic University in Islamabad. A corollary has been the increasing deviation from traditional Kazakh Sufi *khoja* Islam of representatives of the new generation of Muslim clergy, as well as of practising and conscious Kazakh Muslims.

Kazakh Muslims versus Muslim Kazakhs

These developments notwithstanding, Kazakhs, along with Kyrgyz, remain the least 'Muslim' Muslims of Central Asia. In this respect they differ significantly from Kazakhstan's more pious Uzbeks, Dungans and Uighurs. True, the vast majority of Kazakhs identify themselves as Muslims, but their actual relationship with Islam is even more problematic and ambivalent than in the case of their Uzbek neighbours. Most Kazakhs have been secular in terms of their world view, lifestyle, dress code and drinking habits, though this has not stopped them from selective or occasional adherence to some Islamicised traditions and rituals. Among these have been *azan shakiru* (the naming of a baby), *sundet* (circumcision) and *janazah* (Islamic burial), all of which required the participation of a mullah, as well as avoidance of eating pork. Other less common Islamicised practices have included *neke* (Islamic marriage) in conjunction with the more important civic marriage; *Salem Qilu* (Islamic greetings); *ziiarats* and the involvement, alongside conventional doctors, of a *khoja*, mullah or *emshi* in cases of severe illness.[54] Unlike in post-Soviet Uzbekistan, where *Hanafi Al-Maturidiia* and indigenous Sufism have retained their centrality in the Muslim cultural matrix as well as in the official national discourse, in Kazakhstan both have had largely a symbolic presence, for several reasons. One relates to the effects of the Stalinist destruction of Kazakh nomadism, which was intertwined with Kazakh *khoja* Sufi Islam. Another, linked with the first, is the deeper level of Kazakhs' cultural and linguistic Russification.[55] All Kazakhs, with a few exceptions among *oralmans*, are Russian-speakers, although many of them have varying proficiency in the Kazakh language. In urban areas the number of ethnic Kazakhs using Russian in the family circle and in public exceeds those who use Kazakh or both languages equally. A considerable number of ethnic Kazakhs, especially among middle-aged professionals, do not know Kazakh at all. The de facto 'mother tongue' status of Russian among Kazakhs is evidenced by the lack of any accent when they speak it. The continuing wide use of Russian by ethnic Kazakhs has also been due to its function as the lingua franca in the multi-ethnic and multilingual Kazakhstani society.[56] Its use has also been perpetuated by the generally higher quality of TV programmes and serials in Russian, compared with those in Kazakh, and the popularity among Kazakhs of the Russian-language social media, *VKontakte* and *Odnoklassniki*, in particular.[57]

The greater cultural Russification of Kazakhs, compared, for example, with Uzbekistan's Uzbeks, has been reflected in their notions of high culture, and in their holiday celebrations, popular music and cuisine. A visiting passer-by in the streets of Almaty, Taraz, Qostanay, Semey, Atyrau or any other major city, would be struck by how ethnically mixed are the groups of children and young people and how they routinely mix Russian, Kazakh and other local languages. Despite the state promotion of Kazakh history, culture and music the level of Kazakh cultural sophistication and refinement continues to be defined by one's knowledge of Alexander Pushkin, Leo Tolstoi and other great Russian poets and writers, as well as by an appreciation of classical Russian ballet and opera and the music of Piotr Tchaikovsky, Modest Mussorgsky, Alexander Borodin, Mikhail Glinka and the other great Russian composers.[58] It is also symptomatic that among the most emotionally charged holidays celebrated by Kazakhs privately and publicly, have been the non-Islamic *Nowruz*, New Year, 8 March – International Women's Day – and 9 May – Victory Day over Nazi Germany in the Great Patriotic War of 1941–5. Other national holidays include the widely celebrated *Qurban-Bairam*, the Orthodox Christmas Day, as well as the newly established civic holidays such as the Day of the First President, Independence Day, Constitution Day, Unity Day, Defender of the Fatherland

Figure 5.4 British and Kazakh students at *Nowruz* at KBTU (photograph by one of the students, Almaty, April 2011)

Day and Day of the Capital. Neither *Ramazan* (*Ramadan*) nor *Oraza-Tutu* (*'Id al-Fitr*) is included in Kazakhstan's public holidays, although they are celebrated informally among a relatively small number of practising Kazakhs and others of Kazakhstan's Muslims. At the same time, the Islamic holiday of *Qurban-Bairam* and the Orthodox Christian holiday of Christmas are often jointly celebrated by the whole neighbourhood irrespective of the formal religious affiliations of its members. A pertinent sign of Kazakhstan's intercultural and inter-confessional nature is the universal observance of the Orthodox Christian Forgiveness Sunday.[59] The intercultural mix is deeply engrained also in Kazakhstani cuisine, characterised by Kazakhs' appropriation of Russian borsch, salad, *bliny* and vodka, and by Russians and other non-Kazakhs of such Kazakh meat dishes as *kuurdak*, *mant* and *beshbarmak*, and Kazakh pastries, *baursak* and *samsa*.

Since independence, the Kazakhs' substantial cultural and linguistic 'Russianness' has been challenged by the strengthening of their ethnonational identity, manifested in their more pronounced *Juz* and clan solidarity. This increased genealogical awareness has been translated into an agency for social and political advancement in relation to Russians and other non-Kazakhs who did not possess similar affiliations.[60] Those in positions of power have begun openly to favour representatives of their clan and *Juz*. For example, it has become a common practice for a newly appointed *akim* of a region to surround him- or herself by representatives of his or her clan and *Juz*. As President Nazarbayev belongs to the *Ulu Juz* and his wife to the *Orta Juz* this has enhanced the positions of representatives of their families and clans in the key political, economic and security sectors. At the same time, the clan-based distribution of spheres of influence has been supplemented by or has overlapped with the fluid cross-*Juz*, cross-clan and extra-clan political and economic alliances that have been centred on personal loyalty and business interests and therefore also included non-Kazakhs.[61]

As noted earlier, due to the eradication of Islamicised Kazakh nomadism, the Islamic component of resurgent Kazakh nationalism has been little influenced by Kazakh Sufi *khoja* Islam. Instead, the Kazakhs' cultural Muslim-ness has been conducive to some proliferation among the young and nationally conscious of 'normative' and *Salafi* Islam, which have been disconnected from the Kazakh Islamic tradition. Meanwhile, the remnants of this tradition, as in the Soviet period, have remained underground. They have been represented by the *mazars* of *avliio/auliie*, Sufi sheikhs/*khojas*, *batyrs* and genealogical ancestors' graves, as well as by Islamicised shamanistic healing practices. The largest number of

Figure 5.5 Dungan wedding (photograph by author, Almaty, April 2011)

mazars are located in the southern town of Turkistan and its surroundings; among those visited by Kazakhs and other Central Asian Muslims have been the mausoleum of *Khoja* Ahmad Yasawi in Turkistan, the Arystan-Bab *mazar* near ancient Otrar about 70 km south of Turkistan and the *mazar*/well of Ukasha-Ata[62] near Atabay about 30 km north of Turkistan.[63]

Although, historically, shamanism had a greater presence in the healing practices of Kazakhs as descendants of shamanist Qipchaks than it did among Uzbeks and Tajiks, in present-day Kazakhstan shamanist practices have retained a very marginal existence compared with conventional medicine.[64] They have been administered by *emshis*, many of whom have been women. Like *baqshis*/*tabibs* in Uzbekistan, *emshis* claim to have spiritual power, which is allegedly passed to them by the *auraq* (spirits) of their ancestors and which allows them to treat a patient's illness spiritually rather medically. They claim to be able to diagnose a person's health problems by simply taking their pulse. Some *emshis* refer to the Qur'an during their healing sessions, while others do not mention it at all.[65] However, some *emshis*, especially of *khoja* lineage, are famous for their 'protective' *tumars* ('amulets') which contain Qur'anic verses. Some Kazakhs hang such *tumars* in their houses and cars in the belief that they will protect them from illness, fire, theft and various other misfortunes. Sometimes they also put in their houses some sacralised flora and fauna items, such as *adiraspan* (steppe sage) and *uki* (owl feathers).[66]

Overall, Kazakhstan has emerged as the most politically stable, economically dynamic and socially coherent country of Central Asia under Nursultan Nazarbayev's continuous leadership. It has asserted itself internationally and benefited from parallel and nuanced cooperation with Russia, China, the West and the Muslim world. The Nazarbayev government has also been consistently committed to Kazakhstan's continuing secular nature and outlook; while the 'Kazakhstan 2050 Strategy', announced by President Nazarbayev in December 2012, named among its priorities the enhancing of Kazakhstan's economic diversity and competitiveness and the aspiration to bring it into the top thirty developed countries; it did not contain any reference to Islam.[67] Up to now the pragmatic and secularist conception of Kazakhstan by the Nazarbayev leadership has remained widely popular.[68] However, as was shown earlier, it has not been entirely congruent to the Islamic dynamic and attitudes towards Islam of some young Kazakhs and others of Kazakhstan's Muslims. There has been a developing trend among young Kazakhs towards the rediscovery of Islam as part of their confused national identity. Compared with the post-Soviet resurgence among the historically sedentary Uzbeks and Tajiks of traditional *Hanafi Al-Maturidiia*-based Islam, as well as both indigenous and non-indigenous *Salafism*, the Islamic reawakening among the historically nomadic Kazakhs, as well as Kyrgyz, has been exclusively defined by non-indigenous perceptions and practices of Islam from other *madhhabs*, including the pro-*Salafi Hanbali madhhab*. At the theological level, this trend has been reinforced by the muftiate's scripture-based interpretation of the Islamic creed and practices and its implicit negation of Kazakh Sufi *khoja* Islam, while claiming its adherence to 'traditional Kazakh *Hanafi* Islam'. It could be argued therefore that the 'Islamic revival' in independent Kazakhstan has taken the form of re-Islamicisation of Kazakhs along new and unfamiliar lines. Among the implications of this process have been the creeping proliferation of moderate *Salafism* among well-off Kazakh professionals and of *jihadism* among those who have been politically alienated and economically and socially disadvantaged.

Notes

1. The movement originated from the ecological and anti-nuclear group of Semipalatinsk, founded in February 1989 by the famous Kazakh writer and politician Olzhas Suleimenov (b. 1936).
2. The official name of the *Alash* group was the Kazakhstan National Independence Party of *Alash*. It was founded by Aron Atabek and Rashid Yutoshev and had some following among the Kazakh intelligentsia. The party claimed to be the successor of the old *Alash* Party that existed in the pre-Soviet period. Like its predecessor, it emphasised Kazakhs' belonging to both the Turkic and Muslim worlds. Karagiannis 2010, p. 30.
3. The name of the group *Zheltoksan* ('December') derived from the anti-Kolbin riots in December 1986.
4. 'Parliament of the Republic of Kazakhstan', available at: http://www.parlam.kz/en/history, last accessed 25 April 2017.
5. 'Ob Itogakh' 1991.
6. Nurmanova and Izbairov 2010, p. 286.
7. Along with Islamic proselytisers, Kazakhstan experienced an influx of Protestant Christian and millenarian missionaries (Pentecostalists, Baptists, Presbyterians, Methodists, Seventh-Day Adventists and Jehovah's Witnesses). Shlymova 2012, p. 44.
8. *Konstitutsiia Respubliki Kazakhstan, 1995*, available at: http://www.constitution.kz, last accessed 2 May 2017.
9. The Assembly has reported directly to President Nazarbayev as its life-long chairman. In 2007, the name of the Assembly was amended from the 'Assembly of Peoples of Kazakhstan' to the 'Assembly of People of Kazakhstan'.
10. Leo Gumilev (1912–92) was an influential Soviet historian and ethnologist. He was the author of the theory of ethnogenesis which links ethnicity and geography. For more on Gumilev's theory of ethnogenesis, see Laruelle 2008, pp. 50–82.
11. See, for example, Abil' 1997; Artykbaev 2001; Bakhti 2004; Daniiarov 2004, Nurtazina 2000; Omarov 1997.
12. The majority of *oralmans* were settled in the southern Kazakhstani region (34 per cent), the Almaty region (over 35 per cent), the Mangistau region (over 10 per cent) and the Jambyl region (6 per cent). *Skol'ko Oralmanov Pribylo v Kazakhstan v 2016 Godu?*, see at: https://tengrinews.kz/kazakhstan_news/skolko-oralmanov-pribyilo-v-kazahstan-v-2016-godu-310929; *Oralmany v Kazakhstane*, see at: http://egov.kz/cms/ru/articles/oralman_rk, last accessed 3 May 2017.
13. The author's field-work findings in Almaty, Taraz, Turkistan and Astana as part of the British Council-funded INSPIRE project, 2011–13.
14. Schatz 2004, pp. 80–1.

15. For more on language policy in Kazakhstan, see Fierman 1998, pp. 1771–86.
16. Rysaliev 2017.
17. See, for example, Orynbekov 2005, p. 186.
18. See, for example, Alsabekov 2009, p. 99.
19. See, for example, Nurtazina 2000.
20. See, for example, Masanov 2007, p. 121.
21. For an in-depth analysis of the energy-related corruption in Kazakhstan and other Central Asian countries, see Cooley and Heathershaw 2017.
22. Mazhitova 2017; Yemelianova 2014, p. 290.
23. The author's observation of mosque-related Islamic book shops and markets in Almaty, Taraz and Turkistan, 2010–13.
24. Fethullah Gulen (b. 1941), a Turkish Islamic preacher and the founder of the transnational Gulen movement *Hizmet* ('Service'), which positions itself as moderate and inclusive. Its members emphasise their altruism and duty of service to the nation and the wider world. Until 2013, Gulen's emissaries acted as de facto agents of Turkey's soft power penetration in Turkic-speaking Muslim countries, as well as in other parts of the Islamic world. Following the break-up between Fethullah Gulen and Turkey's President Recep Erdoğan in 2013, Gulen has been pursuing his proselytising projects independently from the Turkish government. In the former USSR, members of Gulen's movement were also active in Azerbaijan and Tatarstan.
25. Nurmanova and Izbairov 2010, p. 306.
26. The university's name was made out of the names of presidents Hosni Mubarak of Egypt and Nursultan Nazarbayev of Kazakhstan. In 2012, in response to political changes in Egypt resulting in the overthrow of President Mubarak in 2011, the university's name was changed to 'Kazakh–Egyptian University *Nur*'.
27. Nurmanova and Izbairov 2010, p. 303; Nysanbai-uly 2000, p. 123.
28. The Ahmadiia Muslim Community is an international Sunni reformist movement that originated in the Punjab, British India, at the end of the nineteenth century. It is named after its founder Mirza Ghulam Ahmad (1835–1905) who proclaimed himself *mahdi*. Ahmadis believe in the spiritual rather than the human nature of the caliphate and see their mission as being the peaceful spreading of the teachings and moral values of Islam across the world. At present there are between 10 and 20 million Ahmadis in 209 countries. Since 1984, the headquarters of the Ahmadiia movement has been in London, and since 2004 their caliph has been Mirza Masroor Ahmed (b. 1960). Ahmadis have been continuously persecuted in Saudi Arabia. For more on the Ahmadiia, see Valentine 2008.
29. Nurmanova and Izbairov 2010, p. 306; Yemelianova 2014, pp. 290, 294.
30. The author's interview with Nasrettin-*qari*, a son of Ishan-Baba sheikh who preceded Ibrahim-Hazrat, Qusshi-Ata, Kazakhstan, 25 April 2012.
31. Yemelianova 2014, pp. 290, 294, 298.
32. The author's research findings in Almaty, Taraz, Turkistan and Astana, 2010–13.
33. Karagiannis 2010, p. 65; Yemelianova 2014, p. 291.
34. Karin 2016, pp. 14–15, 69–71; Yemelianova 2014, p. 291.
35. '150 Kazakhstanok Voiuiut v Riadah IGIL', *Tengrinews*, 18 November 2014, available at: https://tengrinews.kz/kazakhstan_news/150-kazahstanok-voyuyut-ryadah-gruppirovki-islamskoe-265425, last accessed 8 May 2017.
36. Although the 1995 Constitution was amended in 1998, 2007, 2011 and 2017, it has retained the article on the democratic and secular nature of Kazakhstan. *Konstitutsiia Kazakhstana*, available at: http://www.akorda.kz/ru/official_documents/constitution, last accessed 8 May 2017.

37. *Zakon Respubliki Kazakhstan o Svobode Veroispovedaniia i Religioznykh Ob'edinenii*, 15.1.1992, available at: http://online.zakon.kz/Document/?doc_id=1000934, last accessed 23 May 2017.
38. 'Spisok Zarubezhnykh Organizatsii Zapreshchennykh po Resheniiu Suda na Territorii Respubliki Kazakhstan', available at: http://dinvko.gov.kz/rus/deyatelnost-upraleniya/religioznye-obedineniya/sepisok-zarubezhnyh-organizatsij-zapreschennyh-po-resheniyu-suda-na-territorii-respubliki-kazahstan.html, last accessed 11 May 2017.
39. Karagiannis 2010, p. 66; Yemelianova 2014, p. 293.
40. *Law of the Republic of Kazakhstan on Religious Activity and Religious Associations of 11 October 2011*, available at: http://www.legislationline.org/Kazakhstan_Law_religious_freedoms_organisations_2011, last accessed 12 May 2017.
41. Lama Sharif 2012; Yemelianova 2014, pp. 290, 294.
42. Yemelianova 2014, p. 294.
43. 'Kazakhstan: Anti-extremism Raid Captures Koran', *Forum 18 New Service*, Oslo, Norway, 22 May 2017, available at: http://www.forum18.org, last accessed 23 May 2017.
44. Muftii Nysanbai-uly's authoritarian style and particular policies met with considerable resentment from some senior Islamic clergy and imams. Among his most outspoken critics were Shukrullo Muhammedzhanov, an ethnic Uzbek and imam-*khatib* of the Chimkent mosque, Imam Ibrahim Mashanlo of Taldykorgan, Deputy Muftii Muhammad Husain Alsabekov, an ethnic Chechen, and Ibrahim Marov, an ethnic Dungan, who was a member of the SDMK's Committee. At the end of 1991, they attempted to overthrow Nysanbai-uly but he managed to outmanoeuvre them, although he renounced his right to be muftii for life. His opponents were forced either to resign or to flee the country. Among the latter was the current Deputy Muftii Muhammad-Husain Alsabekov, who left for Chechnya where he had served as muftii under President Dudayev, during which period he adhered to the *Shafi'i madhhab* which is dominant in Chechnya. Nurmanova and Izbairov 2010, pp. 286–8.
45. Nysanbai-uly 2000, p. 123.
46. Nurmanova and Izbairov 2010, p. 297.
47. Nysanbai-uly 2000, pp. 6, 142.
48. Since 2014 the Islamic University has been headed by Zhuda 'Abd al-Gani Basiuni (b. 1946), an Egyptian graduate of *Al-Azhar*.
49. The *Nur-Mubarak* University offered BA and MA programmes in Islamic theology. Among its compulsory courses were Arabic, *'aqeeda*, *fiqh*, *hadith*, *seerah* and *tajweed*. The best MA graduates of the university were provided with scholarships to continue their education at *Al-Azhar* University in Cairo. The curriculum of the Institute for Islamic Clergy presented a simplified version of the curriculum in the *Nur-Mubarak* University. The length of study at the institute has been two years for male students and short-term Qur'anic courses for female students. Nurmanova and Izbairov 2010, pp. 298–9, and the author's findings, 2010–13.
50. This assertion is based on the author's interviews with members of both groups, Qusshi-Ata and Almaty, Kazakhstan, April 2012.
51. Matveev 2012.
52. Ex-Muftii Derbissali returned to academia as Director of the Suleimenov Oriental Studies Institute in Almaty.
53. Between 2006 and 2008 Yerzhan Mayamerov worked at the *Fatwa* department in the muftiiate in Egypt.
54. Privratsky 2001, pp. 94–7.
55. From the 1980s, the phenomenon of the overwhelming Russification of Kazakhs, along with Kyrgyz, has been known under the term *mankurtizatsiia*. The term 'mankurt', which defined a person who has lost his or her language and consequently ethnic identity, was first

introduced in 1980 by the Soviet Kyrgyz novelist Chingiz Aitmatov to describe a person who has lost his or her past. Dave 2007, pp. 50–1.

56. The Russification of Kazakhs and other non-Russian peoples of Kazakhstan was mirrored by the considerable cultural 'kazakhisation' of Kazakhstan's ethnic Russians and other non-Kazakhs. Many Russian migrants who left Kazakhstan for central Russia in the early 1990s acutely experienced their 'Kazakh-ness' in relation to local Russians.
57. The author's ethnographic observations, 2011–13.
58. Ibid.
59. Forgiveness Sunday (Lat. 'Quinquagesima') is the seventh Sunday before Easter in Orthodox Christianity when believers ask each other's forgiveness for any wrongdoings in the past.
60. For a fuller discussion of the clan politics in post-Soviet Kazakhstan, see Schatz 2004.
61. Olcott 2002, pp. 186–7.
62. It is worth noting that while the number of visitors to the mausoleum of Ahmad Yasawi has been notable, the number of pilgrims to Arystan-Bab and Ukasha-Ata has remained negligible.The author's findings, April 2012.
63. Privratsky 2001, pp. 162–4.
64. For more on the history of shamanism among Kazakhs, see Basilov 1991.
65. For example, *emshi-moldas* ('emshi-masters') recite the Qur'an during their healing sessions, *emshi-tawips* ('emshi-doctors') only refer to it occasionally, while *emshi-palshis* ('emshi-fortune tellers') and *emshi-baksis* ('emshi-shamans') do not refer to it at all. *Emshi-palshis*, who are predominantly females, specialise in prognosis of a patient's illness. *Emshis*' 'healing' methods include meditation, spiritualised breathing, 'pressure on a patient's heart', manipulation with knives and horse whips, and the administering of herbal remedies. Privratsky 2001, pp. 194–5.
66. Privratsky 2001, pp. 194–5, 200–1.
67. *The Kazakhstan 2050 Strategy*, official website of the President of the Republic of Kazakhstan, available at: http://www.akorda.kz/ru/official_documents/strategies_and_programs, last accessed 17 May 2017.
68. Burova and Kosichenko 2013, p. 99.

Selected reading

Primary sources

Constitution of the Republic of Kazakhstan of 1995, available at: http://www.constitution.kz/english, last accessed 12 May 2017.

Law of the Republic of Kazakhstan on Religious Activity and Religious Associations of 11 October 2011, available at: http://www.legislationline.org/Kazakhstan_Law_religious_freedoms_organisations_2011, last accessed 12 May 2017.

Secondary sources

Cooley, A. and J. Heathershaw (2017), *Dictators without Borders: Power and Money in Central Asia*, New Haven, CT: Yale University Press.

Cummings, S. N. (2012), *Understanding Central Asia: Politics and Contested Transformations*, London: Routledge.

Dave, B. (2007), *Kazakhstan: Ethnicity, Language and Power*, London: Routledge.

Khalid, A. (2007), *Islam after Communism: Religion and Politics in Central Asia*, Berkeley: University of California Press.

Karin, E. (2016), *The Soldiers of the Caliphate: The Anatomy of a Terrorist Group*, Astana: KazISS.

Malashenko, A. (2008), *Islam in Central Asia*, Reading: Ithaca Press.

Matveev, D. (2012), 'Mechet' 'Nurdaulet' Pytaiutsia Zakryt' Cherez Sud', *Evrika*, 21 April.

Melvin, N. (2000), *Transition to Authoritarianism on the Silk Road*, Amsterdam: Harwood Academic.

Nurmanova, A. Sh. and A. K. Izbairov (2010), 'Islamic Education in Soviet and post-Soviet Kazakhstan', in M. Kemper, R. Motika and S. Reichmuth (eds.), *Islamic Education in the Soviet Union and its Successor States*, London: Routledge, pp. 280–312.

Olcott, M. (2002), *Kazakhstan: Unfulfilled Promise*, Washington, DC: Carnegie Endowment.

Privratsky, B. G. (2001), *Muslim Turkistan: Kazak Religion and Collective Memory*, Richmond: Curzon Press.

Roy, O. (2000), *The New Central Asia: The Creation of New Nations*, London: I. B. Tauris.

Rysaliev, A. (2017), 'Kazakhstan Takes Decisive Step toward Adopting the Latin Alphabet', *Eurasianet.org*, 12 September, available at: http://www.eurasianet.org/node/85111, last accessed 6 December 2017.

Schatz, E. (2004), *Modern Clan Politics: The Power of 'Blood' in Kazakhstan and Beyond*, Seattle, WA: University of Washington Press.

Yemelianova, G. M. (2014), 'Islam, National Identity and Politics in Contemporary Kazakhstan', *Asian Ethnicity* 15(3): 286–301.

CHAPTER 6

Muslims of Kyrgyzstan

The effects of *perestroika*

At the onset of the Gorbachevian *perestroika* the political and economic trajectories of Kyrgyzstan (Kirghizia)[1] were not very different from Kazakhstan, which was ethnically and culturally close to it. Thus, in 1985, the Brezhnev-era Kyrgyzstan Communist Party First Secretary Turdakun Usubaliyev (1919–2015, in office 1961–85) was ousted from office and replaced by the reform-minded Absamat Masaliyev (1933–2004, in office 1985–91), who had previously occupied the post of First Secretary of the Communist Party of Issyk-Kul' *oblast'*. Masaliyev initiated a number of political and economic reforms which had the effect of stimulating some anti-establishment civic, ethnic and religious activism. From 1988, the opposition movement in Kyrgyzstan acquired its own momentum and became increasingly radicalised. Particularly active was the party of national revival *Asaba* ('Banner'), which campaigned for the raising of the status of the Kyrgyz language, the rehabilitation of leading Kyrgyz historical figures and the revival of Kyrgyz national traditions and customs. It established links with national-democratic forces in the Baltic republics, which had been in the vanguard of the anti-Communist and anti-Soviet movement in the USSR. Other opposition pro-democracy organisations included the centrist democratic party *Ashar* ('Ten'), the radical 'Democratic Party of Free Kyrgyzstan', the left-centrist organisation the 'People's Unity', the internationalist organisation 'the Union of Civic Accord' and the 'Agrarian Party'.[2] The common demands of the opposition were the cleansing of the Party, state and government structures of the supporters of Turdakun Usubaliyev, the transfer of power from the Communist Party to the Soviets, the strengthening of Kyrgyzstan's economic independence and a resolution of the acute housing problem among young people. By 1989, the opposition had achieved notable representation in the Supreme Soviet and in September, under its pressure, the latter adopted a Law on the State Status of the Kyrgyz Language.

Between December 1989 and February 1990 opposition activists orchestrated a series of mass protests under democratic and anti-Communist slogans at Lenin Square in the capital city of Frunze (Bishkek). They also encouraged homeless young people to illegally occupy land for private housing on the outskirts of the capital. By May 1990, the Kyrgyz opposition had consolidated into the Kyrgyzstan Democratic Movement (KDM), which challenged the weakened political monopoly of the Communist Party under Absamat Masaliyev. Masaliyev's authority was fatally wounded by his reluctance to address the acute housing issue, which in June 1990 escalated into a bloody Kyrgyz–Uzbek ethnic conflict in the overpopulated southern region of Osh.[3] The conflict was politicised by the ethnically Uzbek party *Adolat* ('Justice') and the largely ethnically Kyrgyz KDM. In September 1990, the KDM challenged the Communist Party and state authorities by issuing a 'Declaration of Sovereignty' of Kyrgyzstan.

In the face of advancing political opposition and rising interethnic tensions in the south of the country Masaliyev, unlike his Central Asian counterparts, was unable to hang on to power by converting himself from the Communist Party first secretary to the president. Instead, in October 1990 he was sidelined by an opposition non-*apparatchik* and ex-president of the Academy of Sciences, Askar Akayev (b. 1944), who aspired to break away from Soviet-era political authoritarianism in favour of Western political and economic liberalism, civil society and civic, rather than primordial, citizenship. In October 1990, Akayev was elected President of Kyrgyzstan by the Supreme Soviet. In order to undermine the institutional political supremacy of the Communist Party, President Akayev created an alternative centre of power – the Presidential Council – which relied on the KDM and consisted of Akayev's supporters from the intelligentsia and professional class. In December 1990, the pro-Akayev parliament changed the name of the country from the Kyrgyz Soviet Socialist Republic to the Republic of Kyrgyzstan.[4] In the same month Akayev restructured the government by bringing in a considerable number of reform-oriented younger politicians, and adopted a programme of political and economic liberalisation and administrative decentralisation of the country. In February 1991, it changed the name of the capital, Frunze, which it had borne since 1926 in honour of the Bolshevik commander Mikhail Frunze, to its pre-Soviet name of Bishkek. Nevertheless, the government's demonstrative radicalism, compared with its Central Asian neighbours, did not transcend the Soviet context. Like other Central Asian leaders, President Akayev did not envisage Kyrgyzstan outside the reformed and democratised USSR. In March 1991, during the national referendum on the preservation of the Soviet Union as a 'reformed federation of equal and sovereign states', he voiced his unequivocal support for the union and his position was echoed by 96.4 per cent of voters supporting the preservation of the USSR.[5]

In April 1991, Akayev strengthened his grip on political power by forcing Absamat Masaliyev to resign as the leader of the Communist Party, although the Communists still continued to dominate central and local government structures. The situation changed as a result of the anti-Gorbachev coup in Moscow on 19 August 1991 during which Akayev, unlike other Central Asian leaders, resolutely opposed the *putschists*. Following the coup's collapse, Akayev quit the Communist Party and embarked on the de-communisation of all state and government structures. On 31 August 1991, in a symbolic move, he proclaimed the independence of the Republic of Kyrgyzstan, and in elections that October Akayev was elected president of the independent republic. Nevertheless, he remained committed to the territorial integrity of the USSR until 8 December 1991 when, having found himself unconstitutionally excluded from the Belavezha Accords on the dissolution of the USSR, he was forced along with other Central Asian leaders to accept the USSR's disintegration.

Kyrgyzstan's 'democratic' experiment

Since 1992, Kyrgyzstan's political, economic and societal development has significantly diverged from other Central Asian states. While the Communist Party leaders in Kazakhstan, Uzbekistan, Turkmenistan and Tajikistan managed to stay in power and ensure considerable continuity in the political system, albeit under a new facade, Kyrgyzstan underwent a self-inflicted regime change under the leadership of President Akayev who declared his adherence to a Western-style economic and political model. In May 1993, Kyrgyzstan became the first Central Asian state to introduce its own currency – the *som* – and to embark on comprehensive market reforms. In the political sphere, Akayev announced his unambiguous commitment to the rule of law, the supremacy of human rights and the civic principles of nation-building. A constituent part of Kyrgyzstan's drive towards economic and political liberalisation was its multifaceted external engagement. It became the first Central Asian state to enter the World Trade Organisation (WTO); and Kyrgyzstan's existing close relations with Russia were counterbalanced by rapidly developing economic and military ties with China, on the one hand, and links with the West, on the other. Thus, in late 1991 Kyrgyzstan joined the Russia-dominated CIS, followed by its membership in 1992 of the CST/CSTO. In 1996, along with Kazakhstan, Tajikistan and Russia, Kyrgyzstan joined the China-speared SCO, while in 2001 it opted for military cooperation with the United States.[6] Similar eclecticism and ambiguity were characteristic of the official policies at the societal and educational level. While retaining close and diverse links with Russian institutions and organisations, Kyrgyzstan also welcomed dozens of Western NGOs promoting democracy, and foreign Islamic, Protestant and other religious funds and missionaries. In 1993, the Akayev government established in Bishkek the Kyrgyz–Russian Slavic University (KRSU) and the Kyrgyz–American University (KAU), which as the names suggest subscribed to different value and polity orientations.[7]

Akayev's nation- and state-building strategy was equally controversial. Given the existence of large Russian and Uzbek minorities and the tense relations between Uzbek and Kyrgyz in the aftermath of the Osh riots in 1990, he tried to keep ethnicity out of politics and stressed his preference for civic nationhood. Thus, the Constitution of 1993 defined Kyrgyzstan as a sovereign, democratic, law-based and secular state. It did not contain any reference to ethnicity and named the people of Kyrgyzstan as the only bearer of sovereignty and the source of state power.[8] Akayev's declared adherence to national harmony was reflected in his ideological project 'Kyrgyzstan is Our Common Home' and the safeguarding of Russian as the country's lingua franca despite the pressure from Kyrgyz nationalists who demanded the introduction of official Kyrgyz monolingualism. Instead, Kyrgyz was officially designated as the state language and Russian as the official language. In 1994, in an attempt to ameliorate Kyrgyz–Uzbek relations, Akayev initiated the opening in Osh of the Kyrgyz–Uzbek University.[9]

In spite of these policies, the Akayev presidency witnessed some resurgence of Kyrgyz clan and regional networks, which acquired a central role in the distribution of pivotal political, economic and military posts and thus contributed to the 'kyrgyzisation' of the government and parliament – the *Jogorku Kenesh* ('Supreme Soviet'). The absence of such networks among Russians and other Slavs inevitably led to their considerable political and economic marginalisation. Another factor was the instrumentalisation of history in favour of an exclusively Kyrgyz heritage. Thus, the flag of independent Kyrgyzstan consists of a Kyrgyz *yurt*, situated on top of a sun with forty rays representing the forty Kyrgyz tribes. Of particular significance was the elevation to the position of forebears of the Kyrgyzstani nation of the heroes of the sixteenth-century Kyrgyz epic *Manas*, named after the Kyrgyz tribal leader who united the forty Kyrgyz tribes.[10] Kyrgyz ethnonationalism was evidenced also in the renaming of streets and squares after Kyrgyz historical figures, the erection of monuments to them and the placing of their images on Kyrgyzstani *soms*.[11] Nevertheless, in comparative terms, the official ethnonational discourse in Kyrgyzstan was less prominent than in other Central Asian republics, mitigated by official Bishkek's adherence to civic nationalism, its greater economic and educational dependence on Russia, its substantial Uzbek population and its precarious relations with Uzbekistan.

By the early 2000s, it had become apparent that Akayev's economic, social and national policies were ineffective and even detrimental for the country. The proclaimed democracy, political pluralism, social justice, open society, market economy and freedom of information were not accompanied by any improvement in the socio-economic conditions of the bulk of the population, which remained dismal. In fact, Akayev presided over the formation of a pseudo-democratic political system that actually functioned through mechanisms of family- and clan-based favouritism, nepotism and endemic corruption, and that was indifferent to the needs of ordinary people. The inner circle of the Akayev regime came to be dominated by people from the Kemin district, the president's homeland, and during his presidency Kyrgyzstani society became polarised between an affluent political, business and foreign NGO-affiliated elite and the extremely poor and desolate majority.

The country's economy was virtually paralysed as a result of a rushed and poorly thought through privatisation and price liberalisation. By the late 1990s, industrial production had plummeted by 63.7 per cent compared with 1990. A similar decline was experienced in agriculture following the introduction of private ownership of land in 1998.[12] The ensuing total destruction of *kolkhozes*, *sovkhozes* and various industrial enterprises deprived the majority of the population of employment. As a result, many working-age people were forced to support themselves through garden farming, bazaar trading, *chelnok* ('trade shuttle') travels between Kyrgyzstan, Uzbekistan, Turkey and China, or by engaging in services and semi-legal or illegal activities including drug trafficking.[13] A large number of men, including those with university degrees, became taxi drivers or joined cartels involved in the shipment of used cars from Europe to Kyrgyzstan. People's everyday life was severely disrupted by regular power cuts and winter blackouts caused by the disintegrating energy supply infrastructure as a result of severe under-investment. The socio-economic situation was particularly desperate in the south of the country, which had suffered from the lengthy political domination of northerners. The tangible socio-economic divide between the more developed north and the disadvantaged south was accompanied by cultural differences related to the south belonging to the historically more Islamicised Ferghana valley.

A corollary of widespread unemployment and socio-economic hardship was the proliferation of alcoholism and drug use, and the increased emigration of young people in search of work and a better life. According to conservative official statistics, in 1993 over 121,000 young Kyrgyz left the country in search of work,[14] their main destinations being Russia and Kazakhstan. On the other side of the same coin, southern Kyrgyzstan – Osh, Batken and Jalal-Abad in particular – turned into the main hub of the illegal drugs trade and trafficking from Afghanistan to Kazakhstan, Russia and Western Europe, as well as the trafficking of women for prostitution purposes to Dubai and other countries of the Gulf and Turkey. A facilitating factor was the involvement of some government officials in this illegal but very profitable business. Such hardships fuelled inter-regional and interethnic tensions and created fertile ground for the proliferation of Islamic radicalism; and the complex domestic ethno-confessional situation was aggravated as a result of the incursions in August 1999 and August 2000 into southern Kyrgyzstan of over a thousand Uzbek IDU fighters from the territory of northern Tajikistan.[15]

Kyrgyzstan's 'democratic' transition was not dissimilar to that in Russia under the leadership of the democracy-oriented Boris Yeltsin (1931–2007, in office 1991–9). In both countries the effects were largely devastating for the society and the state. In the economic sphere, they led to the complete destruction of the Soviet economic infrastructure, which was the major employer, causing the drastic impoverishment of the bulk of the population and pushing a considerable number of highly skilled professionals and young people out of the country in search of work and a better life. In the case of Kyrgyzstan, an aggravating factor was the scarcity of natural resources, which might have been exchanged for cash and used to cushion the post-Soviet transition, as was the case in oil- and gas-rich Russia, Kazakhstan, Turkmenistan and Azerbaijan.

In March 2005, the people's frustration with the Akayev regime prompted mass protests orchestrated by the coalition of opposition forces under the joint leadership of Kurmanbek Bakiyev (b. 1947),[16] a representative of the south, and General Felix Kulov (b. 1948), a long-term northern adversary of Askar Akayev.[17] Subsequently, these protests became known as the Tulip Revolution in association with other 'coloured revolutions' across the post-Soviet space.[18] The driving forces of the Tulip Revolution were ethnic Kyrgyz from the southern regions of Osh and Jalal-Abad, which were particularly badly hit by Akayev's 'reforms'. To a considerable extent the Tulip Revolution reflected the country's socio-economic, political and cultural divide into the dominant north and the disadvantaged south. During the revolution Akayev[19] was ousted and superseded by a new president, Kurmanbek Bakiyev (in office 2005–10), who sought to change the regional power balance in favour of the southerners. In particular, he abolished the post of prime minister, occupied by his former ally and northerner, Felix Kulov; brought into top government positions his relatives[20] and friends from the south; and changed election rules to enhance the greater parliamentary representation of the south.[21] Externally, the Bakiyev government attempted to increase Kyrgyzstan's engagement with the Muslim world; in 2006, it signed an agreement with the Islamic Development Bank (IDB) on the introduction of Islamic principles in some sectors of the banking system of Kyrgyzstan. Several dozen *halal* shops were established across the country. More broadly, however, the Bakiyev government did not produce any notable positive changes, and the country became a de facto failed state on the brink of regional disintegration and interethnic strife.

In spring 2009, the authorities failed to prevent ethnic clashes in Chui *oblast'* in the north of the country, involving Russians and Karachais, on the one side, and Kurds, on the other.[22] In April 2010, Bakiyev was confronted with violent mass protests in Bishkek and was forced to flee to Jalal-Abad, where his presence reignited the Kyrgyz–Uzbek conflict in May 2010. In June 2010, clashes between the Kyrgyz and Uzbeks spread to Osh, which for four days was subjected to savage killings and looting, resulting in the deaths of 295 Uzbeks and 123 Kyrgyz.[23] Having lost control over the rapidly deteriorating political situation, Bakiyev fled to Belarus, while the country succumbed to political chaos under a sequence of interim leaders.[24] Kyrgyzstan's spiralling decline was halted in October 2011 with the arrival of the new president, Almazbek Atambayev (b. 1956, in office 2011–17).[25] Atambayev's government began Kyrgyzstan's gradual reversal from 'the democratic transition' towards a

Figure 6.1 Men at the Andarak mosque (photograph by Zumrat Salmorbekova, Batken, Kyrgyzstan, April 2003)

more familiar Eurasian economic and political path, an approach that received a further boost as a result of Kyrgyzstan joining the Eurasian Economic Union (EAEU) in 2015. Importantly, he undertook concerted steps towards national and regional reconciliation by co-opting representatives of the south into key political and economic positions. In 2016, he appointed Sooronday Zheenbekov (b. 1958), a representative of the south,[26] as prime minister, and in November 2017 Zheenbekov (in office 2017–present) succeeded him as Kyrgyzstan's new President.

The 'Islamic revival'

From the late 1980s onwards Kyrgyzstan, like other Muslim-majority regions of the USSR and for the same reasons, experienced an 'Islamic revival', which was more prominent in the south of the country. Still, compared with neighbouring Uzbekistan and Tajikistan, the Islamic dynamic in Kyrgyzstan was less intensive and more comparable with that in Kazakhstan. As in Kazakhstan, the main reasons for this were the Kyrgyz nomadic heritage, the ethnic and confessional diversity[27] of the country, and the more intensive Kyrgyz secularisation and Russification. Other contributing factors were the large emigration of young Kyrgyz to predominantly Orthodox Christian Russia and the particularly liberal religious legislation in Kyrgyzstan. In December 1991,

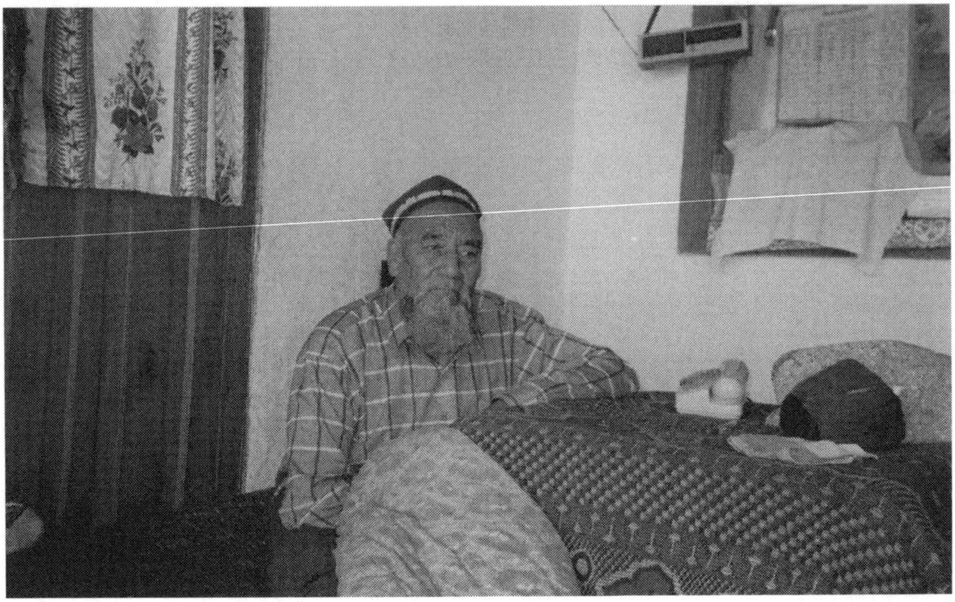

Figure 6.2 Baisanov-*mullo* (photograph by Zumrat Salmorbekova, Isfana, Kyrgyzstan, April 2003)

the Kyrgyzstani parliament adopted the 'Law on the Freedom of Religion and Religious Organisations', which removed any restrictions on Islamic and other religious activities by locals and foreigners in Kyrgyzstan. As a result, this small mountainous country attracted a disproportionately large number of foreign religious preachers and educators, especially of Islamic and Protestant orientation. Among the far-reaching implications of this Law was the establishment of a relatively large number – given the size of the country – of Islamic foundations, organisations and educational institutions from Pakistan, Turkey, Egypt, Jordan, Saudi Arabia and the Gulf states. They invested generously in advancing their particular strands of Islam, while de facto treating the Kyrgyz version of Central Asian Islam as *bid'a.*

In the conditions of state non-interference in the religious sphere the foreign Islamic assistance was the primary source of the rapid growth in the number of mosques, *madrasahs,* Arabic-language centres and other Islamic institutions in Kyrgyzstan, especially in the south. Saudi, Pakistani and other foreign Islamic universities provided numerous scholarships for young Kyrgyz.[28] Secondary sources of the 'Islamic revival' included donations by wealthy locals, whose sudden piety was often related to their rapid enrichment in not entirely Islamic ways, and, to a lesser extent, the collective donations by villagers or members of neighbourhood communities. Between 1991 and the mid-1990s the total number of registered and unregistered mosques rose from 39 to over 2,000; for example, in the border market town of Kara-Suyu a dozen registered mosques co-existed with over 100 unregistered mosques.[29]

The fast rise in the number of mosques created a large deficit in qualified imams and mullahs. In the rural areas newly opened mosques were dominated by elderly imams and mullahs, Soviet-era *kolkhozniks*, who were largely illiterate in Islamic theology but committed to the local understanding and practices of *Hanafi* Islam, referred to as 'the tradition of imam Azam'. These mosques, attended by Muslims from different age groups, had distinctive ethnonational characters and often catered for exclusively Kyrgyz, Uzbek, Dungan, Uighur or Tatar worshippers. Alongside, there emerged a relatively small number of mosques which acquired younger imams who were trained either in Islamic institutions abroad or by foreign Islamic *mudarrises* at home. These were competent in the Qur'an, *hadith* and *shari'a* and attracted predominantly young Muslim worshippers of different ethnic backgrounds who sought qualified theological guidance on vital questions in their lives. Inevitably, the young imams' judgements often clashed with the entrenched local Muslim perceptions of good and evil, true and false. They denounced local Muslim customs, especially the spending of large amounts of money on funeral and wake ceremonies.[30]

By the late 1990s, there were over 200 *madrasahs* and over a dozen Islamic institutes in Kyrgyzstan. The vast majority of Kyrgyz village *madrasahs* had poor educational standards in spite of their claim to belonging to 'imam Azam's tradition'. They were largely inferior to the Kyrgyz *madrasahs* in urban areas, as well as to Uzbek and Tajik *madrasahs* in neighbouring Uzbekistan and Tajikistan. However, some newly opened Islamic institutes and *madrasahs* in Osh, Jalal-Abad and Bishkek began to offer a structured Islamic education by employing *mudarrises* from Egypt, Jordan, Saudi Arabia, Syria, Pakistan and Turkey who used the curricula of their original institutions, which inevitably reflected their regional versions of *Shafi'i*, *Maliki*, *Hanbali* or *Hanafi madhhab*. The largest among them were the Islamic institute of Hazrati Umar in Bishkek and the Islamic University in Osh. Unlike neighbouring Uzbekistan and Tajikistan, Kyrgyzstan acquired co-educational as well as exclusively female *madrasahs*.[31] In comparative terms, there were more female students in Kyrgyzstan's *madrasahs* than in the *madrasahs* of neighbouring Uzbekistan and Tajikistan, where young women who were interested in Islam continued to favour home Islamic education overseen by *bibi-otuns*.[32] In the Jalal-Abad *oblast'* a main provider of Islamic education for girls became the Pakistan-based *Tablighi Jama'at*, which treated local Islamic traditions as corrupt and instead promoted 'normative' Islam. It ran a network of *madrasahs* where girls were required to wear the *hijab*, which historically was alien to nomadic Kyrgyz women.[33]

Throughout the 1990s the Uzbek population in southern Kyrgyzstan was not entirely immune to the propaganda and recruitment mobilisation of Uzbek Islamists from *Adolat*, *Barakah*, *Tawba*, *Islam-Lashkarlari* and, subsequently, the

Figure 6.3 Students at the female *madrasah* in Batken (photograph by Zumrat Salmorbekova, Batken, Kyrgyzstan, April 2003)

IDU. Some of the local Uzbeks were sympathetic to the ideas and political agenda of Uzbek militants from the IDU who crossed into southern Kyrgyzstan from Tajikistan in August 1999 and August 2000. In the 2000s, the HTI acquired some presence in the Jalal-Abad, Osh and Batken regions. Although the majority of *Tahriris* there were ethnic Uzbeks, they did also include some ethnic Kyrgyz. In the 2010s, in the context of the globalisation of Islamism and *jihadism*, the number of ethnic Kyrgyz Islamists and *jihadists* began to rise. Ethnic Kyrgyz were noted among members of the IIJ and the Islamic Movement of Turkestan; and, in 2010, the Kyrgyzstan intelligence sources reported the uncovering of the first Kyrgyz-centred jihadist *jama'at* – the *Jaish al-Mahdi* ('Army of the Righteous Ruler')[34] under the leadership of Amir Sovetbek Islamov (b. 1972), an ethnic Kyrgyz from Chui *oblast'*. It was alleged that the *jama'at* consisted of fifteen members who predominantly originated from the north of the country.[35] The increasing involvement of ethnic Kyrgyz in the international *jihadist* network was evidenced by their presence among ISIS fighters in Iraq, Syria and Turkey; in 2015, over 200 ethnic Kyrgyz were reported to be fighting for ISIS in Iraq and Syria.[36] In June 2016, Kyrgyz suicide bombers were involved in the bombing of the Atatürk airport in Istanbul, which killed 45 and wounded 239.[37]

State–Muslim relations

Following independence, Kyrgyzstan, along with other post-Soviet and post-atheist Central Asian states, adhered to the principles of secularism. State secularism was enshrined in its consecutive constitutions of 1993, 2007 and 2010, all of which defined Kyrgyzstan as a democratic, sovereign and secular state. President Akayev, like other Central Asian leaders as well as the majority of Kyrgyzstan's population, regarded Islam as part of the Kyrgyz ethnocultural heritage, rather than as a religion or an ideology per se. In 1994, following the example of other post-Soviet Muslim leaders, Akayev conducted the *hajj* to Mecca and Medina. As elsewhere in post-Soviet Muslim Eurasia, he made the Islamic holidays of *Orozo-Ait* (*'Id al-Fitr*) and *Qurban-Ait* (*'Id al-Adha*) official holidays of Kyrgyzstan and sanctioned the introduction of Islamic or Islamicised symbols and themes into the public domain.

But beyond this formal symbolic respect towards its traditional religion Akayev's actual interest in Islam was marginal. As mentioned earlier, this was due to the historically complex relationship of the nomadic Kyrgyz with Islam, the polyethnicity of Kyrgyzstan, the high level of secularisation and cultural Russification, as well as – in President Akayev's case – his ideological Westernism. As a result, during his presidency state regulation of religion was minimal; the Soviet-era system of state–Muslim relations was effectively abandoned and the Islamic sphere was largely hijacked by foreign Islamic foundations, proselytisers and educators. Particularly assertive were emissaries of the Turkish Gulen movement *Hizmet* and the Pakistani *Tablighi Jama'at* who promoted a stricter version of Islam of the Deobandi School.[38] The former established the Kyrgyz–Turkish University 'Manas' in Bishkek and formed a network of Kyrgyz–Turkish lycées across the country, while the latter created a chain of *Tablighi madrasahs* in the south of the country. In addition, Kyrgyzstan attracted Islamic missionaries from Saudi Arabia, the Gulf states and other countries of the Middle East. Compared with neighbouring Uzbekistan and Tajikistan, the governments of which in the late 1990s stopped sending young people to study in Islamic institutes abroad, the Kyrgyzstani authorities and the muftiiate continued to send young Kyrgyzstani Muslims for further Islamic education to Egypt, Saudi Arabia and Syria until the early 2010s.[39]

The lack of state support coupled with foreign Islamic dominance accounts for the particular weakness of the Kyrgyzstani muftiiate, which was established in 1991 on the basis of the former SADUM's *qaziiate* of Kyrgyzstan. The first muftii of Kyrgyzstan was Kimsanbai-*aji* Abdurahmanov (b. 1940),[40] who was one of the 'young imams'. Having negated the Soviet-era SADUM, Muftii Kimsanbai-aji, like his counterparts in other Central Asian republics, used it as a template for the Kyrgyzstani muftiiate – the Spiritual Directorate of Muslims of Kyrgyzstan (SDMK) – which acquired similar administrative structures and launched its own periodical, *Ummah*. However, the SDMK's economic, financial and cadre situation, as well as its authority among ordinary Muslims, was significantly inferior to that of its Soviet predecessor. Muftii Kimsanbai-*aji* and his successors,[41] as well as other official Muslim clergy, were preoccupied

Figure 6.4 Children in the Ala-Too Mountains (photograph by author, Kyrgyzstan, June 2017)

by internal rivalries and squabbling over the attention and favours of various foreign Islamic funders.

Theologically, most Kyrgyzstani muftiis have lacked an adequate knowledge of Central Asian Islamic scholarship and tradition and have been dependent on external expertise which tended to be of *Salafi* nature. As a result, they produced *fatwas* which denounced traditional lavish funerals, involving the distribution of meat and other food among numerous relatives and guests as well as the practice of burying the deceased three or four days after the death and, instead, instructed worshippers to bury their deceased on the day of the death as required by 'normative' Islam (i.e.,*Salafi* – G.Y.).[42] The current Muftii Toktomushev, as a graduate of a Pakistani *madrasah*, has been supportive of the activities in Kyrgyzstan of *Tablighis* who treated local Islamic practices as *bid'a*.[43] Some of the muftiis' religious and public credentials suffered from their involvement in political or public scandals,[44] as well as in unscrupulous businesses related to the organisation of *hajj*,[45] the selling of counterfeit *halal* licences and of bottles of '*zamzam* water'.[46] It is not surprising therefore that some young Kyrgyzstani Muslims have given up on the official Islamic clergy and have begun to seek guidance from various unofficial Islamic preachers, including those of *Salafi* and *jihadist* orientation, as well as from online and social media Islamic and Islamist sources. Until the early 2010s, unofficial Islamic leaders were especially active in Jalal-Abad *oblast'*, where they served as imams in unregistered mosques and as *mudarrises* in unregistered *madrasahs*. They were much younger than traditional imams and mullahs and were mostly foreign-educated; they were also more approachable and were prepared to discuss wider issues than Islamic ritual. They were, however, critical of Sufism which was central to Kyrgyz Islam and regarded it as *bid'a*.

Since the 2010s the government has moved towards reasserting its control over the religious sphere. In particular, it revised the registration procedures for mosques and Islamic educational institutions, leading to the closure of a large number which did not comply with the newly introduced criteria. As a result, the number of registered *madrasahs* was reduced from over 200 to just over 60.[47] A special Anti-Terrorist Centre (ATC) was created within the State Security Committee; its central task has been the monitoring of Kyrgyzstani nationals involved in Islamist and *jihadist* activities inside and outside the country. Of particular concern have been the Kyrgyz *jihadist* organisation *Jaish al-Mahdi* and the Kyrgyz *jama'at* within ISIS. Following Kyrgyzstan's accession to the EAEU in 2015, there has been growing coordination between Kyrgyzstan and Russia, Kazakhstan and Tajikistan in the sphere of Islamic education and counter-radicalisation.[48] Still, in comparative terms, state control over Islam remains significantly weaker than in other Central Asian countries or in Azerbaijan or Russia. In 2017, despite its small size and the relatively weak religiosity of its population, Kyrgyzstan had 1,700 registered mosques, nine Islamic institutes

Figure 6.5 Kyrgyz girls at the leavers' party (photograph by author, Bishkek, June 2017)

and sixty *madrasahs* – much more than in its larger and historically more religious neighbours Uzbekistan and Tajikistan.[49]

Popular perceptions and practices of Islam

The post-Soviet transitional trauma and widespread disillusionment with the ability and willingness of the political class to deliver promised reforms forced many Kyrgyzstanis to seek moral refuge in their families, in clan and tribal solidarity, and in Islam. The resurgence of the clan and tribal network among the Kyrgyz was facilitated by their retention of their genealogical history as a national defence mechanism as they experienced the Stalinist destruction of nomadism, the influx of Russians and other non-Kyrgyz into the country, and the high level of linguistic and cultural Russification. Most Kyrgyz, like most Kazakhs, preserved their knowledge of their ancestors through seven generations. The process of rediscovery of people's Muslim-ness has occurred in different forms and has been conditioned by their geographical habitat, history, ethnicity, education and age. It has been more intensive in southern Kyrgyzstan, which is administratively divided into Osh, Batken and Jalal-Abad *oblasts*. This has been due to the region's lengthier and deeper Islamicisation, its existence within various sedentary Islamic and semi-nomadic Islamicised polities, including the Uzbek-dominated Islamic Kokand khanate, and its substantial Uzbek community who constituted over 40 per cent of the region's population. Under the Uzbeks' Islamicising influence the southern Kyrgyz turned out to be more 'Muslim' than the Kyrgyz elsewhere in the country in terms of their observance of Islamic norms, dress codes, dietary requirements and gender relations. Despite this cultural and religious 'Uzbekisation' of the southern Kyrgyz the relations between Kyrgyz and Uzbeks have been difficult, as evidenced by their violent clashes in 1990 and 2010.[50]

For these reasons, the Islamic dynamic in southern Kyrgyzstan has been more congruent to the rest of the Ferghana valley than to Kyrgyzstan as a whole. It has been manifested by both the resurfacing of traditional Islamicised pilgrimages to over 400 *mazars* scattered across the region, and the advance of mosque-based Islam. The largest number of *mazars* are natural sites (mountains, rocks, lakes, springs and trees);[51] other *mazars* include the *mazar* of Kyrgyz's forefather-*Manas*, which is located in the Talas valley; the Tash Rabat, which is the well-preserved remnants of the *caravansarai* of the Silk Road, situated not far from the Kyrgyz–Chinese border in At-Bashin district of the Naryn region; and *mazars* related to *sahaba*, such as Dzhany-Nookat in Osh *oblast'*, and Kojo-Kaiyr and Kojo-Bilal in Jalal-Abad *oblast'*, as well as other remnants of the early Islamic period.[52] Simultaneously, the region has witnessed the proliferation of mosques, *madrasahs* and other attributes of 'normative' Islam. Until the early 2010s some of them were funded and run by *mudarrises* from Pakistan, Saudi Arabia and Turkey and provided a more comprehensive Islamic education, albeit along their own methodological and doctrinal lines. Its students and graduates have been more visible because, in case of men, they wore beards and skull caps, prayed five times a day, abstained from drinking alcohol, fasted during the month of *Ramadan*, while, in case of women, they wore the *hijab* and have retreated into the traditional secluded lifestyle based on family and household. There has also been the sporadic proliferation of Islamism among younger people, especially Uzbeks who sympathised with the IDU and the HTI.

By contrast, the resurgent Islam among the nomadic and semi-nomadic Kyrgyz in the mountainous regions has retained its predominantly syncretic character, with a strong reliance on shamanism, Zoroastrianism, animism

Figure 6.6 A Kyrgyz *samsa*-maker (photograph by author, Kyrgyzstan, June 2017)

and Kyrgyz tribal rulings. As in the past, the people's belief system has been dominated by the spirits of horses and ancestors, magic, fire and nature worship. Local Muslims tend to view Islam as a logical continuation of their ancestral traditions which include numerous non-Islamic practices, such as, for example, the *ala kachuu* (kidnapping of a girl for marriage). They therefore regard visitation of historic, natural and, to a lesser extent, Islamic *mazars* as being more important than mosque attendance. Among the most common reasons for a pilgrimage, which are accompanied by chanting what they believe to be Qur'anic sayings, lighting of candles and burning wool. The historical prevalence of *ziiarat* practices has accounted for an inferior status of mosque imams or mullahs compared with *moldo* (unofficial Muslim authorities), sheikhs and various healers – *bakshi, bubu* or *demchi.* Nevertheless, this tradition has been increasingly challenged by the growing number of mosques and male *madrasahs* which opened in the mountainous area of Naryn and the Naryn *oblast'* after independence.[53] Most of newly founded *madrasahs* have been externally funded and taught along the 'normative' Islamic lines, thus causing identity confusion among its Kyrgyz students.

Compared with the more religiously pious dwellers of the Ferghana valley and the religiously syncretic inhabitants of the mountains the vast majority of the residents of Bishkek and other urbanised northern regions have been characterised by a high level of secularisation and cosmopolitanism. In terms of dress code and attitudes to alcohol and food they are largely indistinguishable from

Figure 6.7 The central mosque in Isfana (photograph by Zumrat Salmorbekova, Isfana, Kyrgyzstan, April 2003)

local Russians and other non-Muslims. Their Muslim-ness has been ethnocultural in nature and reducible to observance of *sunnet*, *janazah*, occasional visits to *mazars* and the avoidance of eating pork. However, in the last two decades the urban areas have also witnessed a limited but steady re-Islamicisation in the form of new mosques,[54] the growing public observance of Islamic holidays, and the number of veiled girls and women in the streets. A contributing factor to this trend has been an influx of migrants from the more Islamicised south as well as surrounding villages.

As noted earlier, the hardships generated by extreme economic and political instability turned a large number of working-age Kyrgyzstanis into labour migrants. Their main destination has been Russia, followed by Kazakhstan, while the offspring of the political and cultural elite often sought to settle in the United States and Europe. Following Kyrgyzstan joining the EAEU in 2015, Kyrgyz migration to Russia and Kazakhstan accelerated even further because Kyrgyzstani citizens no longer needed to obtain Russian work permits.[55] As a result, in January 2016, the number of Kyrgyzstanis working in Russia exceeded half a million.[56] The relations of diaspora Kyrgyz with Islam have varied significantly, depending on their origins, the nature of their employment, and the level of their social and cultural integration. Because of their higher level of Russification and cosmopolitanism Kyrgyz migrants were more successful than their Uzbek and Tajik counterparts in competing in the Russian job market. They became well represented at low managerial, administrative and shop assistant levels. Kyrgyz women became widely employed as hospital and GP nurses and carers, while men were especially present in the spheres of communication and transport. Compared with Uzbek and Tajik male labour migrants, who favoured seasonal migrations while leaving their families at home, Kyrgyz migrancy has involved both men and women. Many of them also migrated as families, while others created families in Russia with the aim of permanent resettlement.[57]

The integration into Russian society of properly employed Kyrgyz migrants, especially from Bishkek and other northern urban centres, has been relatively smooth though not entirely problem-free due to the element of hostility to migrants and Islamophobia in Moscow, St Petersburg and other large Russian cities, which developed in response to the large-scale post-Soviet immigration from Muslim Central Asia and the Caucasus. Even so, a considerable number of Kyrgyz migrants, especially young men from the villages of southern Kyrgyzstan, have been unable to find stable employment and have ended up in dire housing and social conditions. They have also been among the most likely targets of xenophobic and Islamophobic mistreatment and abuse. Their ensuing social marginalisation and cultural alienation has served only to intensify their socialisation along Islamic lines. The main sites for their Islamicised solidarity were a limited number of historically Tatar mosques and a larger

Figure 6.8 *Bibi-otun* Badabaeva (photograph by Zumrat Salmorbekova, Andarak, Kyrgyzstan, April 2003)

number of recently established prayer houses. Alongside the Kyrgyz, these migrant Muslim networks also included ethnic Uzbeks, Tajiks, Azerbaijanis, Chechen, Ingush, Avars and some other historically more 'Muslim' migrants of the former USSR.[58] Yet another implication of the Islamicised social alienation of some Muslim Kyrgyzstanis and other Central Asian and Caucasian migrants has been their Islamic radicalisation. For example, in the Urals Kyrgyzstan citizens have been recorded among members of HTI, the Islamic Party of Turkestan, the *Tablighi Jama'at* and ISIS.[59] It is symptomatic that the suicide bomber Akbarjon Zhalilov, who in April 2017 killed sixteen and injured over fifty in the St Petersburg metro, was a native of southern Kyrgyzstan.

Overall, the nature and trajectory of the 'Islamic revival' in Kyrgyzstan, as in neighbouring Kazakhstan, has been affected by the Kyrgyz's poor knowledge of book-based Islam due to their nomadic past, and the theological weakness of their official Islamic clergy. Given a lengthy period of unregulated foreign Islamic proselytism in post-Soviet Kyrgyzstan, such inadequate Islamic knowledge has acted as a major factor in the particular susceptibility of some young Kyrgyz Muslims to foreign Islam (i.e., *Salafi* – G.Y.), which has often been uncritically accepted as the 'true Islam'. Moreover, the diversity of Islamic teaching provision has created some doctrinal confusion among those young Kyrgyz who sought to rediscover their historical Muslim-ness. As a result, there has been a division of the Kyrgyzstani Muslim community into followers of various foreign Islamic teachings, most of which denounced Kyrgyz Islamic traditions as non-Muslim. Another theologically and politically de-stabilising factor has been the increasing exposure online and through social media of young Kyrgyz in Kyrgyzstan and the diaspora to globalised *Salafi* Islamic messages.

Notes

1. The territory of Kyrgyzstan covers 199,951 km^2. It is a small, landlocked and mountainous country that borders Kazakhstan, Uzbekistan, Tajikistan and China. According to the 1989 USSR census, the total population of Kyrgyzstan was 4,257,755 with the Kyrgyz making up 2,229,663 of the population. Among Kyrgyzstan's largest ethnic minorities have been Russians (916,558), Uzbeks (550,096), Ukrainians (108,027), Germans (101,309), Tatars (70,068), Dungans (64,000), Uighurs (36,778), Turks (21,294) and Koreans (18,355). In 2017, Kyrgyzstan's population was estimated at 6,089,859 people. 'Natsional'nyi Sostav Kirgizskoi SSR', *Demoscope Weekly*, 1–21 May 2017, available at: http://demoscope.ru/weekly/ssp/sng_nac_89.php?reg=1, last accessed 26 May 2017.
2. *Vremia Vostoka*, available at: http://www.easttime.ru/countries/topics/1/4/22.html, last accessed 27 May 2017.
3. The housing problems in the Osh region were aggravated by the recent influx of ethnic Kyrgyz into predominantly Uzbek areas. In June 1990, a group of ethnic Kyrgyz seized farmland that had been claimed by Uzbeks. The dispute over land soon evolved into violent clashes between ethnic Uzbeks and Kyrgyz leaving between 300 and 600 people dead and over 500 houses burnt down. The riots were stopped by the intervention of Soviet airborne troops. For more on the 1990 Osh conflict, see Asankanov, 1996; Montgomery 2007; Rotar 2007.
4. In 1993, the name of the country was changed to the Kyrgyz Republic.
5. 'Ob Itogakh' 1991.
6. Thus, in 2001, in the context of the US-led global war on terror, the Akayev government agreed to the stationing on Kyrgyzstan's territory of the American airbase 'Gansi'. It was located at Manas international airport, 23 km southwest of Bishkek. In 2003, the Kyrgyzstani authorities made similar arrangements for the establishment of a Russian airbase in Kant, 20 km east of Bishkek. In 2014, upon the expiry of the lease, the American base was closed down, while the Russian base remained intact. Marat 2010, p. 110.
7. In 2004, the KRSU was co-funded by the Yeltsin Foundation and offered a wide range of familiar Soviet-style Russian-based undergraduate and postgraduate programmes in the sciences, engineering, medicine and the humanities. By contrast, the KAU, which was funded by the US government and George Soros' Open Society, focused on English-based American liberal arts programmes in the social sciences and humanities. In 1997, the KAU was renamed the American University in Kyrgyzstan (AUK), which in 2002 changed its name to the American University of Central Asia (AUCA).
8. *Constitution of the Kyrgyz Republic*, 1993, available at: http://www.gov.kg/?page_id=263&lang=ru, last accessed 1 June 2017.
9. In 2011, in response to the renewed Uzbek–Kyrgyz violence in Osh in 2010, the Kyrgyz–Uzbek University was renamed the Osh State Social University.
10. The teaching of *Manas*' seven commandments – patriotism, humanism, harmony with nature, aspiration to gain knowledge and skills, unity of the nation, international cooperation and defence of the state – was included into the school curriculum. In 1995, the Akayev

government organised a countrywide celebration of the 1,000th anniversary of Manas' birth. Cummings 2012, p. 111; Montgomery 2007, p. 184.

11. Those images included, for example, images of a Kyrgyz tribal leader Kurmanzhan Datka (1811–1907), a *manaschi* Sayakbay Karalayev (1894–1971), an *aqyn* Toktogul Satylganov (1864–1933), poets Togolok Moldo (1860–1942) and Alykul Osmanov (1915–50), a composer Abdylas Maldybayev (1906–78), a ballerina Bulbusara Beyshenaliyeva (1926–73) and a scientist and politician Kasym Tynystanov (1901–38). The most spectacular Kyrgyz monuments were those of *Aykol Manas* ('Magnanimous Manas') and *Batyr Kaba Uuly Kozhonkul* in Bishkek.
12. Koychuev, Mokrynin and Ploskikh 1999, pp. 97–8.
13. Until 1999 the major centre for transregional trading activity was a bazaar in Kara-Suyu, situated on the border between Kyrgyzstan and Uzbekistan. For more on transregional drug- trafficking, see Bohr and Price 2015, p. 16.
14. Koychuev, Mokrynin and Ploskikh 1999, p. 104.
15. In order to isolate the Uzbek militants the Kyrgyzstan authorities created a separate administrative unit – the Batken *oblast'*. The IDU invasion was rebuffed by the joint government troops of Kyrgyzstan, Uzbekistan and Russia.
16. Kurmanbek Bakiyev originated from southern Kyrgyzstan. Prior to becoming President of Kyrgyzstan in 2005 he served as *akim* of Jalal-Abad region (1995–7), head of administration of Chui region (1997–2000) and prime minister of Kyrgyzstan in 2000–2 and 2005. He was one of the founders of the opposition movement *Ata-Jurt* ('Fatherland').
17. Felix Kulov was born in Frunze (Bishkek). In the 1990s he occupied the powerful positions of Minister of Interior, Minister of National Security and Mayor of Bishkek. In 1999, he founded the political party *Ar-Namys* ('Dignity'). In 2000, after he revealed his presidential ambitions, he was charged with abuse of power in the past and imprisoned. He remained in prison until 2005.
18. For a detailed analysis of the Tulip Revolution, see Heathershaw 2007.
19. President Akayev, who feared for his life, fled first to Kazakhstan and then to Moscow, where he reverted to his academic career as professor of mathematics at the Moscow State University.
20. Kurmanbek Bakiyev ran the country as a family business, employing his brothers and sons in key political and economic positions. Thus, his brother, Zhanysh Bakiyev, was appointed Deputy Director of National Security; his other brother, Zhusup Bakiyev, became Governor of the Jalal-Abad *oblast*; another brother, Kanybek Bakiyev, was put in charge of the Suzak district authority. Kurmanbek Bakiyev's son, Marat Bakiyev, was appointed as Kyrgyzstan's ambassador to Germany, and his other son, Maxim Bakiyev, was made president of the lucrative newly established Central Agency for Development, Innovations and Investments.
21. According to Kyrgyzstan's new Constitution of 2007, designed by Bakiyev, two-thirds of the parliament were to be elected from party lists, while one-third was to be from territorial districts. In this way, during the parliamentary elections in December 2007, Bakiyev secured a majority for his newly established party, *Ak Jol* ('Light Path').
22. The conflict, which had deep economic and cultural causes, was provoked by mass Russian protests against the alleged rape of a four-year-old Russian girl by a Kurdish man. It escalated into violent clashes and resulted in the eviction of Kurds from the region.
23. Megoran 2012, p. 4.
24. For a short period Kyrgyzstan was headed by Rosa Otynbayeva (b. 1950), who originated from northern Kyrgyzstan. Previously she had served as a senior Communist Party functionary in Frunze (Bishkek, 1981–6), Minister of Foreign Affairs (1986–9), as Kyrgyzstan's Ambassador to the United States and Canada, Minister of Foreign Affairs (1994–7) and

as Kyrgyzstan's Ambassador to the United Kingdom (1997–2002). In 2005–7 she headed the political party *Asaba* and in 2007–9 she was one of the leading figures in the Social Democratic Party (SDP).

25. Almazbek Atambayev originated from northern Kyrgyzstan. Previously he had served as prime minister (2010–11) and as Minister of Industry, Trade and Tourism (2005–6). Atambayev's presidency, like that of his predecessors, has not been free from controversy and public scandals related to his authoritarian tendencies and the financial improprieties of members of his inner circle.
26. Sooronbay Zheenbekov was born in Biy-Murza of the Osh *oblast* where he previously served as Governor (2010). During the Presidential elections in October 2017 he represented the SDP.
27. There are thirty officially registered confessions in Kyrgyzstan. Tokmakov 2011.
28. For example, in 2003 over 600 Kyrgyz students studied in *Al-Azhar* University and some other Islamic universities in Egypt and Saudi Arabia. Salmorbekova and Yemelianova 2010, p. 229.
29. Salmorbekova and Yemelianova 2010, pp. 228–9.
30. Ibid.
31. Among co-educational Islamic institutions were, for example, an Islamic institute in the town of Tash-Kumyr, a *madrasah* in the town of Suzak and a *madrasah* in the village of Kulundu in the Lailak district. The author's findings within the Nuffield Foundation-funded project on 'The Growth of Islamic Radicalism in Eurasia', 2002–5.
32. Salmorbekova and Yemelianova 2010, pp. 228–9.
33. Eshenkulova 2017; Tokmakov 2011.
34. The sources on this group are not verified. It is possible that it is a virtual organisation, constructed by the security services during the Second Kyrgyz Revolution in April 2010 against President Bakiyev. It is also strange that Sunni Kyrgyz chose the name 'Jaish al-Mahdi', which has obvious Shi'a connotations.
35. Karin 2016, pp. 135–6.
36. 'Pochemu IG Verbuet Uzbekov i Kyrgyzov dlia Ispolneniia Terroristicheskikh Aktov', *Sputnik News*, 19 January 2017, available at: http://ru.sputniknews-uz.com/analytics/20170119/4624834/Pochemu-IG-verbuet-uzbekistancev.html, last accessed 2 August 2017.
37. 'Istanbul Airport Attackers Russian, Uzbek and Kyrgyz', *BBC News*, 30 June 2016, available at: http://www.bbc.co.uk/news/world-europe-36670576, last accessed 2 August 2017.
38. Deobandism is an Islamic teaching that originated in the madrasah *Dar al-'Ulum* in the city of Deoband in India in the 1860s. It represented a form of Islamic revivalism aimed at cleansing Islam of allegedly corrupting influences associated with British colonialism.
39. For example, the Islamic Centre in Osh over two decades had been sending their graduates for further training to *Al-Azhar* University in Cairo and the International Islamic University in Medina. Salmorbekova and Yemelianova 2010, p. 229.
40. Muftii Kimsanbai-*aji* was a native of Batken. In 1959 he graduated from the *Mir-i Arab Madrasah* in Bukhara. In 1976-80 he studied at the Shari'a faculty at the Islamic University in Jordan. Upon his return to Central Asia he occupied a number of senior positions in SADUM.
41. In 1996, Kimsanbai-*aji* was forced out of office by Moldo Abdusatar-*aji* Majotov, who was in charge of the muftiiate for four years. In 2000, he lost again to Kimsanbai-*aji*, who remained in office till 2002. Between 2002 and 2010, the SDMK was headed by Muftii Murataaly-*aji* Zhumanov, who was replaced by Muftii Chubak-*aji* Zhalilov. In 2012, Muftii Chubak-*aji* was succeeded by Muftii Rahmatullo-aji Egemberdiyev. Since 2014, the muftiiate has been headed by Maksatbek-*aji* Toktomushev (b. 1973), a native of Osh. He does not have higher

Islamic education, having graduated from the Institute of Agriculture, followed by a *madrasah* in Pakistan. For this reason, his eligibility for the post is questionable.

42. Diushenbieyev 2011.
43. Eshenkulova 2017.
44. Thus, in 2010, Muftii Zhumanov was abducted and beaten to death, while in 2014 Muftii Egemberdiyev resigned due to his involvement in a sex scandal.
45. Almost all successive muftiis and other senior official Islamic clerics have personally profited from the *hajj* business which amounted to over US$9 million a year. The *hajj*-related profits were among the reasons for the tense relations between the SDMK and the State Commission for Religious Affairs, the officials of which were also eager to profit from them. See 'Igry Shaitana: Sledui Propovediam Mully, no ne Sledui Ego Postupkam', *Kyrtag*, 14 January 2014, available at: http://kyrtag.kg/standpoint/igry_shaytana_sleduy_propovedyam_mully_no_ne_sleduy_ego_postupkam, last accessed 27 July 2017.
46. The well *Zamzam* is situated within the *Masjid al-Haram* ('the Sacred Mosque') in Mecca. Its water is regarded as sacred by Muslims who seek to drink it during the *hajj* or *'umrah.*
47. Nasritdinov 2017.
48. 'Otkrytie Mecheti v Bishkeke', *Minbar Islama*, No 3(257)–4(258), March–April 2017.
49. Nasritdinov 2017.
50. In other parts of Kyrgyzstan and Central Asia, as well as in the diaspora, relations between the Kyrgyz and Uzbeks have been less problematic and mixed Kyrgyz–Uzbek marriages have been quite common. Montgomery 2007, p. 129.
51. Among venerated natural sites are, for example, the sacred lakes of Kyz-Kol, Kuptan-Ata, Kol-Tulpar-Ata, Uch-Kol and Ai-Kol. Other important natural *mazars* have been the 'sacred' springs of Kulunda-Ata, Urkyz Bulagy, Mazar Bulak, Tamchy and Tash-Bulak, and the 'sacred' caves of Emchek-Ungkur, Dunduromo and Chil-Ustun. Aitpaeva 2013, pp. 9, 12–18; Montgomery 2007, p. 57.
52. Aitpaeva 2013, pp. 6–7, 9; Montgomery 2007, p. 57.
53. The education in these *madrasahs* consists of learning the Arabic alphabet and memorising, although without properly understanding, some Qur'anic *surahs* and *ayats*, as well as a selection of *hadiths.*
54. In April 2017, the grand cathedral mosque of Mahmud al-Kashgari for over 5,000 worshippers was opened in Bishkek.
55. The rise in Kyrgyz migration to Russia occurred alongside a decline in labour migration to Russia from Uzbekistan and Tajikistan, related to the decreased value of the Russian rouble following a drastic drop in oil prices in 2014.
56. According to the Russian Federal Migration Agency, in January 2016 there were 553,910 registered Kyrgyzstani citizens working in Russia. 'Kolichetvo Trudovykh Migrantov iz Kyrgyzstana Rastet, a iz Uzbekistana i Tajikistana Snijaetsia', *Fergana News*, 13 January 2016, available at: http://www.fergananews.com/news/24330, last accessed 31 July 2017.
57. This assessment is based on the author's ethnographic observations and interviews with Kyrgyz migrants in Moscow in the period between 1999 and 2017.
58. The influx of Kyrgyz and other Central Asian and Caucasian Muslims in the mosques of Moscow and other Russian cities has had major implications for their traditionally Tatar outlook. In particular, it has led to the mosques' changing demographics, the replacement of the language of prayer from Tatar to Russian and the development of mosque-centred informal religious activities performed by Central Asian folk mullahs or north Caucasian *dhikrists.* Oparin 2017.
59. Malashenko and Starostin 2015.

Selected reading

Primary sources

Constitution of the Republic of Kyrgyzstan, 27 June 2010, Bishkek, available at: http://www.gov.kg, last accessed 10 December 2017.

Law on the Freedom of Religion and Religious Organisations of the Kyrgyz Republic, new edn, 19 November 1997, Bishkek, available at: http://www.legislationline.org/ru/documents, last accessed 10 December 2017.

Secondary sources

Aitpaeva, G. (ed.) (2013), *Sacred Sites of Southern Kyrgyzstan: Nature, Manas, Islam*, Bishkek: Aigine Cultural Research Center.

Cummings, S. N. (2012), *Understanding Central Asia: Politics and Contested Transformations*, London: Routledge.

Karin, E. (2016), *The Soldiers of the Caliphate: The Anatomy of a Terrorist Group*, Astana: KazISS.

Malashenko, A. (2008), *Islam in Central Asia*, Reading: Ithaca Press.

Marat, E. (2010), *The Military and the State in Central Asia: From Red Army to Independence*, London: Routledge.

Megoran, N. (2012), *Averting Violence in Kyrgyzstan: Understanding and Responding to Nationalism*, Russia and Eurasia Programme Paper: 2012/13, Chatham House, London.

Montgomery, D. (2016), *Practicing Islam: Knowledge, Experience and Social Navigation in Kyrgyzstan*, Pittsburgh, PA: University of Pittsburgh Press.

Rotar, I. (2007), 'Under the Green Banner: Islamic Radicals in Russia and the Former Soviet Union', *Religion, State and Society* 30(2): 89–153.

Roy, O. (2000), *The New Central Asia: The Creation of New Nations*, London: I. B. Tauris.

CHAPTER 7

Muslims of Tajikistan

Perestroika and the 'Islamic revival'

In Tajikistan the 'Islamic revival' acquired a political dimension from the onset. The main reason for this was Tajikistan's only partially Sovietised secularisation and its consequent higher degree of Islamic traditionalism compared with its neighbours. Among other reasons were the country's weak political and societal cohesion and strong regionalism; its deficient economy, which had been highly subsidised by Moscow; and its geographical and ethnolinguistic closeness with war-torn Islamic Afghanistan. Tajikistan was also the region's only Persian-speaking polity within externally imposed political borders, outside of which were left both a large number of Tajiks and their historical and cultural centres – Bukhara and Samarqand. The country constituted two distinct zones: the economically and politically dominant and more secularised north, and the disadvantaged and more Islamicised south. The origins of this divide go back to the 1860s when the north was incorporated into the Russian Empire, while the south remained under the rule of Bukhara emirs. As a result, the north became more developed and Russified than the south. During the Soviet period, the higher degree of Islamicised traditionalism in the south was perpetuated by the organisation of *kolkhozes* along the lines of existing Islamicised clan-based communities or *qavms* (solidarity networks). The north–south divide was complicated by multiple sub-regional and sub-ethnic divisions with numerous overlaps, as well as by the inclusion of Uzbekistan-based Samarqandis and Bukharans in the north. The north was widely associated with the regions of Khujand-Leninabad, Ura-Teppe, Samarqand, Bukhara, Isfara, Panjikent and, subsequently, Kulyab, and the south with the regions of Qurghan-Teppe, Darvaz and particularly Karategin (Gharm), which in the 1950s became the centre for state-orchestrated mass resettlement of people during the construction of the Vakhsh River valley irrigation project. From the late 1930s all leaders of the Communist Party of Tajikistan were natives of the Khujand-Leninabad region in northern Tajikistan. The functional division in Soviet Tajikstan was reflected in the folk saying: 'Leninabad rules, Kulyab guards, Pamir dances and Karategin trades'. This regional fragmentation was aggravated by the complex ethno-religious composition of Tajikistan's population, including the existence of sizeable Uzbek communities in the Khujand-Leninabad, Hissor and Qurghan-Teppe regions.[1]

The Gorbachevian political liberalisation and the ensuing drastic reduction of central investment and funding had a particularly detrimental impact on Tajikistan, especially in the south, which became the epicentre of Islamic resurgence. This resurgence had been preceded by the activities of various underground Islamic groupings that had begun to form on the territory of Soviet Tajikistan in the early 1970s. Originally, they largely followed the non-political Islamic reformist path of Muhammadjon Hindustoniy (*Hajjee* Domla) and focused on spreading knowledge of Arabic, the Qur'an and *hadith*. Prominent among them was the Islamist youth educational organisation *Nahzat-i-Javononi Islomii Tojikiston* ('Revival of the Islamic Youth of Tajikistan'), formed in 1973 in the southwestern town of Qurghan-Teppe by Sayyid Abdulloh Nuri (1947–2006),[2] who was a native of Gharm. Its members also studied 'normative' Islam (i.e., *Salafi* – G.Y.), with special emphasis on the teaching of Hasan al-Banna, the founder of the Muslim Brotherhood in Egypt. A major catalyst for Tajik Muslim reformers' politicisation was the Soviet invasion of neighbouring Afghanistan in December 1979, which they resolutely opposed and which turned them away from the quietist teaching of Muhammadjon Hindustoniy towards political Islam. Particularly influential on them were Sayyid Qutb's *Ma'alim fi al-Tariq* (*Milestones*) and his Qur'an commentary *Fi Zilal al-Qur'an* (*In the Shade of Qur'an*).[3]

In June 1990, politically conscious Tajik Muslim reformers took part in the establishment of the IPV in Astrakhan. In October 1990, at a clandestine gathering in a mosque on the outskirts of Dushanbe, the IPV Tajik activists, Sayyid Abdulloh Nuri and Muhammad Sharif Himmatzoda (1951–2010), created the IPV Tajik branch[4] – the *Islamskaia Partiia Vozrozhdeniia Tajikistana* (IPVT), which, unlike in other Central Asian republics, under the leadership of Sayyid Abdulloh Nuri turned into a major political and Islamist force. The IPVT's proclaimed objectives included the involvement of Tajikistani Muslims in the political, economic and spiritual life of the country and the promotion of Islamic norms and values in Tajikistani society. In terms of its membership, the IPVT was dominated by natives of the Karategin region, which historically belonged to the Bukhara Emirate.[5]

The growing political activism of the IPVT occurred in the context of the unravelling political and economic crisis in the country. From the beginning of 1990, the Tajikistan Communist Party leadership under Qakhor Mahkamov (1932–2016, in office 1985–90),[6] a native of economically and politically dominant Khujand-Leninabad in northern Tajikistan, was increasingly challenged by pro-democracy and nationalist political opponents, who were mainly from the traditionally disadvantaged southern and mountainous regions and who were behind a series of anti-government protests and demonstrations in the capital Dushanbe. Particularly damaging for Mahkamov were the violent anti-government riots which erupted in Dushanbe in February 1990, in which twenty-two people lost their lives.[7] On 30 November 1990, in an attempt to strengthen his eroded authority, Mahkamov also assumed the titles of president and prime minister of Tajikistan. However, his unequivocal support for the anti-Gorbachev coup on 19 August 1991 sealed his fate as Tajikistan's leader; on 31 August, in response to growing pressure from the opposition, he resigned from all his posts. Following his departure the country was plunged into political turmoil involving multiple changes in the country's leadership and direction, high-profile assassinations and politicised violence. It was in these precarious conditions that on 9 September 1991 the Supreme Soviet of Tajikistan proclaimed the country's political independence.

The political crisis accentuated Tajikistan's regional divisions and led to the emergence of the two camps who contested the leadership of the country. One was headed by the Khujand-Leninabad and Kulyab-based members of the Communist Party and Soviet establishment, while the other was made up of members of various strands of the opposition from the predominantly southern and mountainous regions of Tajikistan. In this context various official and unofficial leaders rallied support from their home towns and regions. In August 1991, the opposition installed Kadriddin Aslonov (1947–92),[8] a native of Gharm, as President of Tajikistan. Aslonov banned the Communist Party, suspended all Party-related activities and ordered the demolition of Lenin's monument in Ozodi ('Freedom') Square in the centre of Dushanbe. After a mere month in office he was ousted by the Khujand-Leninabad and Kulyab-based Communist *apparatchiks* under the leadership of Rahmon Nabiyev (1930–93), a native of Khujand,[9] who reverted to Soviet-type oppressive policies. During the presidential elections in November 1991 Nabiyev reasserted himself as Tajikistan's president by defeating the opposition candidate Davlat Khudonazarov (b. 1944),[10] a native of politically and economically disadvantaged Gorno-Badakhshan in the Pamir Mountains, who was backed by the Democratic Party of Tajikistan (DPT) which had been established in August 1990 by democratically and liberally-minded intellectuals of anti-Communist and secularist orientation under the leadership of Shodmon Yusupov and Mahmadruzi Iskandarov, both natives of Gharm.[11] Following the dissolution of the USSR in December 1991, Rahmon Nabiyev became the first president of the independent Republic of Tajikistan.[12] In late December 1991, Tajikistan, along with Uzbekistan, Kyrgyzstan, Kazakhstan, Turkmenistan, Azerbaijan and Armenia, joined the Russia-speared CIS, and in May 1992 joined the CST (CSTO). In April 1996, it became a member of the China-dominated Shanghai Five group (SCO), which also includes Russia, Kyrgyzstan and Kazakhstan.

The Tajik war: the inter-Tajik regional dimension

President Nabiyev's heavy-handed stance escalated anti-government protests orchestrated by the opposition. Dushanbe became engulfed in violent clashes between pro-government activists and the opposition, which included members and supporters of the IPVT, the DPT, the popular movement *Rastokhez* ('Revival') and the *La'li Badakhshon* ('Ruby of Badakhshan') party. The *Rastokhez*, founded in September 1989 by an economist, Tokhir Abdujabbor (1949–2009),[13] united nationalistically oriented members of the Tajik intelligentsia from the politically marginalised mountainous regions with students from Dushanbe and some other parts of Tajikistan. They advocated Tajikistan's greater autonomy within a reformed USSR, revival of Tajik Islamic culture, a return to the Arabic-Persian alphabet, the restoration of the pre-Soviet names of Tajikistan's cities and streets, and greater cultural autonomy for Tajiks in Uzbekistan.[14] The *La'li Badakhshon*, which was founded in March 1991 by political activists from the Gorno-Badakhshan Autonomous *Oblast'* under the leadership of Atobek Amirbekov, campaigned for the Pamiris' wider representation in government, especially in law enforcement structures.[15]

In March 1992, the conflict escalated as a result of mass anti-government demonstrations in the Shohidon ('Martyrs', formerly Lenin) Square in Dushanbe, which were organised by DPT activists in response to the authorities' persecution of their leaders. They were soon joined by *La'li Badakhshon*-led Pamiris, who demanded the resignation of Safaraly Kenjayev (1942–99),[16] the chairman of the Supreme Soviet. The joint opposition demands included the dissolution of parliament and a new constitution. In response, the government rallied its supporters in Ozodi Square. The regional nature of the confrontation was evidenced by the regional codes on the number plates of the buses and other vehicles that brought protesters to the capital. Thus, Shohidon Square gathered together Gharmis, dwellers of Qurghan-Teppe, Pamiris, and natives of Darvaz, Kofarnikhon and Zarafshan, while on the other side, Ozodi Square brought together people from Kulyab, Khujand-Leninabad, Hissor, Shahrinav, Tursunzoda, Lenin and Varzab.[17] This intrinsically regional and clan-driven conflict acquired an ideological dimension and was framed by its protagonists and external actors as a war between Communists and Islamists.

In May 1992, the confrontation between the two camps in Dushanbe turned into armed clashes as a result of the proliferation of firearms among its participants. The violence spread from Dushanbe to Qurghan-Teppe, Kulyab and other parts of the country. President Nabiyev attempted to rescue the situation by forming a government of national reconciliation which included eight representatives of the opposition, a measure that temporarily defused the tension in the capital while the rest of the country descended into fully-fledged warfare. In June 1992, over three thousand armed IPVT and DPT supporters and militants attempted to establish control over the strategically important Vakhsh valley in north-central Tajikistan. President Nabiyev reacted by introducing a state of emergency, entrusting the 201st Russian Motor-Rifle Division with the protection of the Nurek hydro-electrical power station on Vakhsh river as well as other major infrastructure, and appealed to the Khujandis, Kulyabis, as well as Uzbeks of Qurghan-Teppe to rise up against the IPVT- and DPT-led forces. The core of the pro-government forces was the Kulyabi-dominated *Sitodi Melli* ('Popular Front') under the leadership of Sangak Safarov.[18] In September 1992, following Rahmon Nabiyev's resignation, Tajikistan was de facto split along the north–south divide, the north being controlled by the Popular Front and the south by the opposition Islamo-democratic forces. In December 1992, the opposition seized Dushanbe; in the same month the Supreme Soviet, which was convened in Khujand, elected Emomali Rahmonov (b. 1952, in office 1992–present),[19] a Kulyabi, as its chairman, and Abdumalik Abdulojonov, a Khujandi, as prime minister.[20]

In early 1993, the fighting intensified even further following the merger of various opposition forces into the United Tajik Opposition (UTO) under the leadership of Sayyid Abdulloh Nuri, Muftii Akbar Turajonzoda (b. 1954, in office, 1988–93),[21] Mohammadsharif Himmatzoda and Davlat Khudonazarov. By the end of 1993 the Popular Front had gained the upper hand and regained control over Dushanbe and most parts of the newly established southwestern Khatlon province with its centre in Qurghan-Teppe, and had invaded the Karategin valley forcing UTO fighters to retreat to the mountains and Afghanistan, though government forces still only controlled 40 per cent of Tajikistan's territory.[22] From 1994 onwards, the war became less intense in other parts of the country due to the relocation of many Islamist militants to northern Afghanistan and active international mediation involving the UN,[23] Russia and Iran.

Between April 1994 and May 1997 representatives of the warring camps had eight rounds of talks in Iran, Afghanistan, Kyrgyzstan, Russia and, finally, in Tajikistan itself. The inter-Tajik dialogue was hindered by the opposing sides' often conflicting perspectives on the future of post-war Tajikistan, as well as multiple and fluctuating internal divisions and separatist alliances. Pro-government negotiators envisaged the future Tajikistan as a secular state, organised along the Soviet model and under the control of Kulyabis and Khujandis. By contrast, the UTO's Islamists sought the creation of an Islamic state in Tajikistan, while democrats pushed for Tajkistan's reorganisation along liberal-democratic and civic citizenship lines. An aggravating factor was the bitter rivalry between the UTO's political leadership and its powerful field commanders who wielded considerable independence. For example, in 1996, parallel to negotiations, hardline Islamists for a short time established a mini-Islamic state in the Karategin valley; local residents were forced to attend mosques, women were veiled, the sale of alcohol was banned and everybody who was suspected of links with Dushanbe was hanged.[24]

The breakthrough occurred in Moscow on 23 December 1996 when President Emomali Rahmonov and Sayyid Abdulloh Nuri, as chief negotiators for the two sides, agreed to end the war on a power-sharing basis. In particular, 4,500 UTO fighters were to be integrated into the government army and police structures, while around 5,500 were to be given amnesty. On 27 June 1997, in Moscow, the General Agreement on the Establishment of Peace and National Accord was signed,[25] according to which the Tajikistani state preserved its secular character while designated UTO members, including Islamists, gained representation in parliament, central and local governments, industrial enterprise management boards, the army and the police. Of particular significance was the appointment of UTO leader and widely respected Islamic authority and former muftii, Akbar Turajonzoda, as deputy prime minister of Tajikistan.[26] However, a considerable number of the opposition field commanders and rank-and-file militants rejected the National Accord Agreement and fled to Afghanistan. In November 1998, one of their hard-liners, Colonel Mahmud Khudoiberdyev (1962–2001)[27] unsuccessfully attempted an anti-government coup with the aim of seizing power in northern Tajikistan. Overall, sporadic outbreaks of resistance persisted until summer 2000 when, in August, Tajik militants were defeated by Uzbekistan government forces when they, together with IDU militants, attempted to invade Uzbekistan from the territory of Tajikistan's Tavildara region.

The Tajik war: the international dimension

The Tajik war was never entirely an inter-Tajik affair. Tajikistan's different regional and clan factions, which assumed Islamist, democratic, nationalist or ex-Communist forms, had their powerful external backers with their own, often clashing, geopolitical agendas. Thus, Russia, with the advantage of being Tajikistan's former Soviet patron, had direct military and political involvement in the war and subsequently in its outcome. Following the outbreak of hostilities Moscow decided to back the government forces, which it perceived as being more congenial to Russia's national and geopolitical interests. Russia was especially concerned over the security of her southern border which was threatened by possible Islamist incursions from Tajikistan, the Ferghana valley and Afghanistan, and the possibility of the latter joining forces with Chechen separatists in Russia's north Caucasus. Russia's other major incentive was the safeguarding of millions of Central Asia's ethnic Russians, who were at risk should the regime change in favour of opposition forces.[28] For these reasons Russian troops, which had been stationed in Tajikistan since the Soviet period, were mobilised to provide vital military backing to the ruling regime. According to the defence agreement signed in May 1993 between the governments of the Russian Federation and Tajikistan, Russian border troops were assigned the task of protecting Tajikistan's borders with Afghanistan and China. These troops remained in Tajikistan until 2005, when the Russian military presence was transformed into a 7,500-strong military base, tasked with 'the defence of the national interests of the Russian Federation in Central Asia'.[29] At the political level, Russia acted as one of the main political brokers and was closely involved in all stages of the inter-Tajik dialogue. In the aftermath of the war it has continued to act as Tajikistan's main security guarantor within the CSTO format.

The other major backer of the government forces was Uzbekistan under President Islam Karimov. Uzbekistan's multifaceted and pivotal involvement in the Tajik war had historical, political, ethnic and security reasons, and was predicated on the two countries' geographical proximity, cultural affinity and ethnic intermingling.[30] Historically, the Uzbeks claimed their political supremacy over the Ferghana valley, including its civilisational jewels Bukhara and Samarqand, which Tajiks regarded as central to their culture and statehood tradition. Official Tashkent therefore was wary of the Tajik nationalists' aspirations towards a new political delimitation and a 'reunification' of Tajik-majority Bukhara and Samarqand with Tajikistan, which would threaten the integrity of Uzbekistan and jeopardise the security of the large Uzbek minority in Tajikistan. The Karimov government was also concerned about the potential effect of an Islamist spill-over from Tajikistan to Uzbekistan and the formation of a joint Tajik–Uzbek Islamist front seeking the establishment of an Islamic state in the whole Ferghana valley. According to some sources, the Karimov regime was directly militarily involved in the combat, reconnaissance and special operations on the side of the government, as well as providing the training and arming of ethnic Uzbeks on the territory of Tajikistan.[31]

On the other side, the UTO received financial, military and political backing from various regional and international Islamist forces, including Afghanistan's *mujahideen*, members of the *Jamiat-e Islamii*,[32] the IDU, Russia's Chechen rebels and, subsequently, from the *Taliban* and *Al-Qaeda*, as well as, indirectly, from the governments of Pakistan, Saudi Arabia and the Gulf states. Throughout the war and afterwards Tajik Islamists were substantially helped by Saudi cash, and received military training and *madrasah* education in Peshawar and other areas of Pakistan. Between 1992 and 1996 vital assistance to the UTO was provided by Tajik Islamists in northern Afghanistan under the leadership of Ahmad Shah Massoud (1952–2001).[33] Another important source of UTO funding came from its members' involvement in the smuggling of drugs (heroin and opium) from Afghanistan.[34]

Due to the civilisational and ethnolinguistic affinity between Tajiks and Iranians, the role of the Islamic Republic of Iran in the Tajik war was important, albeit ambivalent. It was determined by Shi'a Iran's concern about the war-related destabilisation of the region and the threat of the proliferation of political Sunni Islam of a *Salafi* nature. This concern increased as a result of the takeover of Afghanistan in 1996 by the Pashtun *Taliban*, who were Sunnis of the fundamentalist Deobandi School. Consequently, Iran consistently lobbied for the de-escalation of the inter-Tajik conflict and acted as one of the key international peace brokers. At the same time, Iran hoped that a war-devastated Tajikistan would enable it to strengthen its economic and cultural presence in Turkic-dominated Central Asia. It was particularly interested in building a direct railway link between Tajikistan and Iran via Afghanistan. However, Iran's official Shi'ism and aggressive anti-Communism prevented it from overt support for either of the warring sides, although it provided asylum to some UTO members in the aftermath of the war. On the whole, Iran preferred indirect methods of involvement in the war through the forging in Tajikistan of pro-Iranian networks, the provision of humanitarian aid and the promotion of Farsi-language media and educational programmes. Of notable influence on the war dynamic in Nagorno-Badakhshan was the international Shi'a Isma'ili Foundation of Aga Khan IV. In 1993, the Aga Khan directly intervened in the fighting in the region by calling upon Pamiri militants, who supported the opposition, to lay down arms. During the war the Aga Khan Foundation provided substantive assistance by organising humanitarian and food convoys from Kyrgyzstan's Osh to blockaded Gorno-Badakhshan.[35]

The war caused enormous human and material losses to Tajikistan, including horrific massacres, rape, torture, collective executions and looting. It is estimated that during the war more than 700,000 Tajikistanis were killed, over a million were internally displaced, and a large number went missing, fled to neighbouring Afghanistan or migrated to Uzbekistan, Russia and some other countries of the former USSR. Over 25,000 women were widowed and over 53,000 children were orphaned. Economic losses exceeded US$10 billion. Over 150,000 houses were burned and over 15,000 were ruined and looted. Particularly devastated were the Vakhsh and Karategin valleys and the region of Qurghan-Teppe, which lost over 80 per cent of its industrial potential. Tajikistan witnessed the return of deadly epidemic diseases that had been eliminated during the Soviet period, and turned into a major regional hub for drug trafficking and other illegal business.[36]

Emomali Rahmon(ov)'s nation-building project

In 1999, during the first post-war presidential elections, Rahmonov, representing the People's Democratic Party of Tajikistan (PDPT) – the party in power, established in 1994 – allegedly gained 97.6 per cent of the vote, while his opponent Davlat Usmon, the IRPT candidate, received 2.1 per cent of the vote. Having won the elections, President Rahmonov was faced with the Herculean task of rebuilding the country's material infrastructure and economic base and, most importantly, of forging a Tajikistani nation out of recent bitter enemies and within territory that was politically disconnected from its historical and cultural centres. Emomali Rahmonov's nation-building strategy consisted of three main components. One was the generating of a Tajik national idea that would unite Tajiks and other Tajikistanis within the existing borders and culturally distinguish them from Uzbeks, other Uzbekistanis, and Afghanistan's Tajiks and Iranians. Second, was the promotion of Rahmonov as the consolidating figure of the new Tajikistani nation, which meant sidelining potential rivals within the former pro-government secular camp and especially from the clans of Khujand-Leninabad. The third component included the gradual demotion and marginalisation of the 'Islamo-democrats' who had taken part in the 1997 National Accord, while appropriating their programme relating to Tajik cultural revival.

The Rahmonov leadership singled out the Tajik language and the Tajik cultural heritage, imbued with Islam, as the main pillars of the Tajik national idea. The 1994 Constitution of Tajikistan designated the Tajik language as the state language, with Russian as the language of interethnic communication. In the official political discourse, media and educational sphere Tajik identity became anchored in ancient sedentary Iranian culture, epitomised in the *Shahnameh* by Firdowsi (940–1020) and the Samanid heritage, as it was endorsed in President Rahmonov's book *The Tajiks in the Mirror of History* (2001). Within this approach the Tajiks were portrayed as the main bearers of Central Asian *Hanafism* and Sufism and civilisationally superior to their historically nomadic Turco-Mongol neighbours.[37] The year 2009 was declared the 'Year of the Great Imam Abu Hanifa', who, alongside the great Kubrawi *pir* Mir Sayyid 'Ali Hamadani (1314–84), were referred to as 'ethnic Tajiks'.[38] Rahmonov began to widely publicise his own Muslim-ness, as well as that of members of his large family, and conducted four *hajjes* to Mecca and Medina. In 1992, Tajikistan joined the OIC and developed its engagement with various Muslim countries. Official Dushanbe's claims to the Islamic legacy of the Samanids, both of whose capitals – Bukhara and Samarqand – are within the border of neighbouring Uzbekistan, inevitably clashed with the post-independence nationalising discourse of official Tashkent and contributed to tensions in their interstate relations, as well as to the personal antagonism between presidents Karimov and Rahmonov.[39]

In March 2007, within the campaign for the return to national roots, Rahmonov called on his compatriots to revert to national names, and dropped the Russian suffix-*ov* from his own surname. Consequently, names of many regions, cities, towns, villages and streets, which related to the imperial Russian or Soviet period, were changed to the original ones.[40] Tajikistan's new currency – the *somoni* – was named after Ismail Samani, with its various banknotes featuring the images of designated forefathers of the Tajik nation such as Abu Abdullah Rudaki, Ibn Sina, as well as renowned Soviet Tajiks such as Sadriddin Aini (1878–1954) and Bobojon Gafurov (1908–77). Monuments to Ismail Samani were erected in Dushanbe, Khujand, Qurghan-Teppe, Gharm and Khorugh, the centre of the Gorno-Badakhshan autonomy.

President Rahmonov's style of leadership and governance followed common Eurasian authoritarian trends, which were exacerbated by the war experience. In the conditions of Tajikistan's acute post-war regional and political fragmentation Rahmonov assumed the role of 'the father of all Tajiks', presiding over a patrimonial regime, centred on a closed group of relatives,[41] friends and representatives of his Kulyabi network, and characterised by the omnipotence of the security forces, the pervasive corruption, nepotism and clientalism, and managerial inefficiency. In September 1999 and June 2003 Rahmonov's leadership organised referenda in order to change the constitution, allowing Rahmon(ov) to extend his presidency until 2020. During the Soviet-style presidential elections in 2006 he was re-elected by 79.3 per cent of the vote; in 2013 he was re-elected yet again by 83.92 per cent.[42] In 2015, Rahmon's cult of personality was legally enshrined when Tajikistan's parliament – the *Majlisi Oli* – passed a law that proclaimed President Rahmon as the life-long leader of the Tajiks, thus joining the ranks of other constitutionally endorsed 'leaders of the nation', such as Nursultan Nazarbayev in Kazakhstan and the late Saparmurad Niyazov in Turkmenistan. President Rahmon was henceforth to be addressed as *Peshvoi Millat* ('Leader of the Nation'), while any public disrespect or criticism of him became punishable by law. In 2016, the parliament passed another law on the status of Rahmon as the 'Founder of Peace and National Unity – the Leader of the Nation', which ensured him life-long presidency and legal immunity. The country has been covered with billboards displaying images of the president, and state media has abounded with panegyrics depicting Rahmon as the 'Father of the Nation', the 'Saviour of the Nation' or the 'King of Kings'. In 2016, a grand monument was erected in Hissor to Rahmon's book *Tajiks in the Mirror of History*, rivalling the monument to the late President Niyazov's sacred book *Ruhnama* in Ashgabat in Turkmenistan, as discussed in Chapter 8.

From the establishment in 1997 of a nominally coalition government Rahmonov sought to marginalise and subsequently destroy his bitter war-time enemy, the Islamo-Democratic opposition. However, during the first post-war years he refrained from direct attack because of his focus on the country's material and societal reconstruction. He also had to tread carefully, domestically and internationally, between Tajikistan's secularism enshrined in the 1994 Constitution and the 1997 National Accord-based legalisation of the IPVT.[43] Indirectly, however, he took steps towards weakening the opposition through the reduction of their parliamentary representation and the appropriation of their programme related to Tajik cultural revival until it was effectively paralysed.

State–Muslim relations

The war introduced a considerable difference in state–Muslim relations in Tajikistan, with the pro-Soviet secularist ideological narrative of the

Figure 7.1 Chairman Ibragimov of the Council of '*Ulama*' of the Sughd *oblast'* of Tajikistan (photograph by Zumrat Salmorbekova, Sughd, Tajikistan, April 2003)

Khujand–Kulyab regional alliance clashing with the Islam-based political and social project of the representatives of the disadvantaged southern and mountainous regions. If, in other parts of Central Asia, representatives of 'official Islam' largely distanced themselves from the anti-establishment Islamic and Islamist opposition and allied with the secular ruling regimes, Tajikistan's muftii and highly respected Qadiri Sufi, *Hojjee* Akbar Turajonzoda (in office 1988–93) joined ranks with Islamists from the IRPT and other opposition forces and became a leading figure within UTO, which was closely involved with Afghanistan's *mujahideen*. Following the 1997 National Accord Agreement, Akbar Turajonzoda, as deputy prime minister (in office 1998–2005), became a leading voice of the opposition in the coalition government and one of the architects of the state religious policy.

In February 2005, President Rahmon(ov) decided to put an end to the government's political ambiguity by sacking Turajonzoda as deputy prime minister in violation of the official status of the IRPT as the guarantor of the 1997 Accord. This act signalled a shift in official religious policy towards a gradual alignment with the state–Muslim relations model across the region. The authorities embarked on the recreation of pro-government Islamic officialdom and the promotion of apolitical 'Tajik traditional Islam'. In October 2005, the parliament introduced a ban on girls and female teachers wearing *hijob/hijab* in state schools. Later on, in 2010, the government recalled over 2,700 young Tajiks studying in Islamic universities and *madrasahs* in Libya, Saudi Arabia,

Iran, Egypt and Yemen. Civil servants were discouraged from attending Friday prayers and the use of loudspeakers in mosques was prohibited.[44] The government also imposed a ban on children under the age of eighteen worshipping in mosques and introduced fines on parents whose children attended mosque. Working-age men were strongly discouraged from wearing a beard, while women were advised to wear national Tajik dress.[45] The authorities launched a campaign against the use of Arabic names and encouraged parents to draw on the *Shahnameh* when choosing names for their newborns.[46]

The main target of official Dushanbe was the IPVT and its influential representatives. Akbar Turajonzoda and the well-respected and independently minded Kulyabi imam Hojjee Mirzo were pushed out of the state-sponsored public space, while politically active IPVT members were marginalised and discredited.[47] During the parliamentary elections in 2015, the IPVT was prevented from passing the required 5 per cent barrier even though it had 40,000 members, and as a result did not gain any seats.[48] A final blow was the decision in September 2015 by the Tajikistani Supreme Court to de-legalise the IPVT and recognise it as a terrorist organisation on the grounds of its alleged involvement in the coup under the leadership of deputy Defence Minister Abdukhalim Nazarzoda. Following this ban, the IPVT's activists were either arrested or put under surveillance, its newspaper *Najod*, website and other media were shut down,[49] and the party's leader Muhiddin Kebir (in office 2006–15) was forced to flee the country.

Along with the sidelining of the IPVT, the Rahmon government tightened its control over Islamic officialdom in the form of the High Council of the 'Ulama' of Tajikistan (HCUT), which was created in 1996 in lieu of the muftiiate. HCUT members were supervised by the Soviet-style State Committee for Religious Affairs (SCRA), which in 2006 was restructured as the Department for Religious Affairs (DRA) within the Ministry of Culture. The SCRA, rather than the HCUT, had the final say on matters related to registering mosques, *madrasahs* and Islamic institutions, organising *hajj*, the contents of imam prayers and *madrasah* curricula, and the attestation of imams and *madrasah mudarrises*. Throughout the 2000s the government has persistently increased the number of congregations required for the establishment of Friday and ordinary mosques. In 2011, the authorities began re-registration of mosques as part of a wider campaign cracking down on 'untraditional Islam'. As a result, a large number of mosques, *madrasahs* and Islamic institutes were closed. By 2015, Tajikistan had one Islamic University (in Dushanbe), 19 *madrasahs* and 3,900 registered Islamic communities, including 300 grand mosques and 27 central city mosques. *Imam-khatibs* were turned into state employees receiving state salaries. Imams were instructed to promote 'Tajik Islam' and were provided with a list of sixty permitted topics for prayers.[50]

Paradoxically, the government's demonstrative assault on 'foreign Islam' has occurred alongside its continuing and substantial reliance on Islamic cash emanating from Saudi Arabia, Qatar and other foreign Islamic countries or non-government Islamic foundations. For example, in 2014, the authorities inaugurated in Dushanbe the Cathedral mosque, the construction of which was funded from Qatar. The Aga Khan Foundation has been particularly active in Gorno-Badakhshan, creating the Aga Khan University in Khorugh and establishing a network of its schools. The authorities' financial dependence on foreign Islamic funders has conditioned state-sponsored endorsement of some 'untraditional' Islamic practices, despite the official trumpeting of 'Tajik Islam'. Thus, the HCUT instructed mosque imams to discourage their worshippers from the traditional practice of lavish wakes on the third, seventh and fortieth days after a person's death, as well as of excessive spending during weddings.[51] In September 2015, the parliament outlawed widespread magical practices as 'non-Muslim' and made them punishable by imprisonment for up to seven years.[52]

Popular Muslim-ness

Tajiks commonly perceive themselves to be more sophisticated and civilised Muslims than their Turkic neighbours. This notion is based on their ancient Iranian roots and especially their western Iranian (Farsi) language, which was used by great Islamic thinkers of the Samanid period and was the main language of Central Asian Persianised Sunni Islamic scholarship and teaching. The Tajiks' Islamic identity is therefore intrinsically linked to the region's historical Islamic centres – Bukhara and Samarqand. In the Soviet period their written Islamic tradition was severely damaged by state atheism and the change from the Arabic to Latin and subsequently Cyrillic alphabets. However, the bulk of Tajiks withstood the Soviet atheist assault and retained their deep Muslim-ness in the form of Islamicised traditionalism, based on oral popular Islam, infused with Sufism and Zoroastrianism. This explains the rather superficial nature of Sovietised secularisation among the majority of Tajiks and the greater role of Islam in their social and political life. However, given their strong regionalism the depth of their Islamicised traditionalism has varied significantly between natives of different parts of the country. It has been greater among the dwellers of the Vakhsh and Karategin valleys, Qurghan-Teppe, Gorno-Badakhshan autonomy and some other rural and mountainous regions, which in the late 1990s constituted three-quarters of Tajikistan's population.[53] It has been weaker among residents of Dushanbe, Khujand-Leninabad and other urban centres in the north of the country. The Tajiks in the north also tend to anchor their ethnic and cultural identity more in their pre-Islamic Sogdian heritage than in Islamic civilisation. The people's Islamicised religiosity and their level of traditionalism have been also influenced by their geographical habitat, social status, education and age. Most representatives of the political and intellectual elite pursue a secular lifestyle; they do not observe all five pillars of Islam and favour Western-style clothing, although, as noted earlier, civil servants are encouraged to wear Tajik national clothes. The least practising Muslims among them are those who belong to the Soviet generations.[54]

By comparison, the rural parts of southern and mountainous Tajikistan, as discussed in Chapter 3, have retained a significant element of Islamicised traditionalism. It was safeguarded by the preservation of the institution of *mahallah* and *qavm* through their integration within Soviet *kolkhoz* and *sovkhoz* system. Among the markers of the post-independence endurance of Tajik Islamicised traditionalism was the greater importance of the Zoroastrian feast of *Nowruz* than of Islamic *Qurban-Bairam* and *Uraza-Bairam*, conspicuous celebrations of circumcision, weddings and funeral wakes, and sophisticated musical and theatrical traditions, as well as widespread belief in ancestor spirits, saints, magic and *jinns*. The *kolkhoz* system also enabled *kolkhoz* members to retain their affiliation to a particular Sufi network, primarily of the Naqshbandi and Qadiri Sufi brotherhoods, by incorporating Sufi *mazars*, which were guarded by undisclosed hereditary *pirs*, within *kolkhoz* structures. For example, the *mazar* of Yaqub Charkhi (1360–1447), a venerated Naqshbandi Sufi, was located on the territory of the Lenin *kolkhoz* in Dushanbe. Consequently, over a hundred *mazars* as well as village mosques were largely preserved, although they were formally transformed into museums or other Sovietised sites.[55]

Pirs, mullahs, *bibi-khalfas/bibi-mullos*, as well as members of their families retained their religious authority and high social status even though they also acquired Soviet jobs as tractor drivers, mechanics, carpenters or ordinary *kolkhozniks*. They continued discreetly to perform major Islamic rites, such as weddings and funerals, and to teach children, outside their state schools, the basics of Islam and Islamic behaviour. Some also acted as traditional healers and practiced *ruqyah*.[56] Their knowledge of Persian and Arabic was limited and they based their teaching mainly on *Chahar-kitab*, copies of which were handed down from fathers and grandfathers. Undisclosed Sufis were well represented within official Islamic structures: for example, Muftii Akbar Turajonzoda was the son of Ishon Turajon, a *murid* of the Qadiri *pir* Hazrat Ishon Khallijon from Qurghan-Teppe; while his successor Muftii Fatullah Khan Sharifzoda (d. 1996) was the son of the Naqshbandi *pir* Damullo Muhammad Sharif from Hissor. Many of Tajikistan's Sufis followed *pirs* outside the country, especially in Uzbekistan.[57]

The rural Tajiks' overall incomplete secularisation accounts for the higher intensity and politicisation of the 'Islamic revival' among them in the late Soviet period and the Islamic dimension of the Tajik war. The war further altered Tajik perceptions and practices of Islam. Economic collapse, mass impoverishment, rising unemployment, and the breakdown of the Soviet socialisation, education, health and social care systems have been conducive to de-modernisation and increased Islamicised re-traditionalisation of local communities. A contributing factor has been the lengthy absences of migrant Tajik men from their families and the resultant increased conditioning of their wives by patriarchal family members and *mahallah*. Among the consequences of this process has been a rising rate of withdrawal of girls from education, and an increase in their early marriages and home confinement. For example, before the war there were over 2,000 women with university degrees and over 3,000 women with college degrees in the Karategin region; after the war their numbers were reduced to less than 200 and 800, respectively.[58] A visible symbol of surging re-Islamicisation has been the return in rural Tajikistan of the veil, which had disappeared in the 1930s in the course of the Stalinist *hujum*.

On the other hand, rural and mountainous areas of post-war Tajikistan have also witnessed notable re-Islamicisation of its inhabitants along *Salafi* lines. The main agents of such non-traditional Islamic influences have been thousands of Tajik men, some of whom directly participated in Islamicised militancy and were exposed to the Islamic practices of *mujahideed* and *Taliban* in Afghanistan; Tajik graduates of Islamic universities and *madrasahs* in Saudi Arabia, the Gulf countries, Afghanistan, Pakistan and Egypt; and foreign Islamic sponsors and preachers who until 2010 freely operated in the country. In the late 1990s, some young Tajiks became attracted to HTI, which had been active in the Ferghana valley from the mid-1990s. A small number of Tajik men within the 2-million strong Tajik labour migrant community in Russia[59] and some other ex-Soviet countries, have been subjected, like their Uzbek and Kyrgyz counterparts, to Islamic radicalisation that has emerged in the context of their social and cultural alienation and increased exposure to digitalised *Salafi* Islamic messaging and Arabic-language courses with *pro-Salafi* content.[60] Since the 2010s Moscow-based Tajiks have played a growing role in the digital *Salafisation* of their compatriots at home. Among the implications of this 'non-traditional' re-Islamicisation has been the increasing confusion among some Tajik Muslim youth about what constitutes 'true Islam' and how it should affect their social and political behaviour, including their relations with other 'improper Muslims' and non-Muslims, as well as their habitual Islamic rituals and dress code. It is worth noting that such confusion has not been restricted to Tajiks and, to varying degrees, has been present among young people across post-Soviet Muslim-majority space.

A different Islamic dynamic has been in evidence in Gorno-Badakhshan, which is home to a 250,000-strong Shi'a *Isma'ili* community. Historically, *Isma'ili* Pamiris maintained their ethnolinguistic and cultural *otherness* within the Sunni-dominated region. However, following Tajikistan's independence, their *otherness* has been at odds with President Rahmon(ov)'s nation-building vision. During the civil war Shi'a Pamiris were divided in their political allegiances. After the war, relations between them and official Dushanbe remained difficult, and during the 2010s have deteriorated even further.[61] The political and cultural 'tajikisation' of Pamiris has also been hindered by their religious loyalty to their imam – Aga Khan IV – as a result of which they have often prioritised the Aga Khan's *firmans* over prescriptions issued by government and official Islamic authorities. At the same time, the promotion among the Pamiris, through educational and humanitarian channels, of the Aga Khan's European 'enlightened Islam' – which includes intrinsically Western notions of civil society, human rights and liberalism – has clashed with President Rahmon(ov)'s intrinsically Eurasian style of governance and his nation-building project.[62]

Official secularism vs Islamic traditionalism and *Salafism*

Twenty years since the signing of the National Accord in 1997, the war's legacy continues to shape Tajikistan's economic, societal and political trajectories. The country has still not regained its pre-war economic capacity and remains one of the poorest in the world. The process of societal recovery has been hampered by enduring animosities and mistrust between former enemies, by widespread poverty and unemployment, by the persistent large seasonal out-migration of Tajik men, and by the advancing Islamicised re-traditionalisation of a substantial part of the population. Nevertheless, the political project of President Rahmon(ov) since 1992 has been relatively successful and the country has been politically stable. The constituent elements of Rahmon(ov)'s governance have been patrimonial authoritarianism; the marginalisation and subsequent destruction of the viable opposition, especially of an Islamist nature; the promotion of secularised Tajik Islamo-nationalism; securitisation of 'foreign Islam'; and reliance on Russia in defending Tajikistan's southern border with politically volatile Afghanistan.

At the same time, continuing economic and social hardships, endemic corruption, political oppression and the state's aggressive religious policy have contributed to the growing, albeit slow, proliferation among young Tajiks of *Salafi* Islam, including of an Islamist and *jihadist* nature. Since the establishment of ISIS in 2014 a growing number of Tajiks, especially from Khatlon province (formerly Qurghan-Teppe and Kulyab regions), have left for Syria. According to official estimates, which are rather conservative, in 2016 around 1,000 Tajiks fought on the side of *Jabhat al-Nusrah* around Aleppo. Among the ISIS commanders of Raqqa was Abu Holid Kulobi, a Tajik from the Kulyab region. Of special concern to the ruling regime was the defection to ISIS in May 2015 of Colonel Gulmorod Halimov, the former OMON Special Police Forces Commander.[63] A considerable factor in the Islamic radicalisation of some Tajik migrants in Russia has been their poor social and cultural integration, their substandard living conditions and the notable Islamophobia of the host society. Natives of Tajikistan have been well represented in *Salafi jama'ats* in Tyumen' and Surgut regions in the Urals.[64] According to ISIS-controlled sources, 80 per cent of their successful Tajik recruitment targets were Tajik migrant workers in Russia.[65]

The creeping *Salafisation* of young Tajiks has also been due to their inadequate Islamic knowledge and their uncritical acceptance of the Islamic teachings of various preachers and online sources, which often treat Tajik Persianised Islam as *bid'a*. Yet another factor has related to the doctrinal ambiguity of Tajikistan's official Islamic clergy. As in the case of Kazakhstan and Kyrgyzstan, the official promotion in Tajikistan of peaceful 'Tajik Islam' and the denunciation of militant 'foreign Islam' has occurred alongside the official Islamic clergy's de facto embracing of *Salafi* Islam. As a result, they have denounced various manifestations of intrinsically syncretic Islam, which for centuries has defined Tajiks' Islamic culture and way of life. Overall, it is not implausible to suggest that through generational change traditionalist elderly imams and mullahs may gradually be replaced by their younger counterparts who are better educated, albeit along normative (i.e., *Salafi* – G.Y.) Islamic lines.

Notes

1. According to expert assessments the actual Uzbek population of Tajikistan is significantly bigger than the official 12.2 per cent and exceeds 25 per cent of the total population. Dagiev 2014, p. 98.
2. Sayyid Abdulloh Nuri was born in the Sangvor *raion* of the Gharm *oblast'* of Tajikistan. He lacked any structured Islamic education and acquired his Islamic knowledge from his father Nuridin Sayidov (1900–82), the chairman of a village council, and Muhammadjon Hindustoniy. In 1973 and 1986, Nuri was arrested on charges of anti-government Islamist propaganda and support for the Afghan *mujahideen*, and he spent 1986–8 in a labour camp in Siberia. Upon his release he worked for a short time as the editor of *Minbari Islam* (*Pulpit of Islam*), the newspaper of the Tajiksitani *qaziiat*. Epkenhans 2010, p. 320.
3. Dagiev 2014, p. 115; Epkenhans 2010, p. 320.
4. For similar historical and political reasons the IPV also acquired political prominence in Russia's Daghestan. Its charismatic founder was Ahmad-*qadi* Akhtayev (d. 1998), a prominent intellectual, theologian and doctor. For more on the IPV in Daghestan, see Yemelianova 2003, pp. 102–5.
5. Naumkin 2005, p. 203.
6. Kakhor Mahkamov was born in Khujand. Having graduated in 1953 from the Institute of Mountain Mining in Leningrad (St Petersburg), he worked within the Soviet and Communist Party structures. Between 1963 and 1982 he occupied the posts of chairman of the State Commission for Planning (*Gosudarstvennyi Planovoi Komitet – Gosplan*) and deputy prime minister of Tajikistan.
7. The riots were provoked by rumours that Mahkamov's government was distributing highly sought-after flats in Dushanbe among Armenian refugees fleeing Baku in the midst of the violent Nagorno-Karabakh conflict of 1988–94. During the riots the initial slogan 'Down with Armenians' transformed into 'Down with Mahkamov'. A. Gusher (1997), 'Voina i Mir v Sovremennom Tadjikistane', 29 November 1997, available at: http://www.xserver.ru/user/vimvs, last accessed 9 August 2017.

8. Kadriddin Aslonov's presidency lasted from 31 August to 23 September 1991. He was murdered in November 1992. It is alleged that Sangak Safarov, the leader of the Popular Front was behind his assassination. According to some sources, Aslanov was found hanged on the Lenin monument in the square of Qurghan-Teppe. 'Aslonov Kadriddin Aslonovich', *Centrasia. Ru*, 1994, available at: http://www.centrasia.ru/person2.php?&st=1013880931, last accessed 9 August 2017.
9. Rahmon Nabiyev was born in Khujand. He graduated from the Institute of Land Improvement and Mechanization Engineers in Tashkent in 1953, and from 1961 he occupied various high-profile posts within the government and the Communist Party of Tajikistan, including Minister of Agriculture (1971–3); prime minister (1973–82) and First Secretary of the Communist Party (1982–5).
10. Davlat Khudonazarov was born in Khorugh in Gorno-Badakhshan. He graduated from the Institute of Cinematography in Moscow in 1966. Between 1966 and 1986 he occupied senior positions at the 'Tajikfilm' studio, and in 1986 became president of the Tajik Cinematographers' Union. Between 1989 and 1991 he was a member of the USSR's Supreme Soviet. In 1990, he was elected president of the USSR Cinematographers' Union, and in 1991 also became a member of the Central Committee of the Communist Party of the USSR.
11. Dagiev 2014, p. 114.
12. The Republic of Tajikistan, which covers 142,000 km^2, is Central Asia's smallest republic, landlocked in the Pamir Mountains. It borders Uzbekistan, Kyrgyzstan, China and Afghanistan in the south. According to the 2010 Census, the total population of Tajikistan was 7,564,502, while according to the 1989 USSR Census, its population was 5,092,000 people. According to the 2010 Census Tajiks constituted 6,373,834 (84.26 per cent of the total population); Uzbeks 1,054,726 (12.2 per cent of the total population); Kyrgyz 60,700 (0.8 per cent of the total population); Russians 34,800 (0.5 per cent of the total population); Turkmen 15,000 (0.2 per cent of the total population), while over 90 per cent of the population of the Gorno-Badakhshan Autonomous *oblast'*, who are predominantly Pamiris, are registered as Tajiks. At the beginning of 2016, Tjikistan's population was estimated at 8,551,200 people ('Chislennost' Naselenia Respubliki Tadjikistan na 1 Ianvaria 2016 goda', *Agenstvo po Statistike pri Presidente Respubliki Tadjikistan)*, available at: http://www.stat.tj/ru/img/7a20337ca019c92e18235196b4e62aaa_1470198679.pdf, last accessed 8 August 2017).
13. Tokhir Abdujabbor was born in Asht in the Leninabad region. He graduated as an economist from the Tajik State University in 1971, and between 1972 and 1990 he worked at the Institute of Economy of the Academy of Sciences of Tajikistan.
14. Epkenhans 2010, p. 319.
15. In particular, the Pamiris were mobilised by their fear of a repetition of 1937, when their politically dominant representatives were purged by the Stalin leadership. Abdullayev and Akbarzadeh 2002, pp. 125–6; Roy 2011, p. 139.
16. Safaraly Kenjayev was a native of the ancient Sogdian town of Panjikent and a law graduate of the Tajik State University (1965), who in 1966–92 worked in the Public Prosecutor's Office. The Pamiris' demand for his resignation related to his alleged public insult of Interior Minister Mamadayez Navjavanov (1942–2015), a Pamiri.
17. Roy 2011, p. 140.
18. Sangak Safarov (Bobo Sangak, 1928–93), like the current president Emomali Rahmonov, was born in the village of Dangara in the Kulyab region. His father and older brother were executed by the Stalinist regime. Before the outbreak of the Civil War Sangak Safarov was a leading figure in the criminal world, spending over twenty years in prison on charges of murder, violence and theft.

19. Emomali Rahmon was born in the Pamir Mountain village of Dangara in the Kulyab region of Tajikistan. Prior to becoming the leader of Tajikistan he worked as the secretary of the management board of the Dangara *kolkhoz* (1976–88) and as the head of the Dangara *sovkhoz* named after Lenin (1988–92).
20. 'Grajdanskaiia Voina v Tadjikistane, 1992–1997', *Sputnik Tadjikistana*, 27 June 2017, available at: http://ru.sputnik-tj.com/country/20170505/1022205182/tadzhikistan-grazhdanskaya-voina.html, last accessed 11 August 2017.
21. *Hojjee* Akbar Turajonzoda was born in Kofarnikhon (Wahdat), situated in the Hissor valley. He came from the family of the highly respected Qadiri *eshon* (sheikh) Turajon. He graduated from *Mir-i Arab Madrasah* in Bukhara, the Islamic Institute in Tashkent and the Islamic University in Amman, Jordan. In 1985–7, he worked in SADUM and in 1988 he became *qazi-kolon* of Tajikistan. In 1990, he was elected to Tajikistan's Supreme Soviet.
22. Epkenhans 2010, p. 322.
23. The UN Mission of Observers was established in Dushanbe on the basis of the UN Security Council's Resolution of 14 December 1994.
24. Rotar 2007, p. 125.
25. 27 June was declared the Day of National Unity and became an official public holiday in Tajikistan.
26. Bobokhonov 2015.
27. Mahmud Khudoiberdiyev was born in Qurghan-Teppe into an Uzbek family. In 1985, upon his graduation from the High Military College in Almaty, he served as commander of a reconnaissance battalion with the Soviet troops in Afghanistan. Between 1992 and 1996 he served as deputy military commissar of Khatlon province and commanded special forces within the 201st army division which was based in Qurghan-Teppe. In January 1996, he organised an anti-government coup in Qurghan-Teppe and for a short period of time controlled the whole Qurghan-Teppe region. In August 1997, having rejected the Reconciliation Agreement, he attempted to capture Dushanbe, but was defeated by government forces and subsequently joined the *mujahideen* in Afghanistan. It is believed that he was killed in 2001 in Meshed in Afghanistan, though according to other sources he is still alive and lives in Uzbekistan. 'V Tadjikistane Osudili Storonnikov Opal'nogo Polkovnika', *REGNUM*, 8 November 2010, available at: https://regnum.ru/news/1343897.html, last accessed 14 August 2017.
28. Around 70 per cent of Tajikistan's ethnic Russians left the country on the outbreak of war. Dagiev 2014, p. 97.
29. Letov 2007, pp. 105–7.
30. On 25 May 1993, Emomali Rahmonov publicly admitted the central role of Russia and Uzbekistan in defeating the opposition and securing the survival of the Tajikistani state. Dagiev 2014, p. 98.
31. Sokolov 2013.
32. The *Jamiat-e Islamii* is an Islamist organisation, which was founded in Afghanistan in 1972 by the theologian Burhanuddin Rabbani (1940–2011), an ethnic Tajik from Afghanistan's northern Badakhshan. His Islamic thinking was strongly influenced by Sayyid al-Qutb. Following the Soviet invasion of Afghanistan in 1979, Rabbani turned to politics and soon became one of the leaders of the US-backed anti-Soviet *mujahideen* movement. Between 1992 and 1996 he was President of the Islamic State of Afghanistan.
33. Ahmad Shah Massoud (1952–2001), an ethnic Tajik, was born in the Panjshir valley in northern Afghanistan. He was a professional engineer, who distinguished himself as a field commander in the anti-Soviet *mujahideen* movement in 1979–89. He became known as the 'Lion of Panjshir'. Ideologically, he was close to Burhanuddin Rabbani. In 1996, following

the rise of the *Taliban*, Shah Massoud fled to Tajikistan's Kulyab and later became one of the leaders of the anti-*Taliban* 'Northern Alliance'.

34. Rotar 2002, pp. 125–6.
35. Bukhari-zade 2015.
36. Kuz'min 1998, p. 238; Roy 2011, p. 140; Salmorbekova and Yemelianova 2010, p. 221.
37. Masov 1991.
38. Malashenko and Niyazi 2014, p. 12.
39. The relations between the two presidents deteriorated in 1994 and remained acrimonious until Karimov's death in 2016. Their personal antagonism aggravated interstate relations, including over the control of the interstate border and water supply. The water conflict was triggered by the decision of President Rahmonov in the early 2000s to construct the Rogun Dam on the Vakhsh river in northern Tajikistan which would ensure the energy independence of Tajikistan, albeit undermining Uzbekistan's lucrative cotton industry.
40. For example, the Leninabad region was renamed as the Sughd region, the Gharm district as the Rasht district, the town of Ura-Teppe as Istaravshan and the town of Chkalovsk as Buston.
41. Members of President Rahmon's large family have been placed in key political and economic positions in the country. For example, in 2016, Rahmon appointed his daughter Ozoda Rahmon as Head of the Presidential administration. Ozoda's husband, Djamoliddin Nuraliyev, has held the powerful position of first Deputy Director of the National Bank of Tajikistan. In 2017, Emomali's son, Rustam Emomali, was made mayor of Dushanbe. Previously Rustam, who became a general at the age of twenty-five, was in charge of the Anti-Corruption Agency of Tajikistan.
42. It is likely that Emomali Rahmon will change the constitution yet again, either to enable him to run for the presidency in 2020 for the fifth time, or to pass the presidency to his son Rustam.
43. According to Tajikistan's 1994 Constitution, 'the Republic of Tajikistan is a sovereign, democratic, law-based, secular and unitary state'. *Constitution of the Republic of Tajikistan*, available at: http://www.president.tj/ru/taxonomy/term/5/112, last accessed 18 August 2017.
44. Egorov 2014, p. 32; Malashenko and Niyazi 2014, p. 12.
45. Ahmadi 2013.
46. Z. Usmonova 2017.
47. Tucker 2016, p. 7.
48. Malashenko and Niyazi 2014, p. 25.
49. 'V Tadjikistane Sud Zapretil' Partiiu Islamskogo Vozrojdenia', *Lenta.Ru*, 29 September 2015, available at: https://lenta.ru/news/2015/09/29/pivt, last accessed 17 August 2017.
50. Popov 2016; 'Tajikistan Government Issues a List of Approved Sermons', 10 January 2011, RFE/RL, available at: https://www.rferl.org/a/tajikistan_government_orders_mosques/2271961.html, last accessed 18 August 2017.
51. Malashenko and Niyazi 2014, p. 11.
52. 'V Tadzhikistane Budut Zhestko Nakazyvat' za Koldovstvo', *Azia-Plus*, 24 September 2015, available at: http://news.tj/ru/news/v-tadzhikistane-budut-zhestko-nakazyvat-za-koldovstvo, last accessed 18 August 2017.
53. Olimova 2000, p. 60.
54. The author's findings within the Nuffield Foundation-funded research project on 'Islamic Radicalism in Uzbekistan, Tajikistan and Kyrgyzstan', 2002–5.
55. Roy 2011, p. 152.
56. Oparin 2017, p. 75.
57. Roy 2011, pp. 146,148–9.

58. Olimova 2000, p. 70.
59. According to official statistics from the Russian Federal Migration Department, in 2015, there were over 1.2 million Tajik migrants in Russia. The actual number of migrants was estimated to exceed 2 million. This constituted over 12 per cent of the total population of Tajikistan and over 25 per cent of its male population between the ages of 18 and 40. Popov 2015.
60. Of notable influence on young Tajiks has been the online Tajik *Salafi* commentator under the name of 'Muhammadi'. 'Moskovskaia Sobornaia Mechet' v Zhizni Musul'man iz Tsentral'noi Azii', *Central Asain Analytical Network*, 23 February 2017, available at: http://caa-network.org/archives/8421, last accessed 18 September 2017.
61. The trigger was an operation by government special forces against alleged separatist leaders in Khorugh, the administrative centre of Gorno-Badakhshan, in July 2012, as a result of which twenty-three civilians and eighteen government troops lost their lives. Bukhari-zade 2015.
62. In addition to the Aga Khan Foundation's considerable involvement in the education system, the Aga Khan also controls Tajikistan's energy company 'Pamir Energy', the mobile phone company *Tcell* and a major hotel in Dushanbe. 'Chto Aga-Khan Delaiet dlia Tadzhikistana', *Sputnik TJ*, 5 May 2015, available at: http://ru.sputnik-tj.com/infographics/20170505/1022225867/aga-khan-prints-tadzhikistan-ismaility.html, last accessed 18 August 2017.
63. Tucker 2016, p. 2.
64. Malashenko and Starostin 2015, p. 14.
65. Tucker 2016, p. 8.

Selected reading

Primary sources

Constitution of the Republic of Tajikistan, 6 November 1994, available at: http://www.prezident.tj/en, last accessed 15 August 2017.

Rahmonov, E. (2001), *The Tajiks in the Mirror of History: From the Aryans to the Samanids*, London: London River Editions.

Secondary sources

Abdullayev, K. and Sh. Akbarzadeh (2002), *Historical Dictionary of Tajikistan*, Lanham, MD: Scarecrow Press.

Cummings, S. N. (2012), *Understanding Central Asia: Politics and Contested Transformations*, London: Routledge.

Dagiev, D. (2014), *Regime Transition in Central Asia: Stateness, Nationalism and Political Change in Tajikistan and Uzbekistan*, London: Routledge.

Epkenhans, T. (2010), 'Muslims without Learning, Clergy without Faith: Institutions of Islamic Learning in the Republic of Tajikistan', in M. Kemper, R. Motika and S. Reichmuth (eds), *Islamic Education in the Soviet Union and its Successor States*, London: Routledge, pp. 313–48.

Erkenhans, T. (2016), *The Origins of the Civil War in Tajikistan*, Lanham, MD: Rowman & Littlefield.

Jonson, L. (2006), *Tajikistan in the New Central Asia*, London: I. B.Tauris.

Naumkin, V. V. (2005), *Radical Islam in Central Asia: Between Pen and Rifle*, Lanham, MD: Rowman & Littlefield.

Malashenko, A. (2008), *Islam in Central Asia*, Reading: Ithaca Press.

Rashid, A. (2002), *Jihad: The Rise of Militant Islam in Central Asia*, New Haven, CT: Yale University Press.

Rotar, I. (2007), 'Under the Green Banner: Islamic Radicals in Russia and the Former Soviet Union', *Religion, State and Society* 30(2): 89–153.

Roy, O. (2000), *The New Central Asia: The Creation of New Nations*, London: I. B. Tauris.

Salmorbekova, Z. and G. M. Yemelianova (2010), 'Islam and Islamism in the Ferghana Valley', in G. M. Yemelianova (ed.), *Radical Islam in the Soviet Union*, London: Routledge, pp. 211–43.

CHAPTER 8

Muslims of Turkmenistan

A preliminary observation

Turkmenistan stands out among post-Soviet Central Asian republics because of its high level of ethnic homogeneity,[1] the Turkmen's Oghuz entholinguistic *otherness*, the country's desert expanses[2] and its direct access to the Caspian Sea. Of particular significance has been the Turkmen's strong tribalism, which has presented a major hindrance to their national consolidation. Historically, nomadic Turkmen have been divided into over thirty tribes, comprising around 5,000 clans. Prior to the Turkmen's inclusion within the Russian Empire at the end of the nineteenth century they did not possess their own statehood tradition and were politically dependent on neighbouring states – the Persian Empire, the Khiva Khanate and the Bukhara Emirate. The Turkmen's tribal genealogical structures withstood even Soviet collectivisation and social engineering, albeit camouflaged by the Communist Party and Soviet exterior. A possible explanation of this bizarre tribal–Communist synthesis is the considerable similarities between the vertical patrilineal organisation of Turkmen tribes and the cult of male ancestors among them, on the one side, and the Communist Party's vertical structure, defined by the principle of democratic centralism and the extreme concentration of power in the hands of the Communist Party's First Secretary, on the other.

For over a quarter of a century, since the collapse of the USSR in 1991, Turkmenistan has been regarded as one of the worst and most secretive of the world's dictatorships, responsible for the banning of freedom of information and the criminalising or suppressing of any unsanctioned manifestations of religiosity. Any field-based research on Turkmenistan which is not related to such innocuous topics as Turkmen rug-weaving technique or its architecture has been problematic, while research on contemporary Islam and Muslims has been practically impossible. Consequently, most information on the Islamic dynamic in post-Soviet Turkmenistan has emanated either from unverified online sources, or from foreign visitors, whose in-depth analysis of the topic has been hampered by the state, or from Turkmen dissidents in exile, whose objectivity has often been compromised by their personal conflict with the ruling regime. As a result, there have been considerable constraints on scholarship on the subject; due to the scarcity of empirical data it is therefore only possible to outline the major trends in the Islamic situation in post-Soviet Turkmenistan.

The effects of *perestroika*

Unlike in other Central Asian republics, the Gorbachevian *perestroika* had a very limited impact on Turkmenistan's elite and society in general. For historical, ethnocultural and political reasons, the positions of Saparmurat Niyazov (1940–2006),[3] the First Secretary of the Communist Party of Turkmenistan (CPT) and other party officials did not falter and remained solid. Throughout *perestroika* Niyazov remained a staunch supporter of the preservation of the USSR and was wary of Gorbachevian liberal reforms which he perceived as Moscow's destabilising meddling in the domestic politics of Turkmenistan.[4] Consequently, pro-democracy activism in Turkmenistan was subdued and restricted to a small number of Russian professionals and members of the Turkmen intelligentsia represented by the national-democratic movement *Aghzy-Birlik* ('Unity'), the Democratic Party of Turkmenistan (DPT) and the liberal club *Paisakh* ('Reason'). In July 1988, the Supreme Soviet of Turkmenistan introduced a ban on politicised meetings and demonstrations, undermining the political capabilities of these organisations.

In January 1990, a group of activists from *Aghzy-Birlik*, in defiance of the official ban, organised a pro-reform demonstration in front of the parliament in the capital city of Ashgabat. The demonstration was dispersed by the police and its organisers were arrested and subjected to a publicised trial. Since then any expression of dissent has been ruthlessly suppressed. At the same time, Saparmurat Niyazov followed the general trend by declaring the republic's sovereignty and introducing the institution of a presidency alongside the CPT. He also incorporated into official policy some of the opposition's demands related to national culture and language. Thus, in May 1990 the Supreme Soviet proclaimed Turkmen as the state language of Turkmenistan. During the first presidential elections, which took place in October 1990 on a non-alternative basis, Niyazov was elected as President of Turkmenistan by 98 per cent of the vote. In the nationwide referendum in March 1991 the same 98 per cent voted in favour of the preservation of the Soviet Union.[5]

During the anti-Gorbachev coup on 19 August 1991 Niyazov lay low and did not take sides. Following the coup's failure, on 26 August 1991 he announced the withdrawal of the CPT, which was renamed the Democratic Party of Turkmenistan (DPT),[6] from the Communist Party of the Soviet Union. In order to secure the political monopoly of the new party of power the Supreme Soviet imposed a moratorium on the establishment of other political parties in the country. On 26 October 1991, the Turkmenistani authorities organised a referendum on the country's independence which was dutifully supported by 94 per cent of the voters; the following day, the Supreme Soviet issued the Declaration of Independence of Turkmenistan. At that stage, however, Turkmenistan's sovereignisation was more symbolic than substantive in nature and Niyazov maintained his support for the USSR. On 13 December 1991, he initiated a meeting in Ashgabat between the leaders of all the Central Asian republics with the aim of overriding the Slavic separatist Belavezha Accords, which had been signed on 8 December 1991. Having failed in his aim, Niyazov opted for international neutrality and for distancing Turkmenistan from the other ex-Soviet republics. This did not preclude him from turning Turkmenistan into a major player in the global energy market. Broadly speaking, Turkmenistan's post-Soviet transition and the role of Islam in it have been determined by its strong tribalism, its Soviet legacy and its extreme authoritarianism, as well as its abundant energy reserves.[7]

Turkmenistan's nation-building

In 1992, Turkmenistan's Supreme Soviet, renamed the Mejlis, adopted a new Constitution that proclaimed Turkmenistan an independent, secular and neutral state, with a presidential form of governance.[8] Having suddenly acquired a state within the Stalin leadership-imposed political borders, President Niyazov was faced with the ominous task of building a Turkmen nation out of numerous Turkmen tribes. His nation-building strategy was shaped by strong reliance on the Soviet/Eurasian political and economic model, the ideological de-Sovietisation and 'turkmenisation' of the public space and, most importantly, by the notion of himself as the consolidating core of the new Turkmen nation. Accordingly, he rejected economic and political liberalisation and preserved the Soviet-era system of free gas, accommodation, education and healthcare, as well as the state's heavily subsidised prices on basic goods and services. In 1994, as a precautionary measure against the potential proliferation of 'destructive' liberal influences from Yeltsin's Russia, President Niyazov blocked all Russian broadcasting on the territory of Turkmenistan.[9] The one-party political system was also retained although under new auspices. The president's DPT assumed the previous role of the CPT, while the omnipotent Committee of National Security (CNS)[10] replaced the KGB, its staffing increasing by more than 60 per cent during the 1990s.[11] Following the KGB's remit, the CNS was entrusted with conducting systematic purges within the top and middle echelons of power, ensuring police control over the population and the flow of information, and suppressing any political or intellectual dissent or criticism of the president and his close associates. As a result, by the mid-1990s, most members of the small political and intellectual opposition had ended up in exile. As in the Soviet period, President Niyazov, who followed tradition in harbouring distrust of his ethnic kinsmen, surrounded himself with aides of Russian, Jewish, Armenian and Azerbaijani ethnic background, supplemented by a number of business advisers from Turkey, France, Germany and Israel.[12]

The power vertical was further strengthened by the establishment in 1992 of a supra-constitutional body – the *Halk Maslahaty* ('People's Council') – headed by the president himself. The Halk Maslahaty was portrayed as the resurrection of the democratic assembly of the period of Oghuz Khan, the mythological ancestor of the Turkmen people. Originally it consisted of 262 persons, including members of the Mejlis, government officials, local governors and some 'independent' deputies, chosen by Niyazov. By 2003, Niyazov had increased its membership to 2,507 by including in it, on the basis of personal loyalty, representatives of the State Council of Elders, the DPT and the *Galkynysh* ('Movement for National Revival'). Through the Halk Maslahaty Niyazov was able to exercise direct rule, bypassing decisions by the Mejlis, government and courts. It enjoyed the exclusive right to declare war, to change political and administrative borders, to ratify international treaties, to run referenda and to define political, economic and social policies, as well as to reverse its own decisions.[13]

In April 1993, within the campaign for Turkmenistan's de-Sovietisation and de-Russification, the Mejlis decreed the switching of schools, universities, the administration and media from the Cyrillic to the Latinised Turkmen alphabet consisting of thirty letters. Soviet-era names were removed from administrative units, streets, political, educational and cultural institutions and replaced either by their pre-Russian/-Soviet equivalents or by newly introduced names related to the president. Banknotes of the new currency – the *manat* – which replaced the Soviet rouble in November 1993, had Niyazov's portrait on one side (where there had been Lenin's portrait on Soviet roubles), and a bizarre mixture of historical personalities[14] and perceived Turkmen 'national' symbols on the other.

An integral part of 'turkmenisation' was the symbolic reassertion of Turkmenistan's Muslim-ness through the introduction of Islamic symbols into the public sphere and its increased diplomatic engagement with the Muslim world. In the summer of 1992, Turkmenistan joined the OIC. In the same year, Niyazov became the first among Central Asian presidents to conduct *hajj* to Mecca. In 1993, he announced that Turkmenistan was returning to Sunni Islam of *Hanafi madhhab*, infused with Sufism, as part of the Turkmen national culture. The Islamic festivals of *Qurban-Bairam* and *Oraza-Bairam* were made public holidays, while the Turkmen translation of the Qur'an was included in the secondary school curriculum. Like his Uzbek and Kazakh counterparts, Niyazov directed considerable resources towards Turkmen nationalisation of over thirty Sufi *mazars* on the territory of Turkmenistan. The mosque and mausoleum of the great Sufi scholar *Khwaja* Yusuf Hamadani in Merv was lavishly renovated and turned into the main official Sufi shrine. The state allocated substantial funds for the erection of mosques which were meant to symbolise the unified Turkmen nation and contracted scores of Turkmen, Turkish and

French architects who built over two hundred of them across the country. The most spectacular new mosques were named after the president and members of his family, the grandest of them being the Saparmurat Hajjee mosque at Fort Geok Tepe for 5,000 worshippers. By 1994 the number of mosques had increased from four in 1991 to over three hundred. But this official reverence towards Islam co-existed with tight Soviet-era control over *hajj* to Mecca and Medina and other forms of Islamic activity. For example, by the mid-1990s, only around 450 Turkmen citizens had been allowed to conduct *hajj* despite the Saudi-allocated annual quota of 4,600.[15]

State-sanctioned selective Islamicisation of the public space went on alongside the promotion of non-Islamic Turkmen symbols and festivals, such as the *Nowruz*, the Turkmen Horse Day, the Turkmen Carpet Day or the Turkmen Melon Day. The Soviet holidays of 8 March – International Women's Day – and of 9 May – Victory Day over Nazi Germany – were preserved, alongside the newly introduced holiday of remembrance of hundreds of Tekke tribe members who were killed during the Russian conquest of Geok-Tepe on 12 January 1881. The flag of independent Turkmenistan, which was adopted in February 1992, contained the distinctive carpet designs of the five largest Turkmen tribes.

Compared with other Central Asian leaders, who have prioritised great 'national' ancestors as the founders of their respective nations, Saparmurat Niyazov made his own personality the main pillar of Turkmen nationhood. In doing so, he exploited his orphaned childhood to portray himself as Turkmenbashi ('Head of All Turkmen') – the benevolent father of all Turkmen, irrespective of their tribal affiliation; in October 1993, Niyazov's Turkmenbashi status was officially endorsed by the Mejlis. Subsequently, Niyazov formulated the Turkmen national ideological triad as *Halk-Vatan-Turkmenbashi* ('Our People-Our Country-Our Leader').[16] It was incorporated into the national oath, which from 1994 became compulsory at morning assemblies in schools, universities and government offices. Mosque imams were instructed to recite it at the end of their sermons. The city of Krasnovodsk was renamed Turkmenbashi, along with airports, universities, mosques, stadiums and streets. The Turkmenbashi's portraits and sayings became ubiquitous in all public spaces, while his profile was placed in the top right corner of the screen on TV channels. University students and army personnel were obliged to wear watches with his portrait. A 75-metre grand golden rotating statue of the Turkmenbashi was placed atop the Neutrality Arch in the centre of Ashgabat, while another golden statue of him with a book, as a symbol of wisdom, was erected in his hometown of Kupchak. The total number of monuments to the 'Head of All Turkmen' exceeded 14,000. The cult of Niyazov was extended to his parents, and the town of Kerki in the east of Turkmenistan was renamed Atamurat, after Niyazov's father.

In 1999, Niyazov was made president for life. In 2000, he published his book *Ruhnama* (*Book of the Spirit*), a collection of his thoughts on Turkmen history, culture and politics.[17] This was soon attributed sacred significance, comparable with that of the Qur'an and the Bible. Ashgabat acquired a monument to *Ruhnama*, while its study was introduced into the school curriculum and quotations from it were displayed on the walls of mosques. In 2001, Niyazov's cult of personality eclipsed that of Stalin when he was proclaimed a national prophet who was sent to the Turkmen people in the third millennium. Niyazov initiated a new calendar, in which months were named after him, his mother Qurban Sultan-eje and the *Ruhnama*, as well as after Turkmen national heroes, symbols and holidays. The first month of the year was naturally called 'Turkmenbashi' and the days of the week were renamed 'main day' (Monday), 'young' (Tuesday), 'suitable' (Wednesday), 'blessed' (Thursday), 'piatnitsa' ('Friday'), 'spiritual' (Saturday) and 'holiday' (Sunday). Opera, ballet, contemporary music and the circus were outlawed on the ground of their alleged incompatibility with Turkmen culture. In Ashgabat, the names of streets, except those related to the Turkmenbashi, were replaced by numbers, starting from '2000', to symbolise the 'millennium of Turkmen'. Niyazov's other eccentric decrees related to the new classification of stages in a person's life; the criminalisation of infectious diseases such as HIV and cholera; and a ban on the use of the internet, on golden teeth caps, dyed and long hair, moustaches and beards on men![18] According to the new classification of a man's life-cycle, a proper life begins after the age of sixty, which inaugurates the 'prophetic age'; and at seventy-three it is comforting to know that a man enters the 'inspired age'.[19]

In 1993, within the context of the de-Sovietisation of the educational sphere, the length of mandatory comprehensive schooling was reduced from eleven to nine years, specialised technical education was discontinued, and Soviet textbooks on history and the other humanities were withdrawn due to their 'anti-national' character. From 2001, the *Ruhnama* became the main textbook in primary schools; and from 2004 the course on 'The *Ruhnama* as the Spiritual Code of the Turkmen People' was also added to curricula in secondary schools and universities. Among other newly introduced courses were 'Political Independence during Saparmurat Turkmenbashi the Great' and 'The Literary Heritage of Saparmurat Turkmenbashi'. These replaced most traditional humanities and natural science subjects, which were discarded on the grounds of their 'obscurity and disconnectedness from reality'. The official assault on Soviet-era universities was accompanied by a drastic reduction of state funding for higher education, as a result of which the number of students plummeted; in 1991 there were around 40,000, but by 2005 their number was reduced to just over 3,000. Between 1993 and 2003 the length of university education was reduced from five to two years, while from 2001 foreign university degrees ceased to be recognised. Additionally, the university teaching of foreign languages was drastically cut and Turkmen was made the sole language of university entrance exams.[20]

Academic research institutes and libraries were equally devastated. In 1998, the Academy of Sciences of Turkmenistan was closed down and replaced by the ideologically prescriptive State Institute of Cultural Heritage of the Peoples of Turkmenistan. The former Institute of History was reorganised along the *Ruhnama*'s lines and subordinated to the presidential apparatus. It was tasked with the rewriting of Turkmen history, which had to be centred on the Turkmenbashi and his book. In 2002, Turkmen historians were prohibited from using Russian-language primary and secondary sources; and in 2005 the Turkmenbashi ordered the closure of all libraries in rural regions because of their apparently low attendance. In any case most Soviet Turkmenistan writers were banned for not being sufficiently 'national'.[21] The Turkmenbashi's reforms of the health and social care services were equally, breathtakingly devastating. All rural and provincial hospitals were closed down and just a few functioning hospitals were left in Ashgabat. In 2006, Niyazov decreed that pensions, the average of which were equivalent to US$50 per month, should no longer be paid to the disabled, former *kolkhozniks* and some other categories of people. As a result, the number of eligible pensioners dropped overnight from 336,000 to 229,000.[22]

The state promotion of everyone and everything Turkmen was combined with the political and social downgrading of ethnic minorities who were prohibited from employment in public services, the police, the security services and the military sector. The Russian-, Uzbek- and Kazakh-language schools were subjected to phased closures. In the early 2000s, several thousands of ethnic Uzbeks were forcibly resettled from the areas bordering Uzbekistan to the desert in the northwest of the country, with the dual aim of preventing their possible irredentism and of populating the desert regions.[23] Overall, the Turkmenbashi's reforms led to the disintegration of the education, health and social care systems, as well as the whole fabric of the Soviet-era Turkestani society.

The sudden death of the Turkmenbashi from cardiac failure in 2006 did little to change the country's internal and external trajectories. His successor, Gurbanguly Berdymuhamedov (b. 1957),[24] has largely retained Niyazov's policies, though with minor modifications. During the presidential elections in February 2007, which were traditionally run on a non-alternative basis, he received nearly 90 per cent of the votes. In February 2012, he was re-elected as president with 97 per cent of the votes in the nominally multi-candidate elections. Unlike his predecessor, in 2011, President Berdymuhamedov assumed the more 'modest' official honorific titles of the Arkadag ('Mountain-like Protector'), the 'Hero of Turkmenistan' and the 'Distinguished Architect of Turkmenistan'. He relocated the grand golden statue of Niyazov to the outskirts of Ashgabat and in its stead, in 2015 a 21-metre high monument to the Arkadag on a horse was built in the centre of Ashgabat, while monuments to the Arkadag's father and grandfather were erected in their hometown. Niyazov's images gradually disappeared from the TV logos, while his name was removed from the state oath and hymn. In 2008, Berdymuhamedov formulated a new national ideology – the 'Era of the Great Renaissance' – which omitted reference to the *Ruhnama*. In 2009, Berdymuhamedov decreed that the teaching of the *Ruhnama* in schools should be reduced to just one hour per week. His own books on Ahal-Tekke horses, carpets and medicinal plants gradually replaced the *Ruhnama* in the offices of civil servants, and at universities and schools. In 2007, Berdymuhamedov reinstated the ten-year-long school education and, in 2012, increased it to twelve years. He also increased the school teaching hours for foreign languages, which now included Chinese and Japanese in addition to the previously offered Russian and English.[25]

Otherwise, the Arkadag has maintained his reliance on the security services, which played a central role in the gradual removal of most of Niyazov's appointees and in the purges within the top and middle echelons of power. Compared with his predecessor, he has increased the number of his family members and representatives of his Ahal-Tekke tribe in the upper ranks of Turkmenistan's officialdom, paving the way for the development of a variety of patrimonialism comparable with that in Tajikistan. In 2012, Berdymuhamedov initiated a new Law on Political Parties, which created a semblance of political pluralism by allowing the formation of the first 'opposition' party, the Party of Industrialists and Entrepreneurs (PIE). However, a genuine opposition has been almost non-existent and has been largely represented by Turkmen exiles in Russia, Turkey and Europe.

State–Muslim relations

State–Muslim relations in independent Turkmenistan have shown many similarities with those in other post-Soviet Muslim-majority regions. They have also exhibited some specific features due to Turkmenistan's extreme political authoritarianism and, in particular, to President Niyazov's prophetic claims in the first decade of Turkmenistan's independence. According to the 1991 Law on Freedom of Religion and Religious Organisations and the 1992 Constitution, Turkmenistan is a democratic, law-based, secular state, which guarantees freedom of religious persuasions. These characteristics were confirmed in the Religious Laws of 2003 and 2016 and all subsequent amended constitutions, which also acknowledge the historical role of Islam in Turkmen history and culture.[26] But under President Niyazov Soviet methods of control over religion were further tightened. In 1994, he created the *Gengesh* ('Council') for Religious Affairs, which was put under his direct control. The Gengesh consisted of the muftii, the deputy muftii, the head of the Orthodox Church and a secular official. All of them were made civil servants, receiving state salaries. Unlike other post-Soviet Central Asian rulers, who backed the upgrading of their Soviet-era *qaziiates* to national muftiiates, President Niyazov preserved the *qaziiate* structure under the leadership of *qazi* Nasrullah ibn Ibadullah,[27] who, like most of Turkmenistan's official Muslim clergy, was an ethnic Uzbek.[28]

Niyazov also, from the first years of independence, exercised thorough control over mosques, *madrasahs* and Islam-related activities. In 1995, he tightened this control further by amending the 1991 Religious Law to make stricter selection rules for Muslim clergy and the requirement for a minimum of 500 signatures in order to register a religious community. Mosques, imams of which were suspected of non-compliance with the Turkmenbashi's vision of Islam, were refused registration and eventually closed down. In 1997, the Gengesh launched a campaign of re-registration of mosques with the aim of de-legalising those mosques deemed to be problematic; this led to the closure of almost half. In 2000, two out of a total of three *madrasahs* were closed down, the only one left functioning being in Ashgabat – though even this one was closed down during Berdymuhamedov's presidency. Advanced Islamic studies were permitted only for a small number of students at the Theology Department at the Makhtumkuli State University.[29] In 2000, the Turkmenbashi ordered the destruction of over 40,000 copies of the Qur'an in Turkmen because of the 'anti-Turkmen commentaries' made by the translator, Hajaahmet Orazklychev.[30]

Turkmenistan's highly respected *qazi* Nasrullah ibn Ibadullah was treated as a civil servant who was expected to follow the ruler's orders rather than provide spiritual leadership to Muslim Turkmen. In 2004, he was sacked and sentenced to twenty-two years in jail for his refusal to recognise the *Ruhnama* as being equal to the Qur'an. Following Ibadullah's removal, all imams were instructed to include excerpts from the *Ruhnama* and praises to the Turkmenbashi in their Friday sermons. In 2006, at the instigation of the Turkmenbashi, the state-run *qaziiate* circulated among provincial governors and imams a compilation of officially recognised Turkmen Islamic practices and rituals which had to be used in mosques. The Niyazov government particularly targeted Shi'a mosques which served Turkmenistan's small Shi'a minority, comprising Azeris, Iranians and Kurds. These mosques were portrayed as being hotbeds of 'wrong' and political Islam and any public reference to Shi'ism was prosecuted. In 2005, the last Shi'a imam of the city of Turkmenbashi was forced out of the country. Along with Shiites, Turkmenistan's other persecuted religious minorities have included the Adventists, Baptists, Pentecostals and some other Protestant groups.[31]

Surprisingly, in the first decade of independence the state's tight control over Turkmen clergy co-existed with its relative laxity towards the activities in the country of Saudi, Pakistani, Iranian, Turkish and some other foreign Islamic funds and educators, as well as towards young Turkmen's studies in foreign *madrasahs* and Islamic institutes. For example, Saudi emissaries were allowed to open an orphanage, where Turkmen children were taught along the stricter *Hanbali madhhab* which is dominant in Saudi Arabia. The Saudis also built a mosque in the village of Keshi, on the outskirts of Ashgabat.[32] The Turkmenistani authorities also welcomed Fethullah Gulen's emissaries and other missionaries and educators from Turkey, who benefited from their ethnolinguistic affinity with the Turkmen. By the mid-1990s, the Gulenists had created in Turkmenistan a network of their schools for around 3,000 students. The Turkish government also funded the establishment in Ashgabat of the Turkish–Turkmen University for 2,000 students and offered dozens of scholarships for its Turkmen students to continue their studies in Turkey.[33] It is important to note that although the Turkish–Turkmen University and Turkish schools provided a superior education in the sciences and IT in Turkish and English, at least compared with Turkmen education, they were not entirely neutral politically and ideologically, and they promoted Turkey-centred pan-Turkism and a Gulenist understanding of Islam, which was at odds with local Islamic tradition based on Sufism and tribal *adats*.

State–Muslim relations have not undergone significant changes since 2007, when Berdymuhamedov became Turkmenistan's second president. Symptomatic among the first actions of the new president was the awarding of the order of *Altyn Asyr* ('Golden Century') to Murat Karryev, the former head of the Gengesh and mastermind of the repressive religious policies. Still, Berdymuhamedov's religious policy has been noticeably less influenced by the *Ruhnama* and more attuned to the general post-Soviet official discourse on Islam, characterised by the dichotomy between 'traditional' and 'untraditional' Islam and the securitisation and suppression of 'untraditional' Islam and other non-traditional beliefs. As elsewhere in ex-Soviet Muslim Eurasia, religious and political opponents of the regime have been routinely accused of foreign connections, extremism, violation of the social order, the propagandising of alien cultural values and the undermining of the Turkmen national Muslim tradition.[34]

In 2011, President Berdymuhamedov decreed the closing down of the Turkmen–Turkish schools and significantly scaled down the involvement of foreigners in the educational and cultural spheres. In 2013, his government launched a de-radicalisation campaign aimed at neutralising local *Wahhabis* and their sympathisers, strengthening even further state control over the Muslim clergy by requesting them to perform surveillance functions. One of the triggers for this campaign was an international news report about the capture by Syrian government forces of a Turkmenistan national, Rovshen Gazakov, known as Abu Abdullah. Abu Abdullah, an *Al-Qaeda* commander, revealed that, together with other young Turkmen, he had been trained by *jihadist* instructors under the command of sheikh Murad in a clandestine camp on the outskirts of Ashgabat.[35]

Popular perceptions and practices of Islam

As in other parts of post-Soviet Central Asia, the majority of Turkmen adhere to popular or 'folk' Islam which is imbued with Sufism, Turkmen *adats* and pre-Islamic beliefs and practices. Nevertheless, its particular manifestations have some distinctive features. Among those is the centrality of the cult of ancestors, spirits and shamanism in the Turkmen's Islamicised belief system. Another is the particularly strong social and ideological role of Sufism due to its merger with tribalism in the form of sacred tribes or *awlat*.[36] Yet another difference specific to the Turkmen is the Iran-related presence of elements of Shi'ism in their Islamic beliefs and practices, even though they formally belong to the *Hanafi madhhab* of Sunni Islam.

Although Islam was brought to the territory of present-day Turkmenistan in the seventh century, the process of Islamicisation of the nomadic and semi-nomadic Turkmen occurred between the fourteenth and eighteenth centuries. The main protagonists of Islam among them were the Sufi *ishans* and *dervishes* who came from present-day southern Kazakhstan and northern Iran. As in other parts of Central Asia, the Turkmen's preference for Sufism, rather than orthodox Islam, was due to its flexibility, which enabled them to continue – albeit in Islamicised form – with their traditional beliefs and ritualistic practices, centred on the veneration of tribal ancestors and spirits. The Turkmen went even further than their Central Asian co-religionists by integrating Sufism into their genealogical lineages through their creation of aforementioned *awlat*. Alongside the common Sufi *sayyid-* and *khoja*-based Islamic sacred lineages, which derived from the Prophet Muhammad and the Four Righteous Caliphs, the Turkmen claimed to have four other lineages, corresponding to their particular tribal formations: the *Ata* ('Forefather'), the *Mujavur* ('Neighbours'), the *Magtym* ('Master') and the *Pakyr Shikh* (named after Pakyr Shikh).[37] The Turkmen *awlat* coexisted or overlapped with dozens of other tribes, the largest of which were the Tekke, the Yomud, the Ersary, the Saryq, the Qara Yusuf and the Kanjyghaly. Historically, the most powerful were the Tekke and the Yomud, the former traditionally dominating in the Ahal-Tekke and Merv oasis, and the Yomud in the areas along the border between Iran and Turkmenistan. The Ersary have prevailed in the border region between Turkmenistan and Afghanistan; the Saryqs in the southernmost corner of the country; the Kanjyghaly along the Kazakh–Turkmen border; and the Qara Yusuf in the Caspian Sea zone.[38]

The sacralised *awlat* have been especially socially and politically influential in the geographical areas of their legendary origins. Thus, the Ata *awlat*'s Turkmen, who claim their descent from the fifteenth-century Yasawi sheikh Gezli-Ata ('Visionary Father'), dominate in the western part of the country. The tomb 'Gezli-Ata', which is situated in the mountainous area to the northeast of Turkmenbashi (Krasnovodsk), remains among the most venerated pilgrimage sites in Turkmenistan. Turkmen from the *awlat* of Dana-Ata reside in the Merv oasis. They derive their origins from a poet and historian Dana-Ata ('Father of Wisdom'), a Yasawi, who lived in the Great Balkhan region in the second part of the sixteenth century. In the early eighteenth century, Dana-Ata Turkmen moved to Khorezm, from where they later migrated to the Merv oasis. The habitat of the Turkmen *awlat* of Magtym (Magsum)[39] is the low Caspian region. The alleged founder of this *awlat* was Muhamedhasan-Magsum who lived in the twelfth century in northern Iran.[40]

Throughout history, the Turkmen's enduring tribal organisation, reinforced by the existence of the *awlat*, safeguarded them in the face of external social and ideological influences and made them less receptive to the book-based Islam of Tatar and Uzbek Islamic preachers. As a consequence, the Turkmen, even more than their nomadic Kazakh and Kyrgyz counterparts, did not develop great enthusiasm for mosques and treated mosque imams and mullahs as inferior to the representatives of sacralised lineages. Individual Turkmen tribes prioritised *adats* in vital matters related to the legitimisation of the authority of tribal leaders, declarations of war and peace, interpersonal relations and economic transactions. In contrast, *shari'a* mainly served the ritual sphere linked to birth, circumcision, marriage and funerals.[41] These attitudes have persisted in Soviet and post-Soviet times, so that, in spite of a significant increase in the number of mosques in the last two decades, they have mainly borne a symbolic function and have been poorly attended. The Turkmen at large have remained aloof from *shari'a* prohibitions, especially those related to the consumption of alcohol and drugs. As a result, there has traditionally been a large number of opium- and hashish-smokers among Turkmen, who cultivated cannabis from at least the sixth century BC. Since independence there has been a persistent rise in the number of heroin and other hard drug-users in Ashgabat and the Merv oasis, which lies on the major drug-smuggling routes from Afghanistan to Russia and Europe.[42]

The Turkmen's religious syncretism has also been evidenced in their Islamicised sacralisation of their political leaders against the backdrop of their disregard for the authority of the *'ulama'*. The roots of this phenomenon go back into distant history when the Turkmen internalised Central Asian Islam as part of their pre-Islamic and non-Islamic beliefs and practices, involving shamanism and the worshipping of ancestors and spirits. Consequently, Turkmen *mazars* have been dominated by tombs and other sacred sites that relate to their pre-Islamic genealogical forefathers and the legendary patrons of various occupations, who were then Islamicised in the later historical period.[43] At the same time, the Turkmen turned some real persons from Islamic history into their pre-Islamic heroes; for example, the aforementioned Yusuf al-Hamadani is widely worshipped as both a Sufi teacher and a patron of *porhans* (shamans). In a similar way, Turkmen often equate shamans with Sufi *khojas* and Iranian *padishahs* and attribute to them the same faculties, such as sacralised wisdom, *arwah* and the ability to cure a person by expelling *jinns*.[44]

In Turkmenistan, then, unlike in the neighbouring Central Asian republics, the Islamic dynamic has been channelled within the state-controlled national discourse, first centred on the personality of Saparmurat Niyazov, and later on Gurbanguly Berdymuhamedov. Although both have pledged their Muslim-ness, they have treated Islam as one of the cultural aspects of Turkmen-ness and their sacralised political leadership. In doing so, they have utilised the traditional Turkmen supremacy of genealogical over religious authority as well as the relative insignificance of book-based Islam among their people. President Niyazov went even further by proclaiming himself a new national Prophet of Turkmen. Under this approach a large number of newly opened and lavish mosques have been designated to supplement the ruling regime rather than to serve as public places for worship, while Islamic education was reduced to a few courses at the State University, thus accounting for the decreased professionalism of Turkmen Muslim clergy. Any independent Islamic thinking and activities have been severely suppressed or entirely prohibited, while the functions of the Islamic establishment have been further curtailed even compared with Soviet times.

It appears that so far the bulk of Turkmen have remained within the tenets of apolitical Turkmen popular Islam which is imbued with local *adats* and Sufism. However, it not impossible that the continued state repressive religious policy and the Muslim clergy's growing theological deficiency may increase the attractiveness among young Turkmen of the Islamic message and Islam-related information disseminated by non-government and underground Islamic and Islamist groups that have been present in the region, as well through the limited and severely censored internet and social media.[45] As some unverified sources suggest, there has been a notable number of young Turkmen who are members of or sympathisers with the HTI, *Tablighi Jama'at*, *Atageldi-Aga*, *Murat-Aga* and other clandestine *Salafi* and Islamist organisations and groupings. They have policed morality and prohibited the consumption of alcohol and the use of satellite dishes, as well as providing material assistance for the poor.[46] It is also reported that there has been a growing number of Turkmenistan's nationals fighting in Iraq and Syria with ISIS.

Notes

1. In 2014, Turkmenistan's population was estimated at 5,171,943 people. Ethnic Turkmen constitute 85.6 per cent, while the main ethnic minorities include Uzbeks (5.8 per cent) and Russians (5.1 per cent). *World Bank: Turkmenistan*, available at: https://data.worldbank.org/country/Turkmenistan, last accessed 29 August 2017.
2. Turkmenistan covers 491,210 km^2 and 85 per cent of it is desert. Turkmenistan borders Afghanistan, Iran, Uzbekistan, Kazakhstan and the Caspian Sea. *World Bank: Turkmenistan*,

available at: https://data.worldbank.org/country/turkmenistan, last accessed 29 August 2017.

3. Saparmurat Niyazov, a member of the Tekke tribe, was born in the village of Qipchak in Ashgabat region into a worker's family. Having lost both parents at an early age, he was brought up in an orphanage. In 1967, he graduated from the Polytechnic Institute in Leningrad (St Petersburg). From 1970 he occupied various positions within the Communist Party. Between 1885 and 1991 he was the First Secretary of the Communist Party of Turkmenistan.
4. Peyrouse 2012, p. 69.
5. 'Ob Itogakh' 1991.
6. By that time the opposition party with the same name of the Democratic Party of Turkmenistan (DPT) was marginalised.
7. Turkmenistan's proven natural gas reserves amount to 17.5 trillion m^3 (January 2014). However, its actual gas deposits are estimated at around 50 trillion m^3. 'Natural Gas in Turkmenistan', available at: http://factsanddetails.com/central-asia/Turkmenistan/sub8_7d/entry-4837.html, last accessed 30 August 2017.
8. The constitutions of Turkmenistan were tailored to the needs of presidents Niyazov and Berdymuhamedov, and amended in 1995, 1998, 2003, 2008 and 2016.
9. Safronov 2000, p. 86.
10. In September 2002 the CNS was renamed the Ministry of National Security of Turkmenistan (MNST).
11. Peyrouse 2012, p. 75.
12. Bohr 2016, p. 24.
13. Peyrouse 2012, pp. 72–3.
14. Among these personalities were, for example, rulers and members of their families from various polities that historically existed on the territory of present-day Turkmenistan, including Il'-Arslan (d. 1172), ruler of Khorezm; Ahmad Sanjar (d. 1157), a Seljuk ruler; and Tiurabek-*hanym* (d. 1388), a daughter of Uzbek-Khan of the Golden Horde.
15. Peyrouse 2012, p. 101.
16. Safronov 2000, p. 82.
17. It is widely believed that the actual author of the *Ruhnama* was the Russian archaeologist Vadim Masson, who belonged to the Turkmenbashi's inner circle. Peyrouse 2012, p. 98.
18. 'Zapretil' SPID, Tsirk i Zolotye Zuby: 15 Reform Saparmurata Niyazova', *Vesti.RU*, 28 December 2013, available at: http://www.vesti.ru/doc.html?id=1173031, last accessed 2 September 2017.
19. Peyrouse 2012, p. 84.
20. Ibid., pp. 95–7.
21. Safronov 2000, p. 88.
22. 'Turkmenbashi Reshil Istrebit' Vsekh Starikov', *NewsRu*, 13 February 2006, available at: http://www.newsru.com/world/03feb2006/turkmenbashi.html, last accessed 3 September 2017.
23. Bohr 2016, p. 33.
24. Gurbanguly Berdymuhamedov, a member of the Tekke tribe, was born in the village of Babarap in the Ashgabat region into the family of a school teacher. In 1979, he graduated from the Faculty of Dentistry of the State Medical Institute in Ashgabat, and between 1980 and 1997 occupied different positions within the dentistry sector. Between 1997 and 2001 Berdymuhamedov served as Minister of Health and Medical Industry, and between 2001 and 2006 as deputy prime minister. Following Niyazov's death his succession was decided at an extraordinary session of the Halk Maslahaty in violation of the Constitution which

required Ovezgeldi Atayev, the chairman of the Mejlis, to become acting president. The latter was charged with criminal offences and imprisoned. Bohr 2016, p. 13.

25. 'S Novogo Uchebnogo Goda v Riade Uchebnykh Zavedenii Turkmenistana Budut Izuchat' Kitaiskii i Yaponskii Yazyki', *Turkmenistan.Ru*, 30 November 2015, available at: http://www.turkmenistan.ru/ru/articles/41317.html, last accessed 4 September 2017.
26. *Zakon Turkmenistana o Svobode Veroispovedania i Religioznykh Organizatsii*, 26 March 2016, available at: ihttp://www.base.spinform.ru/show_doc.fwx?rgn=84971#A000000043, last accessed 7 September 2017.
27. Nasrullah ibn Ibadullah was educated at *Al-Azhar* in Egypt. In the late 1980s he was one of the leaders of Central Asia's 'young Imams'.
28. Nuryev 2011.
29. Safronov 2000, p. 89.
30. Kalishevskii 2014.
31. Peyrouse 2012, pp. 99, 100–2.
32. Safronov 2000, p. 86.
33. Peyrouse 2012, p. 97.
34. Kalishevskii 2014.
35. Ibid.
36. The Turkmen term *awlat* derives from the Arabic *awlad* which is the plural of *walad* meaning 'a son'.
37. For a detailed analysis of Sufism among the Turkmen, see Demidov 1978.
38. For more on the geography of Turkmen tribes, see Vasilieva 2002.
39. The terms *magsum* and *magtym* represent colloquial forms of the term *makhdum*, meaning 'master' in Arabic.
40. In the nineteenth century, descendants of the Magtym lineage 'deepened' their *shezheres* by linking them to the Prophet Muhammad, the Righteous Caliphs ('Dortcharyya' or 'Four Friends') and Adam. It is likely that this was done in order to strengthen their religious credentials and to secure special privileges such as personal immunity, immunity for their dwellings and cattle especially during tribal internecine strife, as well as exemption from heavy communal work on the irrigation system. Tyson 1997.
41. Bohr 2016, p. 51.
42. Hays 2008.
43. Particularly venerated among these are the *mazars* of Baba-Daikhan and Baba-Gambar.
44. Basilov 1970, pp. 12, 60, 64.
45. At the time of writing, at least three Turkmen-run social sites on Islamic matters have been available through the Russian social network *VKontakte*.
46. Kalishevskii 2014.

Selected reading

Primary sources

Constitution of the Republic of Turkmenistan, Ashgabat, 18 May 1992, available at: http://www.uta.edu/cpsees/TURKCON.htm, last accessed 15 December 2017.

Secondary sources

Bohr, A. (2016), *Turkmenistan: Power, Politics and Petro-Authoritarianism*, London: Chatham House.

Cummings, S. N. (2012), *Understanding Central Asia: Politics and Contested Transformations*, London: Routledge.

Edgar, A. L. (2004), *Tribal Nation: The Making of Soviet Turkmenistan*, Princeton, NJ: Princeton University Press.

Khalid, A. (2007), *Islam after Communism: Religion and Politics in Central Asia*, Berkeley: University of California Press.

Peyrouse, S. (2012), *Turkmenistan: Strategies of Power, Dilemmas of Development*, Armonk, NY: M. E. Sharpe.

Safronov, R. (2000), 'Islam in Turkmenistan: The Niyazov Calculation', in R. Sagdeev and S. Eisenhower (eds), *Islam and Central Asia: An Enduring Legacy or An Evolving Threat?* Washington, DC: Center for Political and Strategic Studies, pp. 73–92.

Conclusion

In the early 1990s there were predictions that formerly Soviet and historically Muslim Central Asia would return to its pre-Russian and pre-Soviet roots by succumbing to the political and economic domination of Turkey and, in the case of Tajikistan, of Iran. A decade later, in the early 2000s, some expected that in the wake of the rising *Taliban* in neighbouring Afghanistan, the Ferghana valley-centred Uzbekistan, Tajikistan and Kyrgyzstan would not withstand advancing Islamic radicalism and *jihadism* and become similarly politically Islamicised. In the second decade of the 2000s these predictions were superseded by expectations that Central Asian states, and Uzbekistan and Kazakhstan, in particular, would join in the 'Arab Spring' and undergo violent regime change along democratic lines. None of these things, at least to date, has transpired.

Instead, for more than a quarter of a century independent Uzbekistan, Kazakhstan, Kyrgyzstan, Tajikistan and Turkmenistan have remained barely affected by powerful regional and international influences and have largely maintained their political and economic viability, their societal cohesion and their adherence to institutional and, to a considerable degree, popular secularism. It could be argued that the remarkable resilience of Central Asian polities and peoples in the face of serious internal and external challenges derives from their intrinsically Eurasian cultural core, which throughout history has shaped their political, economic and cultural trajectories. As shown in Part I, the cornerstones of the Eurasian core were Central Asians' Sogdian cultural diversity and openness rooted in the ancient Silk Road's cosmopolitanism, their Persianised Islamicisation, their sedentary–nomadic synthesis, their lengthy existence within the pan-Eurasian Genghizid/Timurid political, economic, cultural and political space, and particularly their distinctly Central Asian Islam. The latter has been characterised by a high content from the Sufi tradition, its intertwining with pre-Islamic Zoroastrian and Tengrian beliefs, shamanism and the cult of ancestors. Doctrinally, it has been defined by *Hanafi*-centred *Al-Maturidiia* which channelled its development along the lines of theological and pragmatic flexibility and adaptability to a succession of major political expediencies. For this reason, compared with the Islamic heartland in the Middle East, Islam in Central Asia has not played the key role in the legitimisation of political authority of Central Asian rulers, who prioritised genealogy over *shari'a,* and it has only rarely provided an ideological framework for Central Asians' political mobilisation.

On the other side, the Central Asian Muslims' Eurasianism has accounted for considerable structural and cultural affinities, notwithstanding substantial differences between them and various peoples of other Eurasian polities, including Russia. Thus, in the political sphere they have shared the propensity for the extreme concentration of power at the centre, the merger of the ruling clan with the state, and the supremacy of personal relations between ruler and subject over any other relations defined by institutional, social or ethnonational affiliation. Their common Eurasianism also charted their state-building along the lines of polyethnic and polyconfessional empires with ill-defined borders which historically contrasted with state-formation process in Europe. In the economic sphere, Eurasianism has manifested itself in the persistence of the tribute–redistributory model between the centre and the periphery, the extreme power of the state and the relative weakness of both private landowners and cities. In the cultural sphere, Eurasianism has accounted for cultural, religious and ethnic diversity; the subordination of ethnicity to the state-defined and cultural and regional identity; the prevalence of spiritual and cultural rather than scriptural perceptions of religion; and the substantial cross-Eurasian mutual borrowings in the field of language, design, cuisine and beliefs.

It is not coincidental therefore that the formerly Genghizid imperial, and subsequently, Soviet Russia was able to exploit the common political and cultural Eurasian matrix of Central Asians and Russians in order to enhance her expansion and governance of the region. As it was shown in Part II, the trans-Eurasian political, economic and cultural commonalities explain the relative suitability in Central Asia of the Soviet system, at both the official and popular levels, and the continuing reluctance of their elites to deviate from it, despite their symbolic negation of Soviet-ness and their ethnonational sovereignisation. Of particular significance has been the persistence in all five Central Asian states of the Soviet model of state–Muslim relations which has entailed constitutionally enshrined secularism and the promotion of state-sponsored apolitical 'official' Islam, rebranded as 'traditional' Islam, which has been integrated into the nationalising discourse; the suppression of any other forms of 'unofficial' and 'untraditional' Islam; and the segregation of local Muslims from their co-religionists abroad. At the grassroots level, the reproduction of distinctive Central Asian Islam has been ensured by the relative autonomy from the state of family- , territory- and common interests-based communities.

However, future sustainability in Central Asia of the Eurasian cultural and ideational model has been increasingly challenged by the continuing socio-economic hardships and political repression within particular Central Asian republics, the inadequate knowledge of Islam in society, combined with the state's securitisation of 'untraditional' Islam, as well as the greater exposure of young Central Asian Muslims who aspire to rediscover their true Muslim-ness to online and social media Islamic messages which treat Central Asian

Islam as *bid'a*. These messages have especially resonated among male Uzbek and Tajik labour migrants in Russia and other non-Muslim majority countries, as well as Kazakhs and Kyrgyz within their respective republics whose Islamicised national identities were severely damaged in the course of their Soviet sedentarisation. In the longer run, the perpetuation of distinct Central Asian Islam will be determined by the ability of Central Asian political elites to ensure the viable economic, social and political development of their respective countries, to overcome ethnonational isolationism in favour of historically productive fully-fledged political and societal interaction across Central Asia and the wider Eurasia, and to substantially improve through the educational system young people's understanding of Islam and Central Asian Islamic tradition, in particular.

Bibliography

Abashin, S. (2015), *Sovetskii Kishlak: Mezhdu Kolonializmom and Medernizatsiei*, Moscow: Novoie Literaturnoie Obozrenie (in Russian).

Abdakimov, A. (2003), *Istoriia Kazakhstana (S Drevneishikh Vremen do Nashikh Dnei)*, Almaty: 'Kazakhstan'.

Abdullaev, I. (1997), 'Islam i Islamskii Faktor v Sovremennom Uzbekistane', *Tsentral'naiia Aziia* 6(12): 87–99.

Abdullayev, K. and Sh. Akbarzadeh (2002), *Historical Dictionary of Tajikistan*, Lanham, MD: Scarecrow Press.

Abduvahitov, A. (1993), 'Islamic Revivalism in Uzbekistan', in D. Eickelman (ed.), *Russia's Muslim Frontier*, Bloomington, IN: Indiana University Press, pp.79–100.

Abramson, D. M. and E. E. Karimov (2007), 'Sacred Sites, Profane Ideologies: Religious Pilgrimage and the Uzbek State', in J. Sahadeo and R. Zanca (eds), *Everyday Life in Central Asia: Past and Present*, Bloomington, IN: Indiana University Press.

Abil', E. (1997), *Etnogenez Kazakhov: Opyt Systemnogo Podkhoda*, Kustanay: n.p.

Abuseitova, M., Klashtornyi and N. Masanov (2001), *Istoriia Kazakhstana i Tsentral'noi Azii*, Almaty: Daik-Press.

Abylkhozhin, Zh. B., M. K. Kozybayev and M. B. Tatimov (1989), 'Kazakhstanskaia Tragediia', *Voprosy Istorii* 7: 58–81.

Ahmadi, M. (2013), 'Roditelei, Deti Kotorykh Posetili Namaz-Tarawih, Oshtrafovali', *RadioOzodi*, 23 July, available at: https://rus.ozodi.org/a/25053926.html, last accessed 24 August 2017.

Ahmedzhanov, G. A. (1995), *Rossiiskaia Imperiia v Tsentral'noi Azii*, Tashkent: FAN.

Aitpaeva, G. (ed.) (2013), *Sacred Sites of Southern Kyrgyzstan: Nature, Manas, Islam*, Bishkek: Aigine Cultural Research Center.

Akiner, S. (1983), *Islamic Peoples of the Soviet Union*, London: Kegan Paul.

Al-Janabi, M. M. (2000), *Al-Ghazali: Mystical Theologico-Philosophical Synthesis*, New York: Edwin Mellen.

Alexander, P. (ed.) (1951), *The Complete Works of Shakespeare*, London and Glasgow: Collins.

Algar, H. (1998), *Sufism: Principles and Practice*, Chandigarh: Islamic Publications International.

Allen, C. and J. Nielsen (2002), Summary Report on Islamophobia in the EU after 11 September 2001, Vienna: EUMC.

Allison, R. and L. Jonson (eds) (2001), *Central Asia Security: The New International Context*, Washington, DC: Royal Institute of International Affairs.

Allworth, E. (ed.) (1994), *Central Asia: One Hundred Thirty Years of Russian Dominance: A Historical Overview*, Durham, NC: Duke University Press.

Alsabekov, M. Kh. (2009), 'Iz Istorii Rasprostraneniia Islama v Kazakhstane', in A. Derbisali (ed.), *Madhhab Velikogo Imama Abu Khanifa i Sovremennost'*, Almaty: Atamura.

Alsambekov, M. Kh. (2005), *Znameniia dlia Liudei Ubezhdennykh*, Almaty: Komplex.

Amrekulov, N. (2000), 'Dzhuzy v Sotsial'no-Politicheskoi Zhizni Kazakhstana', *Central Asia and the Caucasus*, Sweden, available at: https://www.ca-c.org/journal/2000/journal_rus/cac09_2000/16.Amrek.shtml, last accessed 23 November 2017.

Arapov, D. (ed.) (2001), *Islam v Rossiiskoi Imperii (Zakonodatel'nye Akty, Opisaniia, Statistika)*, Moscow: IVRAN.

Arapov, D. (ed.) (2010), *Islam i Sovetskoe Gosudarstvo (1917–1936). Sbornik Dokumentov*, vol. 2, Moscow: Mardzhani.

Arapov, D. (ed.) (2011), *Islam i Sovetskoe Gosudarstvo (1944–1991). Sbornik Dokumentov*, vol. 3, Moscow: Mardzhani.

Artykbaev, Zh. (2001), *Materialy k Istorii Praviashchego Doma Kazakhov*, Almaty: n.p.

Asadulin, F. (2015), *Mir Islama v Obshchestvenno-Kul'turnom Prostranstve Moskvy*, Moscow: IVRAN.

Asankanov, A. (1996), 'Ethnic Conflict in the Osh Region in Summer 1990: Reasons and Lessons', in K. Rupesinghe and V. Tishkov (eds), *Ethnicity and Power in the Contemporary World*, Paris: United Nations University, pp. 116–24.

Atanova, S. (2017), 'Tsentral'naia Aziia – Konstruirovanie Obraza i Granits v Kolonial'nom Diskurse', *CAAN*, 8 August, available at: http://caa-network.org/archives/9860, last accessed 12 April 2018.

Babadzhanov, B. (2004), 'Russian Colonial Power in Central Asia as Seen by Local Muslim Intellectuals', in B. Eschment and H. Harder (eds), *Looking at the Colonizer: Cross-Cultural Perception in Central Asia and the Caucasus, Bengal, and Related Areas*, Würzburg: Ergon, pp.80–90.

Babadzhanov, B. (2006), 'Husainiia', in S. M. Prozorov (ed.), *Islam na Territorii Byvshei Rossiiskoi Imperii*, vol. 1, Moscow: Voctochnaia Literatura, pp. 431–2.

Babadzhanov, B. (2010), *Kokandskoe Khanstvo: Vlast', Politika i Religiia*, Tokyo-Tashkent: TIAS.

Bakhti, A. (2004), *Shumery, Skify, Kazakhi*, Almaty: n.p.

Bakiev, M. I. (2000), 'Istoriia Prosvetitel'skogo Dvizheniia i Svobodomysliia v Srednei Azii: konets XIX-nachalo XX vekov', PhD résumé, Dushanbe, available at: http://www.dissercat.com/content/istoriya-prosvetitelnogo-dvizheniya-i-svobodomysliya-v-srednei-azii-konets-khikh-nachalo-khk, last accessed 11 January 2017.

Bali, W. A. (2004), *Sword against Black Magic & Evil Magicians*, London: Al-Firdous.

Bariev, R. (2005), *Volzhskie Bulgary: Istoriia i Kul'tura*, St Petersburg: Agat.

Barth, F. (1993), *Balinese Worlds*, Chicago, IL: University of Chicago Press.

Bartol'd, V. V. (1965), 'Tuzemets o Russkom Zavoevanii', *Sochineniia*, vol. 2, Moscow: Nauka, pp. 333–59.

Bartol'd, V. V. (1965), 'Teokraticheskaia Idea i Svetskaia Vlast' v Musul'manskom Gosudarstve', *Sochineniia*, vol. 3, Moscow: Nauka, pp. 262–6.

Basilov, V. (1970), *Kul't Sviatykh v Islame*, Moscow: Mysl'.

Basilov, V. (1991), *Islamizirovannoe Shamanstvo Narodov Srednei Azii i Kazakhstana*, Moscow: IEA RAN.

Bassin, M. (1999), *Imperial Visions: Nationalist Imagination and Geographical Expansion in the Russian Far East, 1840–1865*, Cambridge: Cambridge University Press.

Bassin, M. (2016), *The Gumilev Mystique: Biopolitics, Eurasianism and the Construction of Community in Modern Russia*, Ithaca, NY: Cornell University Press.

Bassin, M., S. Glebov and M. Laruelle (eds) (2015), *Between Europe and Asia: The Origins, Theories and Legacies of Russian Eurasianism*, Pittsburgh, PA: University of Pittsburgh Press.

Beissembayev, S. (2016), 'Religious Extremism in Kazakhstan: from Criminal Networks to Jihad', *The Central Asia Fellowship Papers*, vol. 15, February, Washington, DC: George Washington University.

Beller-Hann, I. (2001), 'Rivalry and Solidarity among Uyghur Healers in Kazakhstan', *Inner Asia* 3: 73–98.

Benn, Ch. (2002), *China's Golden Age: Everyday Life in the Tang Dynasty*, Oxford: Oxford University Press.

Bennigsen, A. and S. E. Wimbush (1985), *Mystics and Commissars: Sufism in the Soviet Union*, London: Hurst.

Bennigsen, A. and S. E. Wimbush (1986), *Muslims of the Soviet Empire*, London: Hurst.

Berger, P. L. (ed.) (1999), *The Desecularization of the World: Resurgent Religion and World Politics*, Washington, DC: Ethics and Public Politics.

Biran, M. (2005), *The Empire of the Qara Khitai in Eurasian History: Between China and the Islamic World*, Cambridge: Cambridge University Press.

Blok, A. (1918), *Dvenadtsat.' Skify*, St Petersburg: n.p.

Bobokhonov, R. S. (2015), *Istoriia Grazhdanskoi Voiny v Tadzhikistane (1992–1997)*, vol. 2, available at: http://www.centrasia.ru/newsA.php?st=1438637640, last accessed 14 August 2017.

Bohr, A. (2016), *Turkmenistan: Power, Politics and Petro-Authoritarianism*, London: Chatham House.

Bohr, A. and G. Price (2015), *Regional Implications of Afghanistan's Transitions: Pakistan, Kyrgyzstan and Tajikistan*, London: Chatham House.

Bregel, Y. E. (2003), *Historical Atlas of Central Asia*, Leiden: Brill.

Bromley, Yu. V. (2008), *Ocherki Teorii Etnosa*, Moscow: LKU.

Broxup, M. (1983), 'The Basmachi', *Central Asian Survey*, 2(1): 57–81.

Brower, D. (2003), *Turkestan and the Fate of the Russian Empire*, London: Routledge.

Bugai, N. (2004), 'Deportatsiia Narodov', *Voina i Obshchestvo, 1941–1945*, vol. 2, Moscow: Nauka, available at: http://scepsis.net/library/id_1237.html, last accessed 21 February 2017.

Bukhari-zade, N. (2015), '1995–2015: Ego Vysotchestvo Aga Khan IV i ego Tadjikskie

Edinovertsy', *FerganaNews*, 26 May, available at: http://www.fergananews.com/articles/8559, last accessed 22 August 2017.

Buldakov, A., S. Shumov and A. Andreev (2003), *Istoriia Srednei Azii*, Moscow: Evrolints-Russkaia Panorama.

Burchuladze, N. (2015), 'The ISIS "Skype Warriors" of Pankisi Gorge', *Georgian Journal*, 25 June–1 July, available at: http://www.georgianjournal.ge/military/30808-the-isis-skype-warriors-of-pankisi-gorge.html, last accessed 6 July 2016.

Burova, E. and A. Kosichenko (2013), *Aktual'nye Problemy Razvtiia Religioznoi Situatsii v Kazakhstane*, Almaty: IPPR.

Burton, A. (1997), *The Bukharans: A Dynastic, Diplomatic and Commercial History, 1550–1702*, Richmond: Curzon.

Casanova, J. (1994), *Public Religions in the Modern World*, Chicago, IL: University of Chicago Press.

Ceraci, R. P. (2008), *Window on the East: National and Imperial Identities in Late Tsarist Russia*, Ithaca, NY: Cornell University Press.

Choueiri, Y. M. (2010), *Islamic Fundamentalism: The Story of Islamist Movements*, 3rd edn, London: Continuum.

Clement, V. (2007), 'Alphabet Changes in Turkmenistan, 1904–2004', in J. Sahadeo and R. Zanca (eds), *Everyday Life in Central Asia: Past and Present*, Bloomington, IN: Indiana University Press, pp. 266–80.

Collins, K. (2006), *Clan Politics and Regime Transition in Central Asia*, Cambridge: Cambridge University Press.

Cooley, A. and J. Heathershaw (2017), *Dictators without Borders: Power and Money in Central Asia*, New Haven, CT: Yale University Press.

Cornell, S. and N. Swanström (2006), 'The Eurasian Drug Trade: A Challenge to Regional Security', *Problems of Post-Communism* 53(4): 10–28.

Crews, R. D. (2006), *For Prophet and Tsar: Islam and Empire in Russia and Central Asia*, Cambridge, MA: Harvard University Press.

Critchlow, J. (1991), *Nationalism in Uzbekistan: A Soviet Republic Road to Sovereignty*, Boulder, CO: Westview Press.

Cummings, S. N. (2005), *Kazakhstan: Power and the Elite*, London: I. B.Tauris.

Cummings, S. N. (2012), *Understanding Central Asia: Politics and Contested Transformations*, London: Routledge.

Cummings, S. N. and R. Hinnebusch (2017), 'Central Asia and the Middle East are still Haunted by their Colonial Past', *Muftah*, 20 April 2016, available at: https://muftah.org/central-asia-and-the-middle-east-are-still-haunted-by-their-colonial-pasts/#.Wd0HdtozWUk, last accessed 9 October 2017.

Curanovic, A. (2012), *The Religious Factor in Russia's Foreign Policy*, London: Routledge.

d'Encausse, H. C. (2009), *Islam and the Russian Empire: Reform and Revolution in Central Asia*, London: I. B.Tauris.

Daftary, F. (1992), *The Ismailis, their History and Doctrines*, Cambridge: Cambridge University Press.

Dagiev, D. (2014), *Regime Transition in Central Asia: Stateness, Nationalism and Political Change in Tajikistan and Uzbekistan*, London: Routledge.

Daniiarov, K. (2004), *O Novoi Istorii Kazakhstana*, Almaty: n.p.

Dave, B. (2007), *Kazakhstan: Ethnicity, Language and Power*, London: Routledge.

De la Vaissiere, E. (2004), 'Sogdian Trade', *Encyclopaedia Iranica*, available at: http://www.iranicaonline.org/articles/sogdian-trade, last accessed 13 June 2016.

Demidov, S. M. (1978), *Sufizm v Turkmenii: Evolutsiia i Perezhitki*, Ashgabat: Ylym.

Demidov, S. M. (1990), *Istoriia Religioznykh Verovanii Narodov Turkmenistana*, Ashgabat: Ylym.

Devonshire-Ellis, Ch. (2015), *The Great Eurasian Game & the String of Pearls*, Hong Kong: Asia Briefing.

DeWeese, D. (1994), *Islamization and Native Religion in the Golden Horde: Baba Tukles and Conversion to Islam in Historical and Epic Tradition*, University Park, PA: Pennsylvania State University Press.

DeWeese, D. (2002), 'Islam and the Legacy of Sovietology: A Review Essay on Yaacov Ro'i's Islam in the Soviet Union', *Journal of Islamic Studies* 13(3): 298–330.

DeWeese, D. (2012), *Studies of Sufism in Central Asia*, Farnham: Ashgate.

Di Cosmo, N. (ed.) (2009), *The Cambridge History of Inner Asia: The Chinggisid Age*, Cambridge: Cambridge University Press.

Diushenbieyev, S. U. (2011), 'Islam v Sovremennom Kyrgyzstane: Sostoianie i Problemy', *Religovedenie* 3: 107–26, available at: http://relig-articles.livejournal.com/33045.html, last accessed 8 June 2017.

Dmitrieva, L. A., D. S. Likhacheva and O. V.Tvorogova (1985), *Slovo o Polku Igoreve*, 3rd edn, Leningrad: Sovetskii Pisatel'.

Dorr, S. (2017), 'The Transregional Impact of the Arab Spring in Kazakhstan, 2005–2015', paper presented at the joint ESCAS–CESS conference, Bishkek: AUCA, 29 June–2 July 2017.

Dzhonov, P. (2010) 'Ekconomika Tadzhikistana- Uspekhi i Tendentsii', 18 March 2010, *Tsentral'naiia Aziia*, available at: http://www.centrasia.ru/newsA.php?st=1268894400, last accessed 17 August 2017.

Edgar, A. L. (2004), *Tribal Nation: The Making of Soviet Turkmenistan*, Princeton, NJ: Princeton University Press.

Egorov, E. N. (2014), 'Bor'ba s Religioznym Exstremizmom v Tadzhikistane: Zakonodatel'nyi Uroven', *Aktual'nye Voprosy Obshchestvennykh Nauk: Sotsiologiia, Filosofiia, Istoriia* 35: 21–44.

Eickelman, D. (1993), 'The Other "Orientalist" Crisis', in D. Eickelman (ed.), *Russia's Muslim Frontiers: New Directions in Cross-Cultural Analysis*, Bloomington, IN: Indiana University Press.

Epkenhans, T. (2010), 'Muslims without Learning, Clergy without Faith: Institutions of Islamic Learning in the Republic of Tajikistan', in M. Kemper, R. Motika and S. Reichmuth (eds), *Islamic Education in the Soviet Union and its Successor States*, London: Routledge, pp. 313–48.

Epkenhans, T. (2016), *The Origins of the Civil War in Tajikistan*, Lanham, MD: Rowman & Littlefield.

Erasov, B. S. (1991), *Kul'tura, Religiia i Tsivilizatsiia na Vostoke. Otcherki Obshchei Teorii*, Moscow: Nauka.

Erturk, K. A. (ed.) (1999), *Rethinking Central Asia: Non-Eurocentric Studies in History, Social Structure and Identity*, Reading: Ithaca Press.

Erturk, K. A. (1999), 'Introduction', in K. A. Erturk (ed.), *Rethinking Central Asia: Non-Eurocentric Studies in History, Social Structure and Identity*, Reading: Ithaca Press, pp. 1–10.

Eshenkulova, K. (2017), 'The Islamization of Kyrgyz Society and the Women's Jama'at', paper presented at the Joint ESCAS-CESS Conference, Bishkek, 29 June–2 July 2017.

Espagne, M., S. Gorshenina, F. Grenet, Sh. Mustafayev and C. Rapin (eds) (2016), *Asie centrale: Transferts culturels le long de la Route de la soie*, Paris: Vendermiaire.

Etnicheskii Atlas Uzbekistana (2002), Tashkent: n.p.

Fierman, W. (ed.) (1991), *Soviet Central Asia: The Failed Transformation*, New York: Westview.

Fierman, W. (1998), 'Language and Identity in Kazakhstan: Formulations in Policy Documents, 1987–1997', *Communist and Post-Communist Studies* XXX(2): 1771–86.

'Foreign Fighters in Iraq and Syria' (2015), *Radio Free Europe*, available at: http://www.rferl.org/contentinfographics/foreign-fighters-syria-iraq-is-isis-isil-infographic/26584940.html, last accessed 16 August 2016.

Frank, A. G. (1999), 'ReOrient: From Centrality of Central Asia to China's Middle Kingdom', in K. A. Erturk (ed.), *Rethinking Central Asia: Non-Eurocentric Studies in History, Social Structure and Identity*, Reading: Ithaca Press, pp. 11–38.

Frye, R. N. (1975), 'The Sāmānids', in R. N. Frye (ed.), *The Cambridge History of Iran, vol. 4: From the Arab Invasion to the Saljuqs*, Cambridge: Cambridge University Press. pp. 136–61.

Geiss, P. G. (2003), *Pre-Tsarist and Tsarist Central Asia: Communal Commitment and Political Order in Change*, London: Routledge.

Golden, P. B. (2011), *Central Asia in World History*, Oxford: Oxford University Press.

Gorshenina, S. (2012), *Asie centrale: l'invention des frontières et l'héritage russo-soviétique*, Paris: CNRS.

Gorshenina, S. (2014), *L'invention de l'Asie central: Histoire du concept de la Tartarie à l'Eurasie*, Paris: Librarie Droz.

Governments Move to Thwart 'Arab Spring' in Central Asia, *Eurasianet*, 28 April 2011, available at: http://www.eurasianet.org/node/63386, last accessed 7 June 2016.

Grousset, R. [1952] (1970), *The Empire of the Steppe: A History of Central Asia*, trans. from French Naomi Walford, New Brunswick, NJ: Rutgers University Press.

Gumilev, L. (1990), *Geografiia Etnosa v Istoricheskii Period*, Leningrad: Nauka.

Hays, J. (2008), 'Drug Use in Turkmenistan: Facts and Details', available at: http://factsanddetails.com/central-asia/Turkmenistan/sub8_7b/entry-4821.html, last accessed 11 September 2017.

'Hearing before the Commission on Security and Cooperation in Europe', 10 June 2015, available at: http://ceriainitiative.org/likepomeps/wp-content/uploads/2015/09/Wanted-Foreign-Fighters-The-Escalating-Threat-of-ISIL-in-Asia.pdf, last accessed 5 July 2016.

Heathershaw, J. (2007), 'The Tulip Fades: "Revolution" and Repercussions in Kyrgyzstan', *Perspective* 17(2): 2–6.

Heathershaw, J. (2009), *Post-Conflict Tajikistan: The Politics of Peacebuilding and the Emergence of Legitimate Order*, London: Routledge.

Heathershaw, J. and D. Montgomery (2014), *The Myth of Post-Soviet Muslim Radicalization in the Central Asian Republics*, London: Chatham House.

Higgins, A. (2004), 'Kharijites, Khawarij', in R. C. Martin (ed.), *Encyclopaedia of Islam and the Muslim World*, vol. 1, London: Macmillan.

Hinnebusch, R. and S. Cumming (2011), *Sovereignty after Empire: Comparing the Middle East and Central Asia*, Edinburgh: Edinburgh University Press.

Hiro, D. (1994), *Between Marx and Muhammad*, London: HarperCollins.

Hopkirk, P. (1992), *The Great Game: The Struggle for Empire in Central Asia*, New York: Kodansha International.

Hopkirk, P. (1994), *On Secret Service East of Constantinople: The Great Game and the Great War*, Oxford: Oxford University Press.

Hosking, G. (1992), *A History of the USSR: 1917–1991*, London: HarperCollins.

Hunter, Sh. T. (2000), 'Iran, Central Asia and the Opening of the Islamic Iron Curtain', in R. Sagdeev and S. Eisenhower (eds), *Islam and Central Asia: An Enduring Legacy or an Evolving Threat?* Washington, DC: Center for Political and Strategic Studies, pp. 171–91.

Hunsberger, A. C. (2003), *Nasir Khusraw, the Ruby of Badakhshan: A Portrait of the Persian Poet, Traveller and Philosopher*, London: I. B. Tauris.

Isaacs, R. (2011), *Party System Formation in Kazakhstan*, London: Routledge.

ISIS Release, 'Shocking New Video of Child Soldiers from Kazakhstan' (2014), Mail Online, available at: http://www.dailymail.co.uk/news/article-2845531/ISIS-release-shocking-new-video-child-soldiers-Kazakhstan-trained-AK47s.html, last accessed 18 August 2016.

Jackson, P. (2005), 'The Mongols and the Faith of the Conquered', in R. Amitai and M. Biran (eds), *Mongols, Turks and Others: Eurasian Nomads and the Sedentary World*, Leiden: Brill, pp. 245–78.

Jonson, L. (2006), *Tajikistan in the New Central Asia*, London: I. B. Tauris.

Kalishevskii, M. (2011), '20 Let GKChP: Sredneaziatskii Rakurs', *FerghanaNews*, 19 August, available at: http://www.fergananews.com/articles/7049, last accessed 25 April 2017.

Kalishevskii, M. (2014), 'Turkmenia: Islam kak Prilozhenie k 'Bashizmu', *Fergana.Ru*, 10

February, available at: http://www.ferganannews.com/articles/8047, (last accessed 8 September 2017.

Kalligulaev, M. (2005), *Doroga k Smerti Bol'she, chem Smert'*, Wolverhampton: Black Quadrat.

Kalyzhnova, Y. (2008), *Economies of the Caspian Oil and Gas Wealth: Companies, Governments, Policies*, Basingstoke: Palgrave Macmillan.

Kamp, M. (2006), *The New Woman in Uzbekistan: Islam, Modernity, and Unveiling Under Communism*, Seattle, WA: University of Washington Press.

Kandiyoti, D. and N. Azimova (2004), 'The Communal and the Sacred: Women's Worlds of Ritual in Uzbekistan', *Journal of the Royal Anthropological Institute* 10: 327–49.

Kappeler, A. (2001), *The Russian Empire: A Multi-Ethnic History*, London: Routledge.

Karagiannis, E. (2010), *Political Islam in Central Asia: The Challenge of Hizb ut-Tahrir*, London: Routledge.

Karin, E. (2016), *The Soldiers of the Caliphate: The Anatomy of a Terrorist Group*, Astana: KazISS.

Kavalski, E. (2012), *Central Asia and the Rise of Normative Power: Contextualizing the Security Governance of the European Union, China and India*, London: Bloomsbury.

Keller, Sh. (2001), *To Moscow, Not Mecca: The Soviet Campaign Against Islam in Central Asia, 1917–1941*, London: Praeger.

Kemper, M., R. Motika and S. Reichmuth (eds) (2010), *Islamic Education in the Soviet Union and its Successor States*, London: Routledge.

Kennedy, H. (2015), *The Prophet and the Age of the Caliphates*, 3rd edn, London: Routledge.

Khalfin, N. A. (1965), *Prisoedinenie Srednei Azii k Rossii*, Moscow: Nauka.

Khalid, A. (1998), *The Politics of Muslim Cultural Reform: Jadidism in Central Asia*, Berkeley: University of California Press.

Khalid, A. (2007), *Islam after Communism: Religion and Politics in Central Asia*, Berkeley: University of California Press.

Khamidov, A. (2013), 'The Lessons of the "Nookat Events": Central Government, Local Officials and Religious Protests in Kyrgyzstan', *Central Asian Survey* 32(2): 148–60.

Khidaiatov, G. A. (1969), *Rossiia i Tsentral'naia Aziia vo vtoroi polovine XIX veka*, Tashkent: TashGU.

Khoroshkevich, A. L. (1980), *Russkoe Gosudarstvo v Sisteme Mezhdunarodnykh Otnoshenii kontsa 15-nachala 16 vekov*, Moscow: Nauka.

Al-Khudayri A. (2012), *The Ruqya Handbook*, Prophetic Medicine Publication, available at: www.Prophetic-Medicine.com, last accessed 1 November 2017.

Khudiakov, M. G. (1996), 'Ocherki po Istorii Kazanskogo Khanstva', in I. B. Muslimov (ed.), *Na Styke Kontinentov i Tsivilizatsii*, Moscow: Insan, pp.531–58.

Knight, N. (2000), 'On Orientalism: A Response to Adeeb Khalid', *Kritika. Explorations in Russian and Eurasian History* 1(4): 701–15.

Konstitutsiia SSSR (1977), Moscow: Politizdat.

Koychuev, T., V. Mokrynin and V. Ploskikh (1999), *Kyrgyzy i ikh Predki*, Bishkek: Raritet Info.

Kreindler, I. T. (1995), 'Soviet Muslims: Gains and Losses as a Result of Soviet Language Planning', in Y. Ro'i (ed.), *Muslim Eurasia: Conflicting Legacies*, London: Frank Cass, pp. 187–204.

Krivets, E. A. (1998), 'Spetsifika Religioznoi Traditsii v Kazakhstane i Kyrgyzstane', in Malashenko, A, (ed.), *Islam v SNG,* Moscow: IVRAN, pp.139–47.

Krivets, E. A. (1999), *Islam v Tsentral'noi Azii*, Moscow: Lenom.

Krivosheev, G. F. (ed.) (2001), *Rossiia i SSSR v Voinakh XX veka: Statisticheskoe Issledovanie*, Moscow: Olma-Press.

Kugelgen, A. von (2004), *Legitimzatsiia Sredneaziatskoi Dinastii Mangytov v Proizvedeniiakh ikh Istorikov (XVIII–XIX vv.)*, Almaty: Dayk-Press.

Kuz'min, A. I. (1998), *Prichiny i Uroki Grazhdanskoi Voiny / Postsovetskaia Tsentral'naia Aziia: Poteri i Obreteniia*, Moscow: Vostochnaia Literatura.

Kuz'mina, E. M. (2007), *Geopolitika Tsentral'noi Azii*, Moscow: Nauka.

Lama Sharif (2012), 'Religioznaia Gramotnost'-Zalog Bezopasnosti Obshchestva', *Kazakhstanskaia Pravda*, 16 November.

Landa, R. (1995), *Islam v Istorii Rossii*, Moscow: RAN.

Landa, R. (2011), *Rossiia i Mir Rossiiskogo Islama*, Moscow: Vostochnaia Literatura.

Lapenko, M. V. (2014), 'The Construction of Central Asia as Region: Internal and External Aspects', *Aktual'nye Problemy Sovremennykh Mezhdunarodnykh Otnoshenii* 3: 1–8.

Laruelle, M. (2008), *Russian Eurasianism: An Ideology of Empire*, Baltimore, MD: Johns Hopkins University Press.

Laruelle, M. (2015), 'US New Silk Road', *Eurasian Geography and Economics* 56(4): 360–75.

Laruelle, M. (ed.) (2016), *Kazakhstan in the Making: Legitimacy, Symbols and Social Change*, Lanham, MD: Rowman & Littlefield.

Laruelle, M. (ed.) (2017), *Constructing the Uzbek State: Narratives of post-Soviet Years*, Lanham, MD: Rowman & Littlefield.

Letov, V. Yu. (2007), 'Istoricheskaia Rol' Pogranichnykh Voisk Rossii v Obespechenii Yuzhnykh Rubezhei SNG', *Proekty Sotrudnichestva i Integratsii dlia Tsentral'noi Azii: Sravnitel'nyi Analiz. Vozmozhnosti i Perspektivy*, Bishkek: n.p.

Lieven, D. (2002), *Empire: The Russian Empire and its Rivals*, New Haven, CT: Yale University Press.

Lindquist, G. (2001), 'Wizards, Gurus, and Energy-Information Fields: Wielding Legitimacy in Contemporary Russian Healing', *Anthropology of East Europe Review* 19: 16–28.

Louw, M. E. (2008), *Everyday Islam in post-Soviet Central Asia*, London: Routledge.

Luong, P. (2002), *Institutional Change and Political Continuity in post-Soviet Central Asia: Power, Perceptions and Pacts*, Cambridge: Cambridge University Press.

Luong, P. and E. Weinthal (2010), *Oil is not a Curse*, Cambridge: Cambridge University Press.

Malashenko, A. (1996), *Musul'manskii Mir SNG*, Moscow: IVRAN.

Malashenko, A. (ed.) (1998), *Islam v SNG*, Moscow: IVRAN.

Malashenko, A. (2008), *Islam in Central Asia*, Reading: Ithaca Press.

Malashenko, A. and A. Niyazi (2014), *Prezidentskie Vybory v Tadzhikistane 2013 g.: Itogi i Perspektivy*, Moscow: Carnegie Center.

Malashenko, A. and A. Starostin (2015), *Islam na Sovremennom Urale*, Moscow: Carnegie Center.

Manz, B. F. (1989), *The Rise and Rule of Tamerlane*, Cambridge: Cambridge University Press.

Marat, E. (2010), *The Military and the State in Central Asia: From Red Army to Independence*, London: Routledge.

Markov, G. E. (2010), *Kochevniki Azii: Struktura Khoziaistva i Obshchestvennoi Organizatsii*, Moscow: KRASAND.

Martin, R. C., M. R. Woodward and D. S. Atmaja (1997), *Defenders of Reason in Islam: Mu'atazilizm from Medieval School to Modern Symbol*, London: Oneworld.

Martin, T. (2001), *The Affirmative Action Empire: Nations and Nationalism in the Soviet Union 1923–1939*, Ithaca, NY: Cornell University Press.

Masanov, N. (1995) *Kochevaia Tsivilizatsiia Kazakhov*, Moscow: Gorizont.

Masanov, N. (2007), 'Mifologizatsiia Problem Etnogeneza Kazakhskogo Naroda i Kazakhskoi Nomadnoi Kul'tury', in N. Masanov, Zh. Abylkhozhin and I. Erofeeva (eds), *Nauchnoe Znanie i Mifotvorchestvo v Sovremennoi Istoriografii Kazakhstana*, Almaty: Dayk-Press, pp. 52–132.

Masov, R. (1991), *Istoriia Topornogo Razdeleniia*, Dushanbe: Irfon

Masud, M. (ed.) (2002), *Travellers in Faith: Studies of the Tablighi Jama'at as a Transnational Islamic Movement for Faith Renewal*, Leiden: Brill.

Mati, H. (2012), 'Tatarskaia Kargala in Russia's Eastern Policies', in U. Tomohiko (ed.), *Asiatic Russia: Imperial Power in Regional and International Contexts*, London: Routledge, pp. 32–80.

Mazhitova, E. (2017), 'Kuda Idet Tsentral'naia Aziia', *Kazakhstan 2.0*, 29 March, available at: http://kz.expert/archives/2319, last accessed 3 May 2017.

Megoran, N. (2012), *Averting Violence in Kyrgyzstan: Understanding and Responding to Nationalism*, London: Chatham House.

Melvin, N. (2000), *Transition to Authoritarianism on the Silk Road*, Amsterdam: Harwood Academic.

Meyer, J. H. (2014), *Turks across Empires: Marketing Muslim Identity in the Russian–Ottoman Borderlands, 1856–1914*, Oxford: Oxford University Press.

Meyer, M. M. (ed.) (2005), *Sredniaia Aziia: Andizhanskii Stsenarii*, Moscow: Evropa.

Miftakhov, Z. Z. (1998), *Kurs Lektsii po Istorii Tatarskogo Naroda*, Kazan: Dom Pechati.

Mohapatra, N. (2007), 'Political and Security Challenges in Central Asia: The Drug Trafficking Dimension', *International Studies* 44(2): 157–74.

Molberly, F. J. (1987), *Operations in Persia 1914–1919*, London: HMSO.

Montgomery, D. W. (2007), 'The Transmission of Religious and Cultural Knowledge and Potentiality in Practice: An Anthropology of Social Navigation in the Kyrgyz Republic', PhD dissertation, Boston University.

Montgomery, D. W. (2016), *Practicing Islam: Knowledge, Experience and Social Navigation in Kyrgyzstan*, Pittsburgh, PA: University of Pittsburgh Press.

Morrison, A. (2008), *Russian Rule in Samarkand, 1868–1910: A Comparison with British India*, Oxford: Oxford University Press.

Muminov, A. (2007), 'Fundamentalist Challenges to Local Islamic Traditions in Soviet and Post-Soviet Central Asia', in T. Uyama (ed.), *Empire, Islam and Politics in Central Eurasia*, Supporo: Slavic Research Center, pp. 254–6.

Muminov, A., U. Gafurov and R. Shigabdinov (2010), 'Islamic Education in Soviet and post-Soviet Uzbekistan', in M. Kemper, R. Motika and S. Reichmuth (eds), *Islamic Education in the Soviet Union and its Successor States*, London: Routledge, pp. 223–80.

Muslimov, I. B. (ed.) (1996), *Na Styke Kontitentov i Tsivilisatsii*, Moscow: Insan.

Nalivkin, V. P. (1886), *Kratkaia Istoriia Kokandskogo Khanstva*, Kazan: TIU.

Nasritdinov, E. (2017), 'Religion, Peace-building, and Education: The Case of Kyrgyzstan's Madrasas', paper presented at the Joint ESCAS-CESS Conference, 29 June–2 July 2017, Bishkek: AUCA.

Natsional'nyi Sostav Naseleniia SSSR (po Dannym Vsesoyuznoi Perepisi Naseleniia 1989 goda) (1991), Moscow: Politizdat.

Naumkin, V. V. (2005), *Radical Islam in Central Asia: Between Pen and Rifle*, Lanham, MD: Rowman & Littlefield.

Northrop, D. (2004), *Veiled Empire: Gender and Power in Stalinist Asia*, Ithaca, NY: Cornell University Press.

Nourse, J. W. (1996), 'The Voice of the Winds versus the Masters of Cure: Contested Notions of Spirit Possession among the Lauje of Sulawesi', *Journal of the Royal Anthropological Institute* (N.S.) 2: 425–42.

Novikov, M. P. (1985), *Soyuz Voinstvuiushikh Bezbozhnikov*, Moscow: Politizdat.

Novikov, V. I. (ed.) (1998), *Russkaiia Literatura XI–XVII vv.*, Moscow: Olimp.

'Number of Fighters per Capita', *Radio Liberty*, 6 July 2016, available at: http://www.rferl.org/contentinfographics/foreign-fighters-syria-iraq-is-isis-isil-infographic/26584940.html, last accessed 6 July 2016.

Nurmanova, A. Sh. and A. K. Izbairov (2010), 'Islamic Education in Soviet and post-Soviet Kazakhstan', in M. Kemper, R. Motika and S. Reichmuth (eds), *Islamic Education in the Soviet Union and its Successor States*, London: Routledge.

Nurtazina, N. (2000), *Islam v Istorii Srenevekovogo Kazakhstana*, Almaty: Farab.

Nurulla-Khodzhaeva, N. (2015), Interview with Professor Nargis Nurulla-Khodzhaeva, Moscow, 2 September 2015.

Nurulla-Khodzhaeva, N. (2016), *Odin iz Fragmentov Istorii Znanii: Dom Mudrosti Abbasidov i o Chernilakh v Reke Tigr*, available at: http://www.mgl.ru/www/library/177/The_Abbasids.html , last accessed 13 June 2016.

Nuryev, A. (2011), 'Islamskie Instituty Sovremennogo Turkmeistana', *IslamSNG*, 10

October, available at: http://www.islamsng.com/tkm/pastfuture/2990, last accessed 7 September 2017.

Nysanbai-uly, R. (2000), *Islam- Istinnaia Religiia Allaha*, Almaty: Rauan.

'Ob Itogakh' (1991), 'Ob Itogakh Referenduma SSSR on 17 March 1991, *Izvestiia*, 27 March.

Obrazovanie i Razvitie SSSR kak Soiuznogo Gosudarstva. Sbornik Zakonodatel'nykh i Drugikh Normativnykh Aktov (1977), Moscow: Politizdat.

Olcott, M. ([1986] 1995), *The Kazakhs*, Stanford, CA: Hoover Institution Press.

Olcott, M. (2002), *Kazakhstan: Unfulfilled Promise*, Washington, DC: Carnegie Endowment.

Olcott, M. (2012), *In the Whirlwind of Jihad*, Washington, DC: Carnegie Endowment.

Olcott, M. and N. Udalova (2000), 'Drug Trafficking on the Great Silk Road: The Security Environment in Central Asia', Washington, DC: Carnegie Endowment Working Papers, vol. 11.

Olimova, S. (2000), 'Islam in the Tajik Conflict', in R. Sagdeev and S. Eisenhower (eds), *Islam and Central Asia*, Washington, DC: Center for Political and Strategic Studies.

Omarov, E. (1997), 'Atilla i Imperiia Evropeiskikh Gunnov', *Vestnik Universiteta* 'Kaynar' 3: 1–15.

Omelicheva, M. (2010), *Counterterrorism Policies in Central Asia*, London: Routledge.

Oparin, D. (2017), 'Migration and Contemporary Muslim Space in Moscow: Contextualizing North Caucasian Loud Dhikr and the Religious Practices of Central Asian Folk Mullas', *Contemporary Islam* 11: 61–80.

Orynbekov, M. S. (2005), *Genezis Religioznosti v Kazakhstane*, Almaty: Daik-Press.

Østbø, J. (2016), *The New Third Rome: Readings of a Russian Nationalist Myth*, Stuttgart: Ibidem.

Ostrowski, W. (2011), *Politics of Oil in Kazakhstan*, London: Routledge.

Overland, I. (ed.) (2011), *Caspian Energy Politics: Azerbaijan, Kazakhstan and Turkmenistan*, London: Routledge.

Peyrouse, S. (2012), 'Drug Trafficking in Central Asia: A Poorly Considered Fight?' *PONARS Eurasia Policy Memo*, vol. 128.

Peyrouse, S. (2012), *Turkmenistan: Strategies of Power, Dilemmas of Development*, Armonk, NY: M. E.Sharpe.

Peyrouse, S. and G. Raballand (2015), 'The New Silk Road Initiative's Questionable Economic Rationality', *Eurasian Geography and Economics* 56(4): 405–20.

Pierce, R. N. (1960), *Russian Central Asia, 1867–1917: A Study in Colonial Rule*, Berkeley: University of California Press.

Ploskikh, B. M. (ed.) (1984), *Istoriia Kirgizskoi SSR*, vol. 1, Frunze: Kyrgyzstan.

Popov, D. (2015), 'Trudovaia Migratsia iz Tadjikistana v Tsifrakh', 29 May, *Russian Institute of Strategic Studies*, available at: https://riss.ru/analitycs/17465, last accessed 17 August 2017.

Popov, D. (2016), 'V Tadjikistane Ottachivaietsia Mekhanizm Regulirovania Religioznoi Zhizni', *Sputnik TJ*, 17 October, available at: http://ru.sputnik-tj.com/analytics/20161017/1020877838.html, last accessed 18 August 2017.

Privratsky, B. G. (2001), *Muslim Turkistan: Kazak Religion and Collective Memory*, Richmond: Curzon Press.

Pulleyblank, E. G. (1955), *The Background of the Rebellion of An Lu-Shan*, Oxford: Oxford University Press.

Radnitz, S. (2010), *Weapons of the Wealthy: Predatory Regimes and Elite-Led Protests in Central Asia*, Ithaca, NY: Cornell University Press.

Rahmonov, E. (2001), *The Tajiks in the Mirror of History: From the Aryans to the Samanids*, London: London River Editions.

Rasanayagam, J. (2011), *Islam in post-Soviet Uzbekistan: The Morality of Experience*, Cambridge: Cambridge University Press.

Rashid, A. (2000), 'Islam in Central Asia: Afghanistan and Pakistan', in R. Sagdeev and S. Eisenhower (eds), *Islam and Central Asia: An Enduring Legacy or an Evolving Threat?* Washington, DC: Center for Political and Strategic Studies, pp. 213–36.

Rashid, A. (2002), *Jihad: The Rise of Militant Islam in Central Asia*, New Haven, CT: Yale University Press.

Read, Ch. (2002), *The Stalin Years: A Reader*, London: Palgrave.

Read, Ch. (2017), *Understanding 1917: A Backward Glance and a Look Forward*, paper presented at the international conference '100 Years since the Russian Revolution', 15–17 November 2017, Granada, Spain: University of Granada.

Reeves, M. (2014), *Border Work: Spatial Lives of the State in Rural Central Asia*, Ithaca, NY: Cornell University Press.

Reeves, M. (2014), 'The Time of the Border: Contingency, Conflict, and Popular Statism at the Kyrgyzstan–Uzbekistan Border', in M. Reeves, J. Rasanayagam and J. Beyer (eds), *Ethnographies of the State in Central Asia*, Bloomington, IN: Indiana University Press, pp. 198–222.

Ro'i, Y. (2000), *Islam in the Soviet Union: From the Second World War to Gorbachev*, London: Hurst.

Rorlich, A. (1986), *The Volga Tatars: A Profile in National Resilience*, Stanford, CA: Hoover Institution Press.

Rotar, I. (2007), 'Under the Green Banner: Islamic Radicals in Russia and the Former Soviet Union', *Religion, State and Society* 30(2): 89–153.

Rowe, W. C. (2010), 'The Wakhan Corridor: The Endgame of the Great Game', in A. C. Diener and J. Hagen (eds), *Borderlines and Borderlands: Political Oddities at the Edge of the Nation-State*, Lanham, MD: Rowman & Littlefield, pp. 58–76.

Roy, O. (2000), *The New Central Asia: The Creation of New Nations*, London: I. B. Tauris.

Rywkin, M. (1982), *Moscow's Muslim Challenge*, New York: M. E. Sharpe.

Safronov, R. (2000), 'Islam in Turkmenistan: The Niyazov Calculation', in R. Sagdeev and S. Eisenhower (eds), *Islam and Central Asia: An Enduring Legacy or An Evolving Threat?* Washington, DC: Center for Political and Strategic Studies, pp. 73–92.

Sagdeev, R. and S. Eisenhower (eds) (2000), *Islam and Central Asia: An Enduring Legacy or An Evolving Threat?* Washington, DC: Center for Political and Strategic Studies.

Sahadeo, J. (2007), *Russian Colonial Society in Tashkent, 1865–1923*, Bloomington, IN: Indiana University Press.

Salih, M. (2005), *The Opponent*, Bodrum: Komen.

Salmorbekova, Z. and G. M. Yemelianova (2010), 'Islam and Islamism in the Ferghana Valley', in G. M. Yemelianova (ed.), *Radical Islam in the Soviet Union*, London: Routledge, pp. 211–43.

Saray, M. (1982), 'Russian Conquest of Central Asia', *Central Asian Survey*, 1(2/3): 1–30.

Saroyan, M. (1997), *Minority, Mullahs and Modernity: Reshaping Community in the Former Soviet Union*, Berkeley: University of California.

Sartori, P. (2013), *Explorations in the Social History of Modern Central Asia (19th–Early 20th Century)*, Leiden: Brill.

Sartori, P. (2016), *Visions of Justice: Sharia and Cultural Change in Russian Central Asia*, Leiden: Brill.

Satoru, K. (2012), 'Sunni–Shi'i Relations in the Russian Protectorate of Bukhara, as Perceived by the Local 'Ulama', in U. Tomohiko (ed.), *Asiatic Russia: Imperial Power in Regional and International Contexts*, London: Routledge, pp. 189–215.

Sattorzoda, A. (2007), 'Sufiiskii Orden Qadiriia v Tadzhikistane', in S. Abdullo (ed.), *Sufizm v Irane i Tsentral'noi Azii*, Almaty: Daik-Press, pp. 95–8.

Schatz, E. (2004), *Modern Clan Politics: The Power of 'Blood' in Kazakhstan and Beyond*, Seattle, WA: University of Washington Press.

Schimmelpennick, D. (2010), *Russian Orientalism: Asia in the Russian Mind from Peter the Great to the Emigration*, New Haven, CT: Yale University Press.

Schmidtz, A. and A. Wolters (2012), 'Political Protest in Central Asia: Potentials and Dynamics', *Stiftung Wissenschaft und Politik*, German Institute for International and Security Affairs, available at: https://www.swp-berlin.org/fileadmin/contents/products/research_papers/2012_RP07_smz_wolters.pdf, last accessed 30 November 2016.

Sergeev, E. (2013), *The Great Game, 1856–1907: Russo-British Relations in Central and East Asia*, Baltimore, MD: Johns Hopkins University Press.

Sharabi, H. (1970), *Arab Intellectuals and the West: The Formative Years, 1875–1914*, Baltimore, MD: Johns Hopkins University Press.

Shlymova, G. E. (ed.) (2012), *Protestantism: Istoriia, Napravleniia i Kazakhstanskie Realii*, Astana: RGU.

Sinor, D. (1969), *Inner Asia. History, Civilization, Languages: A Syllabus*, Bloomington, IN: Indiana University Press.

Sinor, D. (1990), *The Cambridge History of Early Inner Asia*, Cambridge: Cambridge University Press.

Smith, J. (2013), *Red Nations: The Nationalities Experience in and after the USSR*, Cambridge: Cambridge University Press.

Soklakov, A. Y. (2013), '400 Years of Ural'sk in the Historiography of the Modern Period', *Nauka. Obshchestvo*, vol. 1, available at: http://www.noo-journal.ru/2013-1-1/article-0007, last accessed 3 November 2016.

Sokol, E. D. (2016), *The Revolt of 1916 in Russian Central Asia*, Baltimore, MD: Johns Hopkins University Press.

Sokolov, A. A. (1969), *Nachalo Voennykh Deistvii Kokandskogo Khanstva, k Voprosu Prisoedineniia ego k Rossii, Trudy TashGU*, vol. 343, Tashkent: TashGU, pp. 31–59.

Sokolov, L. (2013), 'Grazhdanskaia Voina v Tajikistane', 5.5.1992-27.0, *Proza.Ru*, available at: https://www.proza.ru/2013/01/11/414, last accessed 12 December 2017.

Soloviev, S. M. (1851), *Istoriia Rossii s Drevneishikh Vremen*, St Petersburg, vol. 1, ch. 1, available at: http://thelib.ru/series/istoriya_rossii_s_drevneyshih_vremen.html, last accessed 29 September 2016.

Soucek, S. (2000), *A History of Inner Asia*, Cambridge: Cambridge University Press.

Sultangalieva, G. (2012), 'The Russian Empire and the Intermediary Role of Tatars in Kazakhstan', in U. Tomohiko (ed.), *Asiatic Russia: Imperial Power in Regional and International Contexts*, London: Routledge, pp. 52–79.

Sultanova, R. (2014), *From Shamanism to Sufism: Women, Islam and Culture in Central Asia*, London: I. B. Tauris.

Terent'ev, M. A. (1906), *Istoriia Zavoevaniia Srednei Azii*, vol. 2, St Petersburg: n.p.

Tokmakov, A. (2011), 'V Kyrgyzstane Stremitel'no Rasprostraniaetsia Islam', *Region. KG*, 24 February 2011, available at: http://region.kg, last accessed 7 June 2017.

Tolybekov, S. E. (1971), *Kochevoe Obshchestvo Kazakhov v XVII–nachale XX veka*, Alma-Ata: n.p.

Tolz, V. (2011), *Russia's Own Orient: The Politics of Identity and Oriental Studies in the Late Imperial and Early Soviet Periods*, Oxford: Oxford University Press.

Tomohiko, U. (ed.) (2012), *Asiatic Russia: Imperial Power in Regional and International Contexts*, London: Routledge.

Tomohiko, U. (2012), 'The Alash Orda's Relations with Siberia, the Urals and Turkestan: the Kazakh National Movement and the Russian Imperial Legacy', in U. Tomohiko (ed.), *Asiatic Russia: Imperial Power in Regional and International Contexts*, London: Routledge, pp. 271–87.

Trimingham, J. S. (1971), *The Sufi Orders in Islam*, Oxford: Oxford University Press.

Tucker, N. (2016), 'Public and State Responses to ISIS Messaging: Tajikistan', *Central Asian Program*, vol. 11, Washington, DC: George Washington University.

Turner, B. S. (2011), *Religion and Modern Society: Citizenship, Secularisation and the State*, Cambridge: Cambridge University Press.

Tursunov, Kh. T. (1962), *Vosstaniie 1916 goda v Tsentral'noi Azii i Kazakhstane*, Tashkent: n.p.

Tursunov, Kh. T. (ed.) (1987), *Hujum Znachit Nastuplenie*, Tashkent: Uzbekistan.

Tyson, D. (1997), 'Shrine Pilgrimage in Turkmenistan as a Means to Understand Islam among the Turkmen', *Central Asia Monitor: Online Supplement*, vol. 1, available at: http://islam.uga.edu/turkmen.html, last accessed 9 September 2017.

Tyuryukanova, E. and R. Abazova (2009), *A Needs Assessment of Women Migrant Workers: Central Asia and Russia*, Almaty: UNIFEM.

Usmanova, D. (1999), *Musul'manskaia Fraktsiia i Problemy 'Svobody Sovesti' v Gosudarstvennoi Dume (1906–1917)*, Kazan: ANRT.

Usmonova, Z. (2017), 'Vlasti Boriutsa ne s Hijabami, a s Religioznym Fanatizmom', *Radio Ozodi*, 17 August, available at: https://rus.ozodi.org/a/28681427.html, last accessed 18 August 2017.

'Uzbekistan: The Hundred Days' (2017), *International Crisis Group, Europe and Central Asia Report*, vol. 242, Brussels.

Valentine, S. (2008), *Islam and the Ahmadiyya Jama'at: History, Belief, Practice*, New York: Columbia University Press.

Validi Togan, Z. (1994), *Vospominaniia*, vol. 1, Ufa: Kitap.

Vambery, A. (1864), *Travels in Central Asia, Being the Account of a Journey from Teheran across the Turkoman Desert on the Eastern Shore of the Caspian to Khiva, Bokhora and Samarcand, Performed in the Year 1863*, London: Murray.

Vasilieva, G. P. (2003), *Istoriia Etnograficheskogo Izucheniia Turkmenskogo Naroda v Otechestvennoi Nauke (Konets 18–20 vv.)*, Moscow: Nauka.

Vsesoiuznaia Perepis' Naseleniia 1939 Goda po Respublikam SSSR, Institute of Demography, High School of Economics, *Demoscope Weekly*, No. 705/706, 14–27 November 2016, available at: http://demoscope.ru/weekly/ssp/sng_nac_39.php?reg=5, last accessed 2 December 2016.

Vsesoiuznaia Perepis' Naseleniia 1989 Goda po Respublikam SSSR: Uzbekskaiia SSR. Institute of Demography, High School of Economics, Demoscope Weekly, No. 717/-18, 20 February–5 March 2017, available at: http://demoscope.ru/weekly/ssp/sng_nac_89.php?reg=4, last accessed 7 March 2017.

Vulpius, R. (2012), 'The Russian Empire's Civilizing Mission in the Eighteenth Century: A Comparative Perspective', in U. Tomohiko (ed.), *Asiatic Russia: Imperial Power in Regional and International Contexts*, London: Routledge, pp. 13–31.

Weber, M. (1966), *Sociology of Religion*, London: Methuen.

Witter, D. (2011), 'Militancy in Pakistan's Tribal Region', *Backgrounder*, Institute for the Study of War, 27 January, available at: http://www.understandingwar.org/sites/default/files/BackgrounderIMU_28Jan.pdf, last accessed 6 March 2017.

Yarlykapov, A. (2015), *Islamskoe Gosudarstvo Stroit v Rossii Podpol'e*, Video-channel Pravda, 27 May, available at: http://www.pravda.ru/news/expert/27-05-2015/1261474-yarlikapov-0, last accessed 6 July 2016.

Yavuz, M. H. (2000), 'Turkish Identity Politics and Central Asia', in R. Sagdeev and S. Eisenhower (eds), *Islam and Central Asia: An Enduring Legacy or An Evolving Threat?* Washington, DC: Center for Political and Strategic Studies, pp. 193–211.

Yemelianova, G. M. (1997), 'The National Identity of the Volga Tatars at the Turn of the 19th Century: Tatarism, Turkism and Islam', *Central Asian Survey* 16(4): 543–72.

Yemelianova, G. M. (2002), *Russia and Islam: A Historical Survey*, London: Palgrave.

Yemelianova, G. M. (2003), 'Islam and Power', in H. Pilkington and G. Yemelianova (eds), *Islam in Post-Soviet Russia: Public and Private Faces*, London: RoutledgeCurzon, pp. 61–116.

Yemelianova, G. M. (2004), 'Gosudarstva Tsentral'noi Azii i Rossiia,' *Istoriia Vostoka*, vol. 4(1), Moscow: Vostochnaia Literatura, pp. 156–61.

Yemelianova, G. M. (ed.) (2010), *Radical Islam in the former Soviet Union*, London: Routledge.

Yemelianova, G. M. (2014), 'Islam, National Identity and Politics in Contemporary Kazakhstan', *Asian Ethnicity* 15(3): 286–301.

Yemelianova, G. M. (2017), 'How "Muslim" are Central Asian Muslims? A Historical and Comparative Enquiry', *Central Asian Affairs*, pp. 243–69.

Zakiev, M. Z. (1995), *Tatary: Problemy Istorii i Yazyka*, Kazan: IYALI.

Zelkina, A. (2000), *In Quest of God and Freedom*, London: Hurst.

Relevant websites

http://caa-network.org: Central Asian Analytical Network –a Washington-based international network of scholars and experts on Central Asia.

http://www.eastview.com: EastView Information Services – analysis by US-based information services.

https://eurasianet.org: EurasiaNet – analytical information on Central Asia, the Caucasus and the Volga-Urals by Harriman Institute, Columbia University, New York.

https://www.rferl.org: Radio Free Europe/Radio Liberty – RFE/RL, Prague-based US government-funded broadcasting on Eastern Europe, Central Asia and the Middle East.

http://www.forum18.org: Forum 18 – a Norwegian Christian human rights organisation dealing with religious freedom in the ex-USSR.

www.hrw.org: Human Rights Watch – a US-based international NGO with a focus on human rights in the former USSR.

http://www.iwpr.net/centasia: Institute for War and Peace Reporting – a London-based independent analytical network with the focus on wars and conflicts across the world.

http://www.crisisgroup.org: International Crisis Group – a Brussels-based international think tank dealing with conflicts and civil wars across the world.

http://central-eurasia.com: Centre for the Study of Central Asia, the Caucasus and the Volga-Urals – Institute of Oriental Studies, RAN.

http://news.ferghana.ru: Ferghana.ru – Russian information agency on Central Asia.

http://www.centrasia.ru – Centralasia.ru (Russian News on Central Asia).

http://islamreview.ru: Islam Review – a Russian information network on Islam in Eurasia.

http://www.harakat.net: *Harakat* – Uzbekistan independent news agency.

http://www.gov.uz: Uzbekistan government official portal.

http://nuz.uz: Uzbekistan News – an Uzbekistan official information news agency.

http://www.islam.uz: Islam Uzbekistan – an official Islamic website affiliated to the Islamic Directorate of Uzbekistan.
http://www.din.gov.kz: an official website of the Religious Affairs Committee of the Republic of Kazakhstan.
http://muftiyat.kg: official website of the muftiiate of Kyrgyzstan.
http://www.region.kg: 'Region.KG' – Kyrgyzstan's analytical centre.
http://kyrtag.kg: *Kyrtag* – Kyrgyz telegraph agency.
http://www.erkin.net: Erkin Net/Free Turkmenistan – UTOD website.

Index